VISITS

from the

AFTERLIFE

SYLVIA BROWNE

with Lindsay Harrison

VISITS

from the

AFTERLIFE

The Truth about Hauntings,
Spirits, and Reunions with
Lost Loved Ones

DUTTON

DUTTON
Published by Penguin Group (USA) Inc.
375 Hudson Street, New York, New York 10014, U.S.A.
Penguin Books Ltd, Registered Offices: 80 Strand, London WC2R 0RL, England
Penguin Books Australia Ltd, 250 Camberwell Road, Camberwell, Victoria 3124, Australia
Penguin Books Canada Ltd, 10 Alcorn Avenue, Toronto, Ontario, Canada M4V 3B2
Penguin Books (NZ) Ltd, Cnr Rosedale and Airborne Roads,
Albany, Auckland 1310, New Zealand

Published by Dutton, a member of Penguin Group (USA) Inc.

 REGISTERED TRADEMARK——MARCA REGISTRADA

ISBN 0-525-94756-6

Printed in the United States of America
Set in Perpetua
Designed by Eve L. Kirch

From Sylvia and Lindsay
to our dads.
This one's especially for you.

Contents

Acknowledgments

To Fern Underwood, our preliminary and grossly underpaid proofreader. I've decided it's not fair that Lindsay has you for a mom and I don't, so adoption papers will follow shortly.

To Bernie Keating, without whom this book would have been released in the year 2012 or so. You're a Godsend in more ways than I can express. And special thanks for the sponge.

To Larry Harnisch. I asked Lindsay to track you down because you've got it right, and you turned out to be patient, compassionate, generous, and a friend as well, with a fierce loyalty to research and accuracy I'll always admire. When your book comes out, Lindsay and I will be first in line to buy it, you can count on it. Until then, one more promise kept: Lindsay and I will be sending a donation, in the name of Elizabeth Short, to a wonderful charity that helps, among others, the homeless and abused women of Elizabeth's hometown, Medford, Massachusetts. If any of our readers would care to do the same, it would be kind and much appreciated. It's Shelter, Inc., P.O. Box 390516, Cambridge, Massachusetts 02139. Thanks, all of you. This will make more sense after you read Chapter Ten.

Acknowledgments

To Brian Tart, our editor on a total of six books now. I truly appreciate that we've become friends in our own right, and I'll never cease to be amazed at the class you showed when, as it turns out, I was sometimes being difficult without knowing a thing about it.

To each of you, from the bottom of my very full heart, eternal thanks.

Sylvia

Introduction

Thousands of people, many of them currently on earth, contributed to this book. There are the spirits and ghosts around the world who've been kind enough to show up and tell me their stories for the last half a century or so. There are the 2,014 visitors to my Web site who had the courage and generosity to e-mail their experiences to me, some of which you'll find in the pages that follow—and let me make it clear right now, I read every single one of those e-mails. Those 2,014 brave people were on the receiving end of some fascinating appearances by spirits and ghosts, some of them deeply comforting and some of them terrifying. There's a victim of an unsolved murder who told me the name of her killer, and there's a Spirit Guide who left her voice on an audiotape, repeating a single word that gave a woman the key to her husband's criminal life. There's a woman who was given strength by a visit with an ex-boyfriend on The Other Side who she didn't know had passed away, and a man who would never have found out he had a stillborn baby sister if her spirit hadn't come to introduce herself when he was four years old.

To the thousands of us collaborators on this particular book, and the many millions who don't question any more than we do that of course there's an afterlife, there are those who will always be ready with a list of handy explanations for what we "think" we're seeing, hearing, and feeling. "Grief hysteria," "oxygen deprivation," and variations on terms for both "mental illness" and "scam" are among the most popular. What these skeptics and "experts" are usually insisting on, though, is the same cynical demand, over and over and over again, which boils down to:

"Prove that there's life after death."

I'm sixty-six years old, and I've never spent one instant doubting that there's life after death. The thousands of us who contributed to this book, on earth and beyond it, don't doubt it. The millions we represent don't doubt it. God certainly doesn't doubt it, since He's the One who told us it's true in the first place, and we take His word for everything. We're not the ones who are having a problem with this. You are. So why do we keep knocking ourselves out trying to prove something we already know with absolute certainty?

Here's my suggestion to the skeptics and "experts," for a refreshing change of pace. We're done proving that there's life after death. We've proven it well past our own satisfaction. From now on, let's do it this way: You prove that there's not.

VISITS

from the

AFTERLIFE

Chapter One

THE TRUTH ABOUT GHOSTS AND SPIRITS

I believe in ghosts, and in the real and magnificent presence of spirits among us from The Other Side.

I believe because, like so many of you, I've seen them, heard them, been startled by them, even smelled the faint familiar fragrance of a lost loved one, urging me to notice, to embrace their assurance that they're not gone at all, they're right here, not some trick of my imagination or wishful thinking, if I'll just open my eyes, ears, mind, and heart and pay attention.

I believe because, surrounded by so much overwhelming evidence of their existence during my sixty-six years on this earth, I'd be insane not to believe.

Most of all, I believe because I know to the core of my being that the majority of the world's great religions are right—we are all eternal, every one of us, as our birthright from God who created us. Our spirits always were and always will be. Our physical bodies are only temporary housing for the essence of who we are, that divine part of us that feels joy and sorrow and love and reverence and holds our truth and our timeless memories and our wisdom intact. Death will take our bodies sooner or later, but it can never, ever destroy *us*. God promised us everlasting lives, and He doesn't break His promises.

And it's precisely because I take God at His word that I can't imagine *not* believing in the existence of ghosts and spirits among us. If our spirits really do transcend death, if they're immortal as we know they are, that means they never cease to exist. So why on earth would we disbelieve the existence of something we agree never ceases to exist? In fact, why not recognize that the presence of ghosts, and of spirits from Home, is actually comforting, even worthy of celebration, proving as it does that eternal life is a beautiful, sacred, God-given certainty?

Don't get me wrong. I'm not saying that the unexpected appearance of a ghost or a spirit can't be scary. You'll read stories throughout the book in which many of you have been frightened, and I'll openly admit to moments of fear during my own stories as well. Some combination of surprise, a cultural insistence that anyone who sees ghosts and spirits is either crazy or lying, and a lack of understanding of what's happening can add up to very real jolts of panic in even the most rational among us.

But please take my word for a few important truths about ghosts and spirits:

For one thing, knowledge really is power. The more I've learned and the more I continue to learn about the spirit world, the more my fear has been replaced by curiosity and fascination, and you'll find the same is true for you; I guarantee it.

For another thing, as so many of you are already aware, it's not just us psychics and other "weirdos" who routinely have perfectly valid encounters with ghosts and spirits. "Normal" people in every corner of every country on earth have come face to face with visitors from the afterlife. These people know what they've experienced, they know they're not crazy, they know the experience was real, and they don't need me or anyone else to validate it for them. And they'd agree with me on this, I'm sure. Just as any scientist would be a fool to get the same result from the same experiment over and over again and refuse to believe it, all of us who have seen, heard, and felt the presence of the spirit world would be just as foolish to refuse to believe what our five physical senses, our minds, and our hearts would swear to.

Finally, as momentarily frightened as I've been by some of my encounters with residents of the afterlife, I can assure you, I've never met a ghost or spirit who could do a fraction of the physical and emotional damage human beings can do. Give me a choice between a confrontation with the world's orneriest ghost or the world's most cunning human sociopath and I'll choose to take on the ghost every time. So while this journey into the spirit world we're about to take together will lead us into territory we might occasionally find scary and unnerving, don't spend one instant wondering whether or not you have enough courage to take the trip. You were brave enough to choose another lifetime as a human being on this rough, confusing, beautiful earth, which makes you brave enough to meet ghosts and spirits, especially since we've all *been* those ghosts and spirits before and will be again when this lifetime ends.

THE SPIRIT'S JOURNEY AFTER DEATH

In order to understand what spirits and ghosts really are and where they come from, it's essential to understand what happens to our spirits when our physical bodies die. I've written about this in great detail in previous books, particularly *Life on The Other Side*, so rather than repeat myself at length, I'll limit this discussion to a few relevant specifics.

When the spirit leaves the body that's provided it with temporary housing for another visit to earth, there are basically three different places it might go. And make no mistake about it, which of those three places the spirit travels to is our decision, not God's. He never stops loving us, never turns away from us, and would never condemn any of us to an eternity of banishment from His presence. It's only when we stop loving Him and turn away from Him that we take such foolish chances with the health and well-being of our souls.

The vast majority of us, who love God by whatever name we call Him and try our best to honor His love while we're here, immediately transcend to The Other Side, that sacred, exquisite, perfect world we came from, where we live joyfully among the Angels, the messiahs, our Spirit Guides, our soul mates and loved ones from an eternity of lifetimes both on earth and at Home. Residents of The Other Side are called spirits, and their appearances in our midst on earth are called visitations.

A much smaller percentage of humankind, those dark, remorseless souls who choose evil over God, travel to an unspeakable unholy void called the Left Door, from which they horseshoe right back into an earthly womb, to be reborn into another Godless incarnation. The Dark Side, as we call those travelers through the Left Door, don't communicate with us or appear among us while they're in vitro.

And then there are those poor trapped souls who, for their own often confused reasons, refuse to acknowledge the very real tunnel leading to The Other Side, illuminated by God's brilliant white light, and remain earthbound. Earthbound souls are called ghosts, and their appearances in our midst are called hauntings.

Understanding the differences between spirits and ghosts, between visitations and hauntings, can help turn an unexpected encounter with the afterlife from frightening to comforting. It can help us tell an earthbound intruder from a beloved visitor from Home. It can answer questions about where a departed loved one went after leaving their body, how they are, and whether or not they're happy. And it can certainly give us fascinating glimpses into the possibilities that lie ahead for us when our current incarnations are complete.

But before I go into any further detail about the brilliant, complex spirit world we're about to explore, I want to address an issue that came up in several of the hundreds upon hundreds of letters my clients and readers were kind enough to send. Antonio, for example, wrote, in the midst of a description of coming face to face with a ghost in his house, "I was especially confused because I knew what I was looking at was absolutely real, but I'd been taught all my life that ghosts and spirits and things like that came from the devil and were to be dismissed." And after telling me about a really gorgeous visitation from her deceased father, Cynthia added, "I confided in my aunt about it, and she admitted that a lot of people in our family have had similar experiences, but she didn't want to talk about it because this sort of thing is evil and it's conspiring with the devil to believe in spirits."

If you know anything about me, you know that I'm passionate about my religion, Gnostic Christianity, and about religions throughout the world, which I've studied all my life. My faith in God is as essential to me as the air I breathe. It empowers me, comforts me, inspires me, sustains me, brings me joy, and diminishes my fears. There's not a doubt in my mind that God wants our reverent devotion to Him to come from adoration, not from intimidation or terror of His wrath, and there's also not a doubt in my mind that nothing He created is or ever could be evil. Evil is a creation of humankind, not of God. Since God, not some mythical devil, created us with souls that are eternal, and ghosts and spirits are manifestations of those eternal souls, the illogic of equating the spirit world with evil really mystifies me.

In fact, depending on which of the twenty-six versions of the Bible you read, Jesus Himself appeared on earth in spirit form between six and ten times after He ascended. Paul's first letter to the Corinthians, for example, in the Revised Standard Edition, Chapter 15, verses 3–8, reads, ". . . that Christ died for our sins . . . , that He was buried, that He was raised on the third day . . . , and that He appeared to Cephas, then to the twelve. Then He appeared to more than five hundred brethren at one time. . . . Then He appeared to James, then to all the apostles. . . . He appeared also to me." With these and other Biblical accounts of the earthly appearances of a Spirit who had very definitely transcended to The Other Side, how and why would someone get the idea that encounters between humankind and the afterlife are evil? I'm certainly not about to give credit to a supposed "devil" for Christ's visitations to this world after His crucifixion, are you?

So, please, whatever your beliefs, whatever you've been taught, whatever you're told, by me or by anyone else, don't accept anything as truth that doesn't make sense in your heart. Just because we don't understand something, or something frightens us, doesn't make it "evil." *Think. Learn.* Knowledge really is power, don't ever doubt that.

All that having been said, and thanks for letting me get it out of my system, let's explore the worlds of spirits and ghosts who, by their very presence among us, prove our God-given eternity to be an absolute, indisputable fact.

SPIRITS

As I mentioned earlier, when our bodies die, most of us experience the brilliantly lit tunnel, not descending from some faraway place in the sky but actually rising from our own bodies and leading much more "across" than "up," at about a twenty- or thirty-degree angle. We travel with gorgeous, weightless freedom through this almost sideways tunnel, never for one instant feeling as if we've died but instead feeling more thrillingly alive than we could ever imagine here on earth. All our worries, frustrations, anger, resentment, and other negativity melt away, replaced by the peace and all-loving, unconditional understanding we remember and are about to reunite with at Home. God's sacred white light waits to embrace us at the end of the tunnel, along with loved ones from every lifetime we've ever lived. Even our pets from every lifetime are there to greet us, so eager with the joy of seeing us that the human spirits have to wait their turn to get to us. And once we've arrived on The Other Side, we resume the busy, active, exquisite lives we temporarily left behind to further our spiritual education in the tough school earth provides.

There's a simple, logical reason that the legendary tunnel takes us more "across" than "up"—our destination, The Other Side, that paradise for which we're Homesick from the moment we leave it until we return, is another dimension located a mere three feet above earth's ground level. This very real, idyllically beautiful place exists at a much higher vibrational frequency than we do here, which is why we don't perceive our intimate proximity to it, any more than the normal human ear can hear the extremely high-frequency pitch of a dog whistle. If you've had encounters with spirits from The Other Side, or talked to or read accounts from those who have, you've noticed that very often the descriptions include the impression that the spirits were "floating" a few feet above the ground. While that's often exactly what it looks like through our eyes, what's really happening is that the spirits are simply moving on their ground level at Home, three feet higher than ours.

To truly understand how to recognize a spirit visitation, and how to distinguish it from other experiences with the afterlife, you have to keep in mind that by the time they've come back to say hello and let us know they're still very much alive, they've already transcended to and been living in a place of emotional and spiritual bliss, not to mention perfect physical health. Any unhappiness they experienced during their latest lifetime on earth, any negativity they carried around, any illnesses or infirmities or injuries they suffered, have all been resolved. What that means is that any entity we encounter who seems to be sad or angry or mean or negative in any way, or who shows any signs of wounds or pain or disease, is something other than a spirit from The Other Side. What it also means, by the way, is that we never need to spend a moment wondering if our deceased loved ones at Home are well and happy. In the blessed perfection of Home, they can't possibly be anything less.

Spirits at Home live in a world unobstructed by our earthly limitations, so there are qualities about them that set them apart from any other kinds of visitors. Because their minds and thoughts are so powerful they can communicate brilliantly with each other, and with us on earth, through the use of telepathy—the immediate transference of information from one entity to another without the use of any of the five physical senses. One of the most common observations you'll hear from people who've had visitations from spirits is that the spirit talked to them without using words or even making a sound.

Another talent spirits have that we'll often experience from them, and that we have to look forward to when we're spirits again, is that they can bi-locate, i.e., be in two places at the same time. It's not unusual for family members or others who were close to a deceased loved one to receive simultaneous visits from that loved one on opposite sides of town or opposite sides of the world, with both visits being completely real and completely unique.

Spirits are invariably eager for us to recognize exactly who they are, which means they'll either appear in a form that's familiar to us, they'll create a scent we'd associate with them, they'll offer a light touch to our hair or the back of our neck or our shoulder that was their habit during their lifetime, or they'll manipulate an object that will offer hints to their identity. They'll repeatedly move a framed photograph of themselves so that it's facing a different direction or lying flat on a table or dresser, play with the flame of a candle we've lit in their honor, superimpose their face on a painting or snapshot, rock their favorite rocking chair, play a music box they gave us—the possibilities are as limitless as the imaginations of our loved ones themselves, and all we have to do is be receptive and pay attention.

Because spirits have to cross back into our dimension in order to visit us, they often attach their energy to such powerful conductors as electricity and water in order to help with their "reentry." Eager to make their presence known, they'll create bizarre behavior in TVs, appliances, telephones, and other objects and electrical devices, and they're especially active between the hours of 1:00 A.M. and 5:00 A.M., when the night air is at its dampest and the dew is at its heaviest. Please don't misunderstand should you experience your telephone chronically ringing with either no one or static on the other end when you answer, or your television set suddenly doing a full rotation of all its channels while its remote control sits idle on the coffee table. Your belongings are not "possessed," any more than they're "possessed" when you use them yourself. Instead, it's very possibly a spirit, simply manipulating something tangible that you'll be sure to notice, to say, "I'm right here, watching over you." (I'm too much of a realist not to add that the spirit world is hardly responsible for every malfunction around the house. Sometimes all you need is a good repairman.)

And speaking of "possessed," don't ever believe that a spirit from

The Other Side, or any other entity from anywhere else, can possess you without your awareness and permission. I promise you, it's impossible, no matter how entertaining exorcist legends, books, and movies might be. As many of you know, I sometimes allow my Spirit Guide, Francine, to occupy my body for short periods of time. It's a matter of pure practicality, and another distinguishing characteristic of spirit visitations—because of the significant difference between The Other Side's vibrational frequency and ours here on earth, Francine's voice, like all other spirits' voices, sounds to our ears like an audiotape played at fast-forward speed. Frankly, it's annoying, hard to understand when you're not accustomed to it, and probably why the majority of spirits communicate telepathically. But when Francine has a lot of information to share, rather than put myself and everyone else through what might resemble a performance by one of the Chipmunks, I'll essentially "step aside" through trance and allow Francine to use my body, or more specifically my vocal cords, for the duration of what she has to say. Without my knowledge, permission, and cooperation, it couldn't happen. Should you hear a high-pitched, tinny, rather distant voice that seems to be coming from out of nowhere, though, as I know so many of you have, you can count on it that someone from Home has stopped by to say hello.

Finally, just as spirits from The Other Side are incapable of negative thoughts and actions, they're also incapable of visiting us for anything but the most positive of reasons. Even though it can be startling to see or hear them when you're not accustomed to it, spirit visitations are never intended to frighten or intimidate or threaten or chase us away. All they want is to love us, comfort us, reassure us that they've never really left us and never will, and most of all to try to prove to us by their very presence, no matter how subtle, that by God's grace, eternal life is a simple, sacred, indisputable fact.

GHOSTS

There is one tragic quality shared by every ghost in every corner of every country around the world: Not one of them has the slightest idea that they're dead. Unlike most spirits who, when their bodies die, eagerly proceed through the tunnel that will take them Home, ghosts turn away from the tunnel, refusing to acknowledge its existence for reasons of their own and, as a result, remain earthbound, desperately confused and lonely, often angry, sometimes aggressive and petulant, trapped in a futile effort to make sense of an existence that by definition makes no sense at all.

Of course, ghosts do leave their bodies like all of us do when our bodies stop functioning, and by leaving their bodies they also leave this earthly dimension. But by rejecting the tunnel and God's loving, healing white light on The Other Side, they don't transcend to the higher-frequency dimension of Home, either, which means that their spirits are left quite literally "neither here nor there." That fact alone makes them very different from spirits from The Other Side in a number of ways:

- Living in neither earth's dimension nor the dimension of The Other Side, ghosts are typically more visible and distinct than spirits. I've used this analogy several times, but it seems effective enough that I'll unapologetically use it again: The easiest way to picture the three dimensions we're talking about—earth's dimension, ghosts' dimension, and the dimension of Home—is to visualize an electric fan. At its slowest speed, the fan's blades are well defined and easy to see. That represents the dimension on earth, the one we all function in and are accustomed to. At the fan's medium speed, the individual blades begin to blur into each other and are harder for our eyes to distinguish. That represents the dimension in which ghosts are trapped. Turn the fan to its highest speed and its blades seem to disappear completely, creating the illusion that the blades aren't there at all, as false an illusion as the idea that The Other Side and its resident spirits don't exist just because we can't readily see them. The fact that some people are able to see and hear ghosts and spirits while others aren't doesn't prove that some people are crazy while others aren't. It just proves that some people's physical senses are more finely tuned than others'.

- Because they haven't yet experienced the love and healing of The Other Side, ghosts will bear visible signs of any injuries or illnesses or deformities that were present when their bodies died. You will *never* see a spirit from Home who's wounded or sick or in any kind of physical or emotional pain.

- When spirits are among us, their ultimate motivation is their love for us, and their efforts to get us to notice them are meant to express that love. Ghosts, on the other hand, are much more complicated. Their reasons for turning away from the tunnel and refusing to accept the fact of their death on this earth are widely varied. Some stay behind out of a confused sense of deep loyalty to a loved one or a property or a job for which they felt responsible during their lifetime. Some stay behind for revenge. Some stay behind to search for or wait for a lost love. Some stay behind out of fear that God is too displeased with them to embrace them into the blessed joy of Home (which is impossible, by the way—He embraces all of us who let Him). Whatever their confused purpose for rejecting the truth that they're dead, they're among us out of a distorted sense of reality. The world through a ghost's eyes is locked in a time warp of their own disturbed creation. From their point of view, *we* are the intruders in *their* world, not the other way around. So we shouldn't be too surprised that in their encounters with us, they're sometimes angry, desperate, resentful, cranky, or annoying. Occasionally, when they realize that someone is seeing, hearing, or acknowledging them in any way, they can be appreciative and even playful, especially with children. But overall, like most unhappy, chronically disoriented beings, they can be unpredictable, not to mention depressing.

• By not transcending to The Other Side, ghosts deprive themselves of the ability to bi-locate. There are no simultaneous appearances of a single ghost as there can be with a single spirit. In fact, by their own design, ghosts are usually too attached to whatever place they're frequenting to wander far away from it anyway.

• Also, having not transcended, ghosts exist in our dimension, not in the dimension of Home three feet above our ground level on earth. That's why, while spirits appear to be "floating" as they move along the ground level of The Other Side, ghosts accurately appear to be functioning on exactly the same level we are.

• As we discussed earlier, spirits, because they're so eager for us to know it's them, will appear in a form that will help us recognize them. Ghosts, on the other hand, couldn't care less whether we recognize them or not, since they're among us out of desperate confusion having nothing at all to do with comforting us. They might show up as very distinct images of their own earthly bodies, they might appear rather faded and unformed, or they might even present themselves as balls of heavy mist, almost as if they were smoke rings with the centers filled in. They have neither the divine skill nor the self-control of spirits from Home, so the physical appearance of ghosts is simply one more way in which they can be frustratingly unpredictable.

Now that we've covered the basics of how and why most souls become spirits and a relative few become ghosts when their bodies die, and the basics of how to tell spirits and ghosts apart, you might think that's pretty much all you need to know to prepare yourself for dealing with any unexpected visitors from the spirit world who come along.

The fact is, though, that we've only just scratched the surface.

Chapter Two

BEYOND SPIRITS AND GHOSTS: MORE VISITORS AND WHERE THEY COME FROM

The worlds of spirits and ghosts are fascinating enough to fill countless volumes all by themselves. But they're only the beginning of the story when it comes to "things that go bump in the night," those welcome and unwelcome intruders who can make us doubt our own eyes, ears, and sanity. As the chapters of this book continue to unfold, you'll be reading one account after another, some mine and some from literally hundreds upon hundreds of you, of encounters with dimensions beyond our own, encounters that I'm only able to fully understand and appreciate after thirty years of research through the Society of Novus Spiritus, the organization I founded in 1974 for the study and exploration of the paranormal. Decades later, I'm still learning, and still mesmerized by the wealth of phenomena around us that can help turn our time on earth from an existence to an adventure if we'll just learn to recognize what those phenomena are, what causes them, and how to deal with them.

TULPA

"Tulpa" is a Tibetan term, and it refers to beings that originate in the mind and then, through intense belief and visualization, actually become physical realities. It's not a case of a person or group of people becoming so convinced, through rumors and legends, that they all imagine the same entity out of some kind of shared hallucination. It's a case of one mind, or several minds, creating a very real, physical, living being that eventually takes on a life of its own, gathering strength as more and more people begin believing in its existence and usually becoming even harder to get rid of than it was to visualize in the first place.

One of the most brilliant explorers into the phenomenon of tulpa creation was a woman named Alexandra David-Neel, who was born in Paris in 1868. She was a fearless adventurer, writer, lecturer, researcher, and scholar who traveled throughout Asia, usually on foot, not just to study but also to experience everything from Eastern mysticism to philosophy to mind-over-matter techniques to the teachings of Buddha. She studied under Indian swamis, became a practicing Muslim in North Africa while studying the Koran, spent four years in a cave with a monk learning Tibetan spirituality, and was even the first Western woman ever to enter the capital, Lhasa, known as "the forbidden city" of Tibet. Her unquenchable thirst for knowledge lasted until her death in 1969 at the age of 101.

One of the concepts of Tibetan culture that enthralled Alexandra David-Neel was the tulpa, the idea that just by mentally conceiving an entity you could actually create it as a physical reality. Like everything else that inspired her curiosity, she wasn't content just to read about the tulpa—she wanted to explore the discipline of creating one herself. In her mind she made up a figure who was a round, pleasant little monk, kind of a Friar Tuck clone, as harmless and friendly as he could be. She then began practicing a routine of intense visualization and concentration, and over time she was able to see the small monk as not just a mental image inside her head but as a living, tangible being, separate from herself, as real as the rest of the world it began to inhabit. The more she continued to visualize him, the more solid and visible her creation became, and, to her increasing concern, the less able she was to control him. He started making appearances at his own convenience, whether she willed him to or not, and within a few weeks, other people around her who knew nothing about her tulpa experiment at all began asking about the diminutive stranger who seemed to be hanging around with increasing regularity.

Most alarming of all to David-Neel, though, was that the longer her creation maintained this life of his own, the more his will began replacing hers. The round, happy little monk began to evolve into a stronger, more slender, more physically fit version of himself, and he became sullen, dark, and almost menacing. Horrified, David-Neel realized that this being she was responsible for creating was becoming dangerous, and she knew she had to take sole responsibility for destroying him, which she could only accomplish by absorbing him back into her own mind where he came from. The tulpa fought her every step of the way, so independent of her by now that he felt completely entitled to exist, and it took well over a month of the same intense concentration that created him for her to eliminate him once and for all. The process was so debilitating that David-Neel's health was almost destroyed right along with the sinister little creature she'd brought into this world.

If you find it hard to believe that a tangible living being can be created simply through the power of the mind, please remind yourself that everything human-made that exists on this earth originated with a single thought. And if you ever question how powerful projected thoughts and emotions can be, gather a group of friends in a room and ask them to agree on a feeling to concentrate on and project— anger, resentment, love, happiness, any well-defined emotion— without telling you which they've chosen or giving you any physical or verbal clues. Then leave the room for a couple of minutes to let them choose the emotion and silently focus their combined energy on it. You'll be amazed at how readily you'll be able to identify the emotion they've chosen as soon as you reenter the room, and how immediately you'll be affected by it, either positively or negatively.

Tulpa, then, are simply those same powerful projected thoughts and emotions that become telescoped into physical forms. The more thoughts and emotions and credibility are invested in the tulpas, the more real and alive they become. It's important to remember that once they've begun to exist on their own, without those who created them controlling when they appear and disappear, they're no longer imaginary, and no longer all that easy to control or get rid of.

The yeti, or "abominable snowman," of the Himalayas is a brilliant example of a tulpa, created by rumor and legend and then given life by increasingly widespread fear of it and belief in its existence. Its huge footprints have been photographed in the deep mountain snow, but even though it has reportedly been seen, fleetingly, from a distance of three hundred yards, its full form has never been captured on film. The native Sherpas of the high Himalayas firmly believe that the yeti lives among them and that it can make itself appear and disappear whenever it chooses, exactly like Alexandra David-Neel's monk, who began to decide for himself when and if he wanted to be seen.

I believe the Loch Ness monster is a tulpa. I also strongly believe that anyone who claims to have seen the devil in physical form has simply allowed fear, negativity, and evil to become such powerful forces in their life that they've created a tulpa that's guaranteed to terrorize them, with no one but themselves to thank.

And speaking of no one but themselves to thank, I also believe that a tulpa, created out of greed and a misguided interest in fame, was the only thing that ever "haunted" the infamous house in Amityville, New York, where the supposed "Amityville Horror" took place.

In case you're not familiar with the whole story of the Amityville house, its real horror took place on November 13, 1974, when a deeply troubled young man named Ronald DeFeo went on a lethal rampage through the three-story home and murdered six members of his family. He was convicted of all six murders and sentenced to twenty-five years to life in prison.

In the summer of 1975, the DeFeo house was bought by George and Kathy Lutz. The young couple and Kathy's three children moved into the house in December of 1975. Within either ten days or twenty-eight days, depending on which of the Lutzes' accounts you choose to believe, they were allegedly driven from the house by ghosts, flying pigs, and other terrifying embodiments of evil. Their accounts of exactly what those ghosts, flying pigs, etc., looked like and did to them continued to change even after their best-selling book with an author named Jay Anson was released in 1977 and the hit movie *The Amityville Horror*, based on that book, leapt onto movie screens around the country in 1979, claiming to be "a true story." To this day the Lutzes can't seem to land on a story they're comfortable with. In one interview, for example, George Lutz said that on their last night in the house, before they ran for their lives, abandoning everything they owned, he was in bed, helpless, unable to move or even cry out, for reasons he couldn't quite articulate, while his wife levitated above the bed and he could hear his children's beds upstairs slamming against the floor as if they were being lifted in the air and then suddenly dropped. In another interview George Lutz said that what happened in that house on their last night there was simply too horrible to describe. The question "So which is it?" leaps to mind.

I need to make it clear before I go on that I've never been to the Amityville house. Warner Bros. Studios offered me a very generous amount of money to go there for a filmed paranormal investigation, but I declined. I believed then and I believe now that, with encouragement from friends and even Ronald DeFeo's lawyer, William Weber, who was writing a book about the murders, George and Kathy Lutz realized that moving into the Amityville house might be their ticket to fame and fortune. I doubt that they meant any harm. Opportunism often starts with innocuous intentions, mixed with a lot of shortsightedness. I'm sure what started out as a potentially profitable publicity stunt kept snowballing until it was out of control and far too late for the Lutzes to gracefully back out of their story, especially with a movie studio determined to include the words "a true story" in their ads for *The Amityville Horror*. But there's no way around the fact that anyone who tries to cash in on someone else's tragedy will always pay too high a price in the long run to make it worth the effort.

One of the psychics who participated in a séance at the Amityville house after the Lutzes moved out called it "the most evil place" she'd ever been. If that were true, how in the world would the people who subsequently bought the house have lived there for years and years without a single problem or paranormal incident?

The bottom line is, I promise you, the only presences in the Amityville house that the Lutzes experienced, *if they experienced any at all,* were tulpas, inadvertently created by them out of a story that started out as fiction but became nonfiction as they became more and more invested in making it true. And those tulpas left the house and its new owners in peace and followed the couple who gave them life, whether the Lutzes are consciously aware of them or not.

The lesson to be learned from the existence of tulpas is that we really do have to take great care with the thoughts we occupy ourselves with and project. The more we let negativity and fear and evil consume our minds, the more in danger we are of creating a tulpa of our own, to haunt us far more relentlessly than any ghost ever could, and we'll have no one to blame but ourselves.

IMPRINTS

An imprint is an intensely concentrated pocket of energy, a site at which some extremely dramatic event or series of events has taken place with such profound impact that the images and emotions from those events literally become a part of the land and the atmosphere at the site itself. Not only do those images and emotions—grief, reverence, rage, terror, or joy, for example—become self-sustaining over the years, but everyone who experiences the powerful effect of the "imprinted" images and emotions and strongly reacts also lends even more energy to the imprint and helps perpetuate it. If you've visited Ground Zero in New York and felt a deep sense of grief and loss, or been overcome with reverent awe during a trip to the Holy Land, you've experienced an imprint and strengthened it with your own reactions.

I learned the hard way about imprints and the images and emotions that characterize them on a drive home from a brief vacation in Palm Springs. Many of you are already familiar with this story from my book *The Other Side and Back*, but please bear with me for the benefit of the newcomers. And keep in mind that at the time this happened, I had never heard of imprints or of the history of a place called Pacheco Pass.

Pacheco Pass is a stretch of Highway 152 in northern California, cutting through the range of mountains between the inland Interstate 5 and Pacific Coast Highway. My then-husband, Dal Brown, had decided to try it as a shortcut to our home in San Jose, and I had no psychic warnings that we were about to drive into one of the most bizarre episodes of my life.

One moment I was gazing idly out the passenger window of the car, silent and bored. An instant later I felt as if I'd suddenly been slammed into a wall of horrific agony. I was so overwhelmed with panic and desperate emotional anguish that it took my breath away. It made me so frantic that I couldn't even follow my instinct to pray my way back to normal because I couldn't remember how.

I heard a deafening flood of voices, screaming, moaning, primal rage and violence, the sounds of torture and cruel death. Then came the relentless assault of images that looked every bit as real as the landscape around us—covered wagons on fire with children trapped inside; Indians, some in chains being beaten, some circling wildly on horseback; Spanish soldiers gathered around a hanging corpse; Mexicans and Caucasians in bloody mortal hand-to-hand combat; thick black smoke rolling from inside poorly built log cabins. I could smell gunpowder and burning flesh. My husband told me later that I grabbed his arm and kept begging, "Help me!" but I have no memory of that at all. I do remember that it seemed to take hours and hours and many miles for me to be released from that awful feeling of doom and near hysteria, and I was in a deep depression for days afterward.

I was determined to find out what on earth had happened to me, partly because I'm a compulsive researcher and partly because I wanted to know whether or not I'd just plain gone completely nuts. First, during an interview on a local radio station, I gave my office number and asked for anyone to call who'd had any kind of unusual experience in Pacheco Pass. The response was astounding. Hundreds of people called to report everything from inexplicable feelings of panic and impending death to actually gaining and losing time while driving through that one stretch of road. We even heard from the California Highway Patrol, whose files confirmed that the number of car accidents, incidents of road rage, and suicides was consistently much higher in Pacheco Pass than anywhere else in their jurisdiction.

In the meantime, I also learned that Pacheco Pass and the land around it had a tragic and violent history. Indians called it "the Trail of Tears" in honor of their ancestors who were tortured and killed by the Spanish feudal empire that ruled the area at the time and kept them as slaves. Once that empire was overthrown and their slaves were released, the Indians were at war for years with the Mexican bandits who'd come to live in the rough mountain range and, later, with the American settlers drawn to California by the gold rush.

The history of Pacheco Pass was so consistent with the images, sounds, and debilitating emotions that had assaulted me on that seemingly uneventful drive that I began reading and exploring everything I could get my hands on about imprints. And the more I learned about them, the less surprised I became at how easily they're mistaken for hauntings. Both imprints and hauntings can evoke very dramatic feelings when we're in their presence, and imprints often include images of people and animals that could easily be mistaken for ghosts.

The important difference, though, is that the people and animals in an imprint are not earthbound, nor are they even "alive." Think of them as three-dimensional holograms in a movie that never ends, never changes scenes, and never releases the participants or the audience from its emotionally charged grip. The actual participants in whatever created the imprint have long since moved on, to The Other Side, through the Left Door, to other incarnations or to stay at Home forever. Only their images remain, no matter how real they might look and behave. But the one thing that will always set an imprint image apart from a ghost is that an imprint image will never,

ever interact with us, any more than a hologram would, while ghosts, believing they're still as alive as we are, will notice us at the very least and probably do a lot more than that, depending on whether they see us as potential allies or as annoying intruders.

ASTRAL CATALEPSY

You awake suddenly from a sound sleep and find yourself unable to move. You're not sure if you're paralyzed or if some awful, menacing, unseen spirit is on top of you, holding you down, pressing you into the bed, making it hard for you to breathe. It might disturb the bed linens around you while it keeps you there, or, horribly, it might begin touching you in lewd, obscene ways while you lie helplessly, wanting to scream but incapable of making a sound. You may hear a loud buzzing, or a whole deafening clamor of harsh, undefinable noises, and strange lights could appear, hovering above and around you. You're terrified and wondering if you're going to survive this nightmare, until finally, and just as unexpectedly, you and everything around you slowly return to normal.

It's easy to see how that surprisingly common experience could be mistaken for a haunting. In fact, cultures around the world have come up with explanations ranging from alien abductions, to a giant devil pinning sleeping people to their beds with its foot, to an old hag sitting on sleepers' chests and trying to strangle them. Dozens of my clients— bright, normal, educated people who've been too embarrassed to tell anyone but me what they've been going through—have assured me that, against all logic, they're sure that a cruel, ominous spirit is essentially stalking them, terrorizing them in their sleep a few times a month, and they almost plead with me to help them get rid of it.

I'd be happy to, except that there is no menacing spirit involved, no alien or giant devil, or old hag, or any other presence except their own. What they're experiencing is a frightening, very uncomfortable, but ultimately harmless phenomenon called astral catalepsy.

Several times a week, whether we're aware of it or not, our spirits leave our bodies while we sleep. It's as normal and natural to us as breathing, an opportunity for our spirits to astrally visit whomever and wherever they want, on earth or on The Other Side. These astral trips are essential to the nourishment of our souls, and glimmering reminders that our eternal spirits don't just live but genuinely thrive both inside our physical bodies and separate from them as well.

In the course of our sleep cycles during the night, there are times when we're very close to consciousness. And of course there are other times when, even when we're deeply asleep, we can get startled into some level of consciousness. In either case, on very rare occasions, the conscious mind can be alert enough to detect the spirit leaving or returning to the body. When that happens, it might panic, instinctively jump to a wrong but understandable conclusion about what it means when the spirit separates from its earthly "vehicle," and send a signal to the physical body that it must be either dying or dead. The feeling of paralysis, the inability to breathe or speak, and the sensations of imminent danger that go along with sudden, disoriented fear—all the classic symptoms of astral catalepsy—are the result of the body receiving and acting on that signal. The loud, confusing noises are simply signs that the spirit has been on a visit to The Other Side and is crossing back from that dimension to this one, essentially the soul's version of a sonic boom.

There's no guaranteed way to permanently "cure" astral catalepsy if it's something you're plagued with. It's guaranteed to help diminish the frequency of astral catalepsy, though, if, as you fall asleep, you ask God to guide your spirit quickly and easily out of and back into your body without your conscious mind's awareness or interference. Praying during an episode of astral catalepsy will help, too, summoning God and your Spirit Guide and your Angels for their protection until your fear passes. Mind you, they're always around you, protecting and loving you anyway, but it will comfort you to remind yourself of their constant presence, and to reassure your frightened conscious mind that you're really in no danger at all.

BLEED-THROUGHS

Bleed-throughs are fascinating and relatively rare experiences in which the past and the present meet with such force that they actually "bleed" into each other and become one event that, like everything else in eternity, is neither past nor present but is simply "now." During a bleed-through, very real traces of history become part of our reality, while we become part of that same history. Bleed-throughs can easily resemble spirit visits or hauntings. But they're unique in that the visitors who enter our reality during them aren't coming from The Other Side, nor are they earthbound. They're from another time and/or another place, just as we're appearing in their reality from *our* time and place.

Leave it to me to essentially miss my first experience with a classic bleed-through. To understand that, you need to know that I sometimes host sessions in which I trance my Spirit Guide, Francine, so that she can speak to groups using my voice instead of the high-pitched, tinny, chirpy voice she's been using to communicate with me since I was eight years old. It's not that Francine "possesses" me. In fact, I don't believe for a moment that anyone or anything can "possess" any of us. All she does is "borrow" my body for the duration of the session. Since she and I can't both occupy my body at the same time, I basically just "step aside" until she's through. The result is that I never have any knowledge or memory of what went on while I was "gone" and have to be filled in on it later by everyone else. So it was actually not me but Francine borrowing my body and voice who fortuitously orchestrated one of the most epic bleed-throughs anyone could hope for.

It was an Easter service, and Francine was telling a large congregation, in great emotional detail, the story of Christ's crucifixion. She's gifted at making people feel like eyewitnesses to whatever she's describing, and I was told afterward that it was a very wrenching evening for everyone, as if they themselves were kneeling at the foot of the cross, although no one made a sound, knowing that the tiniest distraction can break my trance. There must have been fifty tape recorders running that night, capturing Francine's voice in an otherwise completely silent sanctuary, which made her slow, deliberate, understated narrative even more powerful.

My phone woke me out of a sound sleep early the next morning. That call was quickly followed by five more. All six calls were from people who'd been in the congregation with tape recorders the night before, and, I established later, none of those six people had talked to each other before calling me. But they were all calling with the same breathless message: "You've got to hear this tape from last night."

Forty-four of the tapes made at Francine's Easter service had recorded exactly what everyone in the room at the time had heard, just Francine's narrative against a backdrop of absolute silence.

On the other six, though, Francine could clearly be heard, but so could a heartbreaking chorus of people crying, sobbing, and moaning in the agony of soul-deep grief as the moment-by-moment account of Christ's crucifixion unfolded. I had never heard anything like it, nor had the six members of the congregation who'd brought their tapes to me. We were all shaken by it, not just because the tape-recorded sorrow affected us so deeply but also because we knew that what we were listening to had absolutely not been audible during the service the night before. We couldn't believe our ears, but we couldn't not believe them either. The sounds of a grieving throng were just far too obvious and powerful to be denied.

To suspect these six people of creating some kind of hoax would mean suspecting that the six of them, four of whom didn't even know each other's names, had left the sanctuary with their two-hour tapes in hand and nothing better to do and, in the five hours between the end of the service and the first phone call I received, created identical audio effects on those tapes and then excitedly dashed over to play them for me. Or, these six tapes might have been the result of some kind of electronic malfunction, which would have required six separate tape recorders with exactly the same malfunction.

I swear, there are few things sillier than the lame, idiotic, and utterly ridiculous theories we come up with when we're insisting that something we don't understand must have a "perfectly logical explanation."

So once I'd exhausted every inane "perfectly logical explanation" I could come up with, I finally turned to the most knowledgeable, reliable source of information at my disposal: I asked Francine. And that's when I first heard of bleed-throughs.

A bleed-through occurs when, through a profoundly emotional telepathic empathy with an event from another time or place, two dimensions—for example, the past and the present—meet with such powerful force that they become one timeless happening, "bleeding through" into each other's realities until there's no difference between them. On the night of the Easter service, Francine's telling of the crucifixion was so extraordinarily effective that the people in our congregation in San Jose, California, and the throngs gathered at Golgotha in Jerusalem two thousand years ago, joined in shared sorrow to mourn Christ's agonizing physical death together.

Bleed-throughs can also occur between the dimensions of earth and The Other Side, as I had the enthralling experience of discovering a few years after that memorable Easter demonstration. Again, my apologies to those of you who've already heard this story, but it's too relevant to pass up, and the newcomers will appreciate your patience.

I've been a licensed master hypnotist for thirty years now, and on occasion, during face-to-face readings, I'll hypnotize a client if we mutually agree that it could enhance the depth of the information they're after. Sometimes, at their request, I'll take clients through past life regressions. Other times, I'll let their subconscious minds go wherever they want, while I simply sit by helping them understand where they are and make sure they get back safely. I tape-record every reading, of course, and in the case of hypnosis sessions the tapes serve two purposes: they provide clients with a lot of information they tend to miss out on while they're "under," and they also clearly establish that I never lead, suggest, or manipulate the directions in which those sessions might go. Whatever comes out originates with my clients and never, ever from me.

A client named Susan wanted to use her hypnosis session to visit The Other Side. She started talking from the moment she was fully hypnotized, thrilled and very articulate about the brilliant sights she was seeing as she traveled Home. One place in particular seemed to take her breath away, and she was silent for several moments. Finally I asked, "Where are you, Susan?"

She described a vast, glistening white marble building, domed, with towering pillars climbing toward an impossibly blue sky. And inside, for as far as she could see in any direction, there were aisles, too many to begin to count, filled with shelves upon shelves upon shelves, all of which were neatly stacked with what seemed to be an infinite number of scrolls.

I knew where she was. I had heard every detail of it from Francine, and I had astrally traveled there myself many times. It's a stunning structure on The Other Side called the Hall of Records. It contains all the great historical and literary works ever written, the chart of each lifetime of each human being who ever lived on earth, and even the sacred Askashic records, which are essentially the written memory of God. I didn't say a word, I just let her keep talking and exploring her awesome surroundings.

This has never happened to me in another hypnosis session, before or since, and to this day I'm still not sure what caused it. Maybe it was my familiarity with the Hall of Records, coupled with Susan's articulate and very emotional description of it as she began to walk through its massive aisles, emotion I found contagious. But whatever the reason, all I know is that suddenly I realized that I wasn't just listening to Susan's trip to the Hall of Records, I was actually there with her, standing beside her among those endless, breathtaking aisles. I caught my breath, but I still kept my mouth shut, even when Susan interrupted her narrative with a pleasantly surprised "You're here with me."

Along for the ride now, I simply followed Susan's lead and let her guide us both through one aisle after another, taking in the splendor of this gorgeous landmark back Home. After several moments I saw a woman, beautiful and dark haired, dressed in blue gossamer. She was walking toward us, and I psychically knew her name was Rachel and she was Susan's Spirit Guide.

"Someone's with us," Susan said. Yes, she and I were definitely taking this trip together.

"Who's with us?" I asked.

"It's a woman," she told me. "She has dark hair. I don't know why, but I think she's my Spirit Guide."

It was then that Susan's Spirit Guide Rachel noticed us. "Susan!" she called out.

Susan gasped. "Did you hear that?"

I asked her what she'd heard.

"She said my name," Susan told me, her voice trembling with excitement.

She was in awe at meeting her Spirit Guide. I was still in awe at the step-by-step validation that somehow I'd been taken along to be an eyewitness to their reunion.

But Susan and I still had one more surprise ahead of us when the session ended. We both wanted to relive that moment when she first saw her Spirit Guide, so I rewound the tape to the point where I said, "Who's with us?"

"It's a woman. She has dark hair," Susan's taped voice repeated. "I don't know why, but I think she's my Spirit Guide."

Our mouths both dropped open when, an instant later, a crystal clear third voice on the tape said, "Susan!"

Another bleed-through—another convergence of two different dimensions—caught on tape. Not a visiting spirit, not a haunting, but a miraculous variation, rare, as I said earlier, but so worth watching for.

ASTRAL TRAVEL

Very early one morning several years ago in California my friend and cowriter Lindsay Harrison was wakened out of a sound sleep by the sound of her mother's voice, insistently repeating her name over and over again. She sat up and looked around, almost surprised not to see her mother standing beside her bed. Her mother, Fern Underwood, was alive and well in Iowa two thousand miles away, mind you, but the voice seemed too real and too present to have been imaginary. After a minute or two of confusion, Lindsay finally decided she must have been dreaming and went back to sleep.

She wouldn't have given it another thought, except that later that morning her mother called her at work and startled her with a simple question: "Did I wake you up this morning?"

Fascinated, Lindsay said, "Yes, actually, you did."

"I'm sorry," Fern replied. "I was meditating about you, and somehow all of a sudden I just knew I'd made contact with you. Did you happen to notice what time it was?"

"Four-thirty, thanks a lot," Lindsay told her, feigning annoyance.

Fern sounded fascinated, but she wasn't pretending. "That's exactly right, it was six-thirty here. I checked. Well, again, sorry. I'll try to be more careful next time."

I know Fern. She's an incredibly spiritual woman. She's also one of the most down-to-earth people I've ever met, and she'd be the first to assure you that she's not psychic, nor does she have special powers of any kind. She just happened to take an astral trip to check up on her daughter without even meaning to.

It's simply a fact that, awake or asleep, deliberately or inadvertently, our spirits prove that they don't have to wait until death to take off from our bodies and go traveling wherever we choose, here on earth, on The Other Side, or anywhere else in the universe. In their natural, God-given state, our spirits are free, able to transport themselves from one place to another by thinking themselves there, able to visit anyone they want whenever they want, able to even bilocate and be in two places at once if they feel like it. Practical as human bodies are for incarnations on earth, they're also very limiting and confining. It's no wonder our spirits insist on escaping their confines from time to time and take off for reunions with people and places they miss. They do it for spiritual nourishment, they do it for the joyful exercise of it, and they do it because nothing comes more naturally to them.

If, while you're sleeping, you dream that you're flying on your own power, and/or that you visited some loved one on earth or at

Home, chances are it wasn't a dream at all, it was an astral trip, your spirit going out to play. If, while you're awake, you're meditating, or in a deep daydream, and return to consciousness feeling as if you actually went away for a few minutes and perhaps even looked in on someone important to you, chances are that's exactly what you did. There's nothing all that strange or mysterious or controversial about it. In fact, I don't even consider astral travel to be "paranormal." Considering that we all came here as spirits from The Other Side and will return there as spirits when our bodies give out on us, I happen to think astral travel is as "normal" as it can be.

Lindsay's and Fern's experience illustrates the truth about a common misconception when it comes to spirit visits and hauntings—namely, that we can miss out on some marvelous and very real spiritual connections if we wrongfully assume that such reunions with loved ones are only possible when one of us is dead. Next time you have the odd feeling that you've been a visitor to someone or somewhere here on earth, or that you've heard, seen, or just perceived a visitor who you know perfectly well is alive, don't be quick to dismiss it as your imagination. (According to my Spirit Guide, Francine, we'd do ourselves a great service by eliminating the word "imagination" from the dictionary, because it's far too easy an excuse for far too many legitimate and significant experiences.) The visit may not always be as clearly announced or as clearly received or as easily validated as Lindsay and Fern's was, but that doesn't make it any less authentic.

Never doubt for a moment, either, that loved ones who are very ill or comatose can pay visits to you and welcome your visits as well. No matter how debilitated our bodies get, or how incapable of conscious communication, our spirits are eternally thriving and able to travel anytime and anywhere they want. Take heart from the story of a client of mine whose husband of forty years is in the last stages of

Parkinson's disease. He'll be hospitalized for the few weeks he has left in his life, he's completely bedridden, he's barely able to speak, and he no longer recognizes her. As a sheer leap of faith, she continues talking to him, reading the news to him, and confiding in him as if he's able to understand every word—which, I've promised her, his healthy, happy spirit deeply appreciates. In the meantime, she's been finding small piles of coins in the most conspicuously impossible places in her house and car, a favorite signal among visiting spirits to get our attention. But in my client's case, it isn't a spirit from The Other Side who's leaving coins for her. It's her husband's spirit, taking off from his helpless shadow of a body, letting her know he's right there with her, reciprocating for all the brave, loving acknowledgment she's giving him.

Again, then, if you've been passing up chances to go visiting, or dismissing signs of a visitation because you know perfectly well that your alleged visitor is alive and well, remember that, thanks to astral travel, by no means do the dead have a monopoly on spirit reunions.

KINETIC ENERGY

You're in your kitchen, making breakfast for your family, when suddenly and shockingly, the cupboard doors begin flying open and slamming shut again on their own. The appliances roar to life, from the garbage disposal to the dishwasher to the toaster oven, as the refrigerator swings open and the food inside is sent hurtling across the room. Frightened, you race into the normalcy of the rest of your house, only to hear the TV come blasting on all by itself and wildly change channels. Lights blink on and off. Your computer shorts out, your printer begins spewing out paper as if it's possessed, and you're desperately reaching for the phone to call for help when it leaps off the desk and falls to the floor, static blaring from the receiver.

A very ornery ghost, trying to chase you out of your house? Maybe. But it's just as likely, if not more so, that you've just witnessed a dramatic display of kinetic energy, caused not by some external force but by you or a member of your family who's either blessed or cursed, depending on how you look at it, with kinetic energy.

Kinetic energy is the unintentional, spontaneous manipulation of inanimate objects through no obvious physical means. It causes its possessor to become kind of a walking force field through no fault of their own. There are several theories about what creates kinetic energy. (And, of course, many skeptics will swear that it doesn't exist at all, which I would be happy to consider if I hadn't witnessed it with my own eyes so many times.) Some believe that kinetic energy can just appear in a person from out of nowhere and then vanish just as inexplicably. Others believe, as I do, that it's a power some people are born with and others aren't, a power that strengthens and weakens in irregular cycles through the course of a lifetime.

Kinetic energy is often at its strongest when the body is going through dramatic hormonal changes—during prepubescence or puberty, for example, or in pregnant or menopausal women. But it can manifest itself in young children, too, as my family, friends, and staff who've known my granddaughter Angelia since she was born can attest to. For several years, starting when she was only three or four years old, we couldn't let her anywhere near office equipment. She could simply walk through a room and leave crashed computers, shorted-out fax machines, and dead copiers in her wake, not to mention a bank of ringing phones with no callers on the other end. She's ten years old now and not nearly as kinetically chaotic as she used to be, but I'm already starting to brace myself for her entrance into her teenage years, which is when my son Paul's kinetic energy hit its peak. In his case, just as he was hitting puberty, he would inadvertently cause all his shoes to zoom around his bedroom like missiles, thudding against the walls, every night as he fell asleep. Today, in his adulthood, Paul's incidents of kinetic energy are virtually nonexistent, and it remains to be seen whether or not they'll return.

And in case you're wondering, Paul and Angelia are the only two members of my family in at least three generations who were born with kinetic energy. Between them and the many other cases I've witnessed and studied, I frankly think it's more likely than not that kinetic energy is *not* an inherited phenomenon, that its occurrence is much more random than that. I almost wish it weren't. If it were more traceable it might be more widely understood and not mistaken so often for either hauntings or, preposterously, satanic possessions.

So if you or someone you know seems to make all hell break loose with inanimate objects by doing nothing more than just walking into a room, remember, it's no one's fault, it's neither a physical illness nor a mental one, it has absolutely nothing to do with evil, it doesn't require an exorcism, and it's not some kind of punishment. It's only a spasm of innate, unintentional kinetic energy, and I guarantee, it will pass.

VISITORS FROM THE HALL OF RECORDS

When we think of spirit visits from The Other Side, we naturally assume that we're being visited either by departed loved ones or by our Spirit Guides, whom our souls recognize even when our conscious minds don't. But there are other spirits from Home who might appear from time to time and thoroughly confuse us, not only because we've never seen them before in our lives but also because their reasons for coming here have nothing to do with us at all.

Earlier I mentioned the magnificent Hall of Records back Home, where our charts are meticulously housed and where every word of written history is preserved. It's a favorite destination of astral travelers from earth, one of the places we get most Homesick for. But it's also one of the most popular sites on The Other Side, the library of libraries, providing access to an infinite wealth of documents, including those whose "originals" have been burned, buried, or destroyed here on earth. Knowledge is one of our passions on The Other Side, and researching our endless areas of interest at the Hall of Records is a perpetual joy.

We have a variety of choices when it comes to researching in the Hall of Records. We can simply read all the documents we want, of course. We can "scan" them, watching their contents unfold before our eyes like a life-sized, three-dimensional hologram. We can listen to them, in an audio version of scanning, essentially radio in "virtual reality" form. Or, we can actually "merge" with the documents themselves, paying a firsthand visit to the events the documents describe, experiencing and assimilating all of the emotional and sensory details that were a reality to every participant in that event. We can live the first moonwalk through the eyes of the astronauts, feeling their exhilarated awe. We can see, hear, smell, and tremble with fear in the chaotic horror of the attack on Pearl Harbor. We can sit in reverent, humble silence listening to the Sermon on the Mount or know to the core of our beings the adrenaline-charged thrill of playing in the first Super Bowl. And because access to the documents in the Hall of Records is unlimited, we can also merge just as easily with the chart of any person who ever lived, from one of our own ancestors to Leonardo da Vinci to Marilyn Monroe to Babe Ruth to Thomas Jefferson.

What's relevant, and fascinating, to those of us on earth about spirits' ability to merge with the documents in the Hall of Records on The Other Side is that the spirits who choose that research option are very likely to put in actual, very real appearances in the charts or events they've chosen to explore. Please don't let the examples I gave mislead you into thinking that the patrons of the Hall of Records are only interested in researching events and people that we here on earth classify as important. In the context of God's creation, there is no such thing as trivial, or unimportant, or "nobodies." Some event of great curiosity to someone on The Other Side could have happened a thousand years ago on the land your house sits on. Someone who's considering an upcoming incarnation with a chart similar to yours might choose to merge with some circumstance in your life as an example of how they might handle it, differently or the same, depending on what they're hoping to achieve. Remember, there are billions of spirits on The Other Side, all of whom are on an eternal quest to learn everything they can about everything there is to know. There's not a person, a place, or a moment here on earth that someone at Home can't learn from, which is why the Hall of Records is so treasured by the "locals." It's also why, no matter who we are, where we go, or what we do, we might catch a glimpse of a strange spirit, or feel their presence, and either mistake them for a ghost or dismiss them because we don't recognize them to be a departed loved one of ours. The truth is, they're just friendly strangers, passionate researchers, dropping in from the Hall of Records on The Other Side to become a momentary part of our reality. And before you let them frighten you, or resent the intrusion, just remember that as soon as you get Home again, you're going to be heading straight to the Hall of Records to do the very same thing. So give them the same greeting you'll want to look forward to.

ANIMALS

Years ago my then-husband and I were living in a second-floor apartment with a large window that faced the street. To my frustration, there was a strict no-pet policy in the building, and believe me, it took every ounce of self-control for me to adhere to that policy in the short time we lived there. So I had very little patience when our landlord suddenly began passing along complaints from a couple of other tenants about our keeping a cat in our apartment. No matter how many times I resentfully assured him that we didn't have a cat, and no matter how many surprise visits he paid in the hope of finding the alleged cat or cat supplies, he continued to insist that we weren't fooling him, he knew we had a cat, because other tenants had seen it, sitting in the window, staring menacingly out at passersby, the end of its tail twitching as if it was ready to pounce right through the glass at any moment.

"What does this cat we don't have supposedly look like?" I finally demanded on his billionth or so complaint call.

"I've never seen it myself," he said, "but according to the people who have, it's a huge black cat with yellow eyes."

It took me a second, but when it hit me I laughed in spite of myself. I tried to imagine his reaction if I'd explained that the "huge black cat" the tenants were so upset about was a panther, in spirit form, just doing its job standing guard and protecting my husband like every other totem does. Needless to say, I didn't bother, I just assured him we'd take care of it, and we did, by moving to a house shortly after that conversation.

When each of us is preparing to come to earth for another incarnation, we choose several protectors to watch over us on our rough journey away from Home. In addition to our Spirit Guides and any number of Angels, we also recruit the animals of our choice to be our loving companions and guardians. Those animals are called our totems. I'd known for years that my husband's totem was a panther, but I'd never seen it, he'd never seen it, and I'd never known of anyone else who'd seen it either. Come to think of it, I owe a long-overdue thanks to those outraged tenants for the unsolicited validation that totems are perfectly real and, to some, perfectly visible.

And then there was a haunting I investigated once at a house in North Carolina. My research team and I explored the entire house for a few hours, and then I set up camp by myself in the room that was rumored to be the hub of all the paranormal activity the owners had allegedly experienced. I locked the door, turned on my ever-present tape recorder, and waited. And waited. And waited. All through a long, boring, uneventful night of complete and total silence.

The next day, on the way home, I decided to play the tape from the night before, planning to kind of half listen to it in case there was some subtle momentary disturbance in the relentless silence that I might have somehow missed. But instead of hour upon hour of silence, I found myself listening to a tape on which, every few minutes, I could hear the loud, agitated, somewhat threatening barking of what sounded like a very large dog. It seemed impossible. I certainly hadn't heard a peep out of a dog, or of anyone or anything else, the whole time I was in that room. There were no two ways about it, though, that persistent barking had been captured loud and clear on tape, as if a dog had spent the night right outside the window a couple of feet away from me.

My research team talked to all the neighbors and even the local police about the barking dog while I talked to the owners of the house I'd investigated. The owners, who had lived in the house for many years, couldn't recall ever having heard a barking dog in the area. Not only had the neighbors heard no barking the night before, but they'd never heard barking there, and to the best of anyone's knowledge, the closest family who even owned a dog lived more than a mile away. There was no earthly explanation for the unmistakable evidence that a big dog with a deep, loud, serious voice had spent the night barking so nearby that my tape recorder caught it while no one else heard a thing. No *earthly* explanation.

And so, of course, I asked for an explanation from Francine instead.

It seems that several lifetimes ago, I owned and very much loved a white bull mastiff, a huge, powerful breed of dog known for its fearless and protective nature. This bull mastiff and I have remained devoted to each other ever since, and according to Francine, he still accompanies me from time to time on potentially risky adventures to warn away anyone who's even thinking about doing me any harm, and he was there taking care of me on that long, supposedly uneventful night in North Carolina.

I wish my conscious mind remembered him, but I can't wait to reunite with him back Home. And there's not a single doubt that I will, just as we'll all find every pet we've ever had and loved, from every life we've spent on earth, waiting to welcome us the instant we emerge from the tunnel back into the blissful, divine love of The Other Side.

Make no mistake about it, not only do animals head straight Home when they die, but they also tend to get there much more quickly and efficiently than we do, unburdened as they are by all the excess emotional baggage we humans carry around. Animals' spirits are perfection, created that way by God and eternally staying that way, which is why they don't reincarnate—they exist in a state of grace, already knowing all they need to know before they ever come here, so they have no need to return to earth again and again and again. They can and do visit us constantly from The Other Side, loving us unconditionally as always and knowing we'll be together again. We should be so lucky as to understand the eternity of the soul with even a fraction of the uncomplicated clarity animals do.

Just as animals don't reincarnate because of their spirits' simple, unquestioning, all-knowing, perfect relationships with God, they also never remain earthbound. There is no such thing as a ghost animal, no such thing as the confusion and mistaken priorities and fear that sometimes frustrate humans' ability to embrace the tunnel and gratefully release another brief time on earth. Animals, every one of them, make it Home in the blink of an eye the instant their spirits leave their bodies, and believe me, that's not just wishful thinking on the part of an impassioned animal lover, it's an absolute promise.

So next time you see or sense the spirit of an animal around you, remember, there's not a chance it's a ghost, there to haunt or frighten you. It might be your totem making itself known. Or it might be the spirit of a beloved pet, from this or some other lifetime, adoring and watching over you with that total, uncompromised acceptance we humans can only aspire to.

Throughout the rest of this book you'll be reading a lot of ghost and spirit-world stories—many of my own, and many that you were generous enough to send. It's my hope that you'll refer back to these first two chapters often, to help you fully understand the extraordinary experiences that will unfold in the upcoming pages, and the experiences you've had and will have that might confuse or frighten you if you don't have enough information to make sense of them. Knowledge really is power, after all, and the more the better.

And so, ideally armed with more knowledge than you had when you first opened the cover of this book, let's explore together our mutual thrilling, fascinating, mysterious, sometimes comforting, and sometimes terrifying visits with the afterlife.

Chapter Three

GHOSTS I'VE KNOWN
AND LOVED

Many of you know the story of my first one-on-one, clear-as-a-bell, no-way-around-it spirit encounter. I was eight years old, alone in my bed one night, when a glow of light cut through the darkness and the slightly vague form of a tall, slender, serene woman with long black hair stepped toward me from the core of the light. "Don't be afraid," she said. "I come from God." I ran screaming to my grandma Ada, who calmly explained that I'd just received a visit from my Spirit Guide. Her name was Ilena, but I changed it to Francine for no apparent reason, and like all Spirit Guides, she's been my closest companion and advisor every minute of every day of my life this time around.

To the best of my memory, though, I don't think I've ever written about my first ghost encounter, a brief introduction to a dimension between earth and The Other Side that would become one of my passions from that moment on.

It was 1945. I was nine years old, and thanks to Francine and Grandma Ada I'd now become fairly accustomed to my ability to see and communicate with the spirit world. My father had moved our family into a wonderful seventy-five-year-old Queen Anne–style house on Charlotte Street in Kansas City, a magical place with an attic, a basement, a butler's pantry, and enough nooks, crannies, and alcoves to seem full of endless secrets. Early one Saturday afternoon a few weeks after we settled in I came bounding out of my bedroom to find an elderly man with a white beard and a handsome gold-braided uniform standing in the hallway. He wasn't quite solid enough to be earthly, but he was more distinct than any spirit I'd run across so far, and I was fascinated by him. He seemed pleased that I could see him and smiled at me. His speech was slower and not nearly as high pitched as the spirit voices, particularly Francine's, that I'd begun hearing on a daily basis when he uttered the single word "Basement."

I was exactly as cautious and circumspect at the age of nine as I am today. In other words, I don't even think my feet touched the stairs as I flew down them to search the basement for any mysterious surprises that might be waiting there. It didn't take long to notice that in the middle of a wall of rough-hewn whitewashed stone was one smooth stone that didn't quite fit and whose mortar looked uneven and hastily applied. I found a small pickax on a wall rack of rusted tools and, with one good solid swing, easily punctured a large hole in the smooth stone, revealing a hollow space behind it. My heart was pounding as I reached into that dark space with one hand, braced to find anything from a chestful of jewels to a hidden stash of money. I let out a quiet gasp as my hand groped its way to a thick bundle of paper. Cash. Piles and piles of paper money. What else could it possibly be? I'm sure I was already trying to decide where to start shopping when I pulled out the first handful and gazed at my own private treasure.

I was crestfallen. It wasn't cash at all. It was nothing more exciting than a stack of folded papers, all but one of which crumbled into dust in the palm of my hand, right along with my dreams of being an independently wealthy nine-year-old.

The one small, fragile document that remained intact seemed to be a handwritten essay, folded in thirds like a pamphlet. What may have once been a title had long since faded into sparse, unreadable pen strokes. But I could still read the name "Captain Frederick Bonneville" in a proud, flowing script. The brief essay that followed, from what I could make out, was an expression of outrage by Captain Bonneville against the violent intolerance of the Ku Klux Klan and a plea for an end to bigotry and injustice. My hero, I thought, smiling, and I hurried back up the stairs to find my grandmother, show her the pamphlet, and tell her about the uniformed old man with the white beard who'd directed me to it.

And that was the day I got my first lesson from Grandma Ada about those poor earthbound souls called ghosts, lonely, trapped, not knowing they're dead, and wondering who all these strange intruders are who keep acting as if they're not even there.

Not long after that we learned from neighbors that the house was originally owned and loved by a sea captain named Frederick Bonneville. A few grainy photos existed of Captain Bonneville standing in front of his house, casually dressed but unmistakably a much younger version of the bearded man in uniform who greeted me in the hallway that Saturday afternoon and gave me such a pleasant, courtly introduction to that dimension between earth and The Other Side where ghosts live, unknowingly waiting to go Home.

Again, that was in 1945, when I was just a very psychic child who wanted nothing more than to be a "normal" wife, mother, and schoolteacher when I grew up. Sooner or later I accomplished the wife, mother, and teacher goals. I've so long since given up on "normal" that I'm not even quite sure what that word means anymore.

But finally, inevitably, I committed my life to what I knew in my heart was the greatest good I could offer: my psychic gifts, infused and elevated by the full force of my spiritual passion. One of the countless results of that commitment was the Nirvana Foundation for Psychic Research, which I created in 1974 to formalize my explorations into the paranormal. And it was through the Nirvana Foundation that I officially hung out my shingle as a "ghost hunter," investigating hauntings around the world, the real, the imagined, and the out-and-out frauds. It's work I love and work I'll continue for the rest of my life, trying to give back some fraction of the enlightenment and affirmation it's given me.

It didn't take long for the requests for haunting investigations to start pouring in. Almost thirty years later, they still haven't stopped.

The Brookdale Lodge

I was asked by *Sightings*, a TV show produced by Henry Winkler, to investigate rumors of paranormal activity at the Brookdale Lodge in northern California. At my request, no one told me the specifics of that activity, but I was filled in on the lodge's fairly chaotic history—from what I understood, it had been burned to the ground, abandoned, and sold, bought, remodeled, sold again, and remodeled again. That wasn't the fault of any ghosts or spirits who might be hanging around, and it certainly couldn't be traced to a curse, since curses don't exist. It was just a curious bit of information I made a mental note of. It's not unusual for perfectly sane, well-meaning people to hear a few odd facts about a place and start filling in blanks of their own at the first sound of a creaking floor or unexpected slam of a door. The truth is, very often floors creak because that's just something floors do, and doors can blow shut in a subtle breeze without a ghost or spirit having anything to do with it.

And so, with a handful of my staff members in tow armed with cameras and tape recorders for our own documentation, I headed off to the Brookdale Lodge with no clue what to expect. I was happy to hear that some of the lodge employees were going to be there to either validate anything I might experience or tell me they didn't know what I was talking about. I can't emphasize enough that I never pretend to see, hear, or feel something I don't actually see, hear, or feel, with or without television cameras rolling. I'd give up my career in a heartbeat if the only way I could keep it going would be to fool people. If you doubt that, just ask anyone who's ever tried to involve me or my name in any kind of scam. I've worked far too hard for far too long and been through far too much to play games with my integrity, let alone sit quietly by while someone else tries to jeopardize it.

The lodge—originally the headquarters of a lumber mill more than a century ago—was charming, nestled in the mountains with giant redwoods standing guard all around it. As we arrived, went through the rounds of introductions, and got our bearings, it seemed like the most benign, restful, undisturbed place on earth. Someone suggested I start in the dining room, known as the Brookroom, where many of the strange noises and unexplained sightings by both employees and guests seemed to be centered, and by the time we reached the doorway I had successfully tuned out all the people and equipment around me, and as far as I was concerned, I stepped into the dining room alone.

No wonder it's called the Brookroom. There's a brook, an actual mountain creek, flowing peacefully right through it, every bit as captivating as it sounds. My sense of being alone quickly vanished when I heard childish laughter and looked to see a little girl, maybe six or seven years old, playfully running beside the creek, a woman I assumed to be her nanny in hot pursuit. Suddenly, to my horror, the child ran too close to the railing of a small footbridge, lost her footing, fell, and very violently hit her head. Aware as I was that I was witnessing a kind of time-warp "instant replay" of an event that had happened many, many years before, the impact was painful to watch.

I glanced behind me just long enough to realize that no one but I could see this child and her nanny, and by the time I turned around again the little girl was standing in front of me.

"Are you all right?" I asked her.

She nodded.

She was far from all right. I knew she had actually just reexperienced the sequence of events that killed her. But before I could explain to her that she was dead and help her go Home, she happily announced, "I'm Sarah, and that's my nanny, Maria." She pointed back toward the creek, to the woman I could no longer see. And with that, she let out a playful giggle and ran away, quickly disappearing among the dining room tables and chairs.

I asked the lodge employees if anyone had ever heard of a little girl named Sarah. Several of them exchanged looks before one of them volunteered that sometime around 1950, a six-year-old child named Sarah Logan, who was the lodge owner's niece, drowned in the dining-room creek.

I assured them that Sarah was still there, probably the source of a lot of noise and mischief like any other six-year-old, and her nanny had stayed behind as well, undoubtedly to take care of her as she had in life. Sure enough, it turned out that countless guests, employees, and owners had been seeing and hearing Sarah for decades in almost every room of the lodge, most especially in the dining room where she died. I appreciated the validation. And then, as directed, I eagerly headed on to what they called the ballroom, another reported source of strange activity in this intriguing place.

I heard music before I even entered the room, distant and indistinct, but swing music, I remember thinking, from the big band era. I asked if a radio or stereo system was turned on anywhere in the lodge but was assured there wasn't. Then I asked the crew and lodge employees around me if anyone heard music. They all listened for a moment and shook their heads, except for one employee, whose eyes widened a little with some combination of recognition and relief.

"I don't hear it now," he said, "but I've heard it late at night, coming from this room, after we close. I never told anyone because I thought it was just me."

"Don't worry, it's definitely not just you," I said, and then I stepped on into the ballroom.

I would love to give you a description of the room itself, but frankly, I didn't notice much about it. I was too focused on the man who was waiting inside, staring at me, expressionless. He was very heavy set, with a moustache, a thick head of hair, and glasses that rested far down on his nose. No one else saw him, although a few crew members felt a sudden cold breeze.

I made eye contact with the man and said hello. He grunted, unsmiling.

"What's your name?" I asked him.

He seemed annoyed, either with the question or with my intrusion in general. Finally he muttered the word "Judge."

"Your name is Judge?" I was trying to sound friendly, but he was having no part of me and wouldn't even grunt a reply. "Or you are a judge? Or you think I'm here to judge you? I give up, what does 'judge' mean?"

"Judge," he said again, and then began repeating that one word over and over again, increasingly impatient. It wasn't the most scintillating conversation I'd ever had, and I wasn't too thrilled with him either. I decided to try warming him up with a kind of we're-all-friends-here approach.

"I met Sarah and Maria earlier," I offered. "Do you know them?"

He nodded. And then, just like that, he disappeared.

When we finished shooting, I assembled a small prayer circle in the center of the ballroom to pray that the spirits of Sarah, Maria, and Judge be released into the white light of the Holy Spirit, to be embraced by God and their loved ones on The Other Side where they belong. All in all, a fairly successful investigation, but definitely not dramatic enough to prepare me for the once-in-a-lifetime experience that followed. And believe me, once in a lifetime was more than enough for me.

My staff and I were headed for the door when something made me look down at myself. To this day I have no idea what that something was, because I certainly didn't feel anything unusual. But there, unmistakably and very conspicuously, covering the whole front of my blouse, was a white sticky substance. It was thick, it was odorless, and it was disgusting. My staff gathered around to gape at it, as mystified as I was about what it was, when it had appeared, and where it could possibly have come from. I hadn't eaten anything. I hadn't had anything to drink. If I'd brushed up against anyone or anything that was covered with whatever this was, there's no way I wouldn't have noticed, and who brushes up against something with nothing but that area between their neck and their waist?

Someone—it might have been my right-hand man, Michael— said out loud what I'm sure the rest of us were thinking: "Don't look now, but I think you've been slimed."

For those of you who didn't see the movie *Ghostbusters*, being "slimed" means finding yourself drenched with ectoplasm from a ghostly encounter.

And what exactly is ectoplasm? According to the dictionary, ectoplasm is "the outer relatively rigid granule-free layer of the cytoplasm usually held to be a gel reversibly convertible to a sol." And cytoplasm, of course, is "the organized complex of inorganic and organic substances external to the nuclear membrane of a cell and including the cytosol and membrane-bound organelles."

Isn't that enough to make you sorry you asked?

Basically, for our purposes, ectoplasm is thought to be the tangible residue of cell energy that's transmitted between a spiritual medium and a ghost. One school of thought is that when ectoplasm is present during or after an encounter between a medium and an earthbound, it's actually emanated by the medium—in other words, something about the energy that passed between me and Judge caused my own ectoplasmic substance to ooze to the surface of my skin, possibly to lend enough power to Judge to help him materialize so clearly. I'm hardly an authority after only one experience with ectoplasm, but I don't believe that theory. I felt then as I feel now that Judge, closemouthed as he was, was a very forceful entity who was still attached enough to our dimension that his energy actually took on the physical form of ectoplasm, and I may have just been standing too nearby when it happened.

So there it was, my first and only exposure to ectoplasm, assuming that's what it was. Everyone who witnessed it that day, including me, has tried unsuccessfully ever since to come up with any other possible explanation for what it was that ruined my blouse. (You don't really think I was going to try to explain to my dry cleaner what those stains were.) But ectoplasm or not, it was real. Several people saw it, touched it, grimaced over it, and could confirm that it was definitely nothing I'd done to myself. Physical proof of ghost encounters being hard as it is to come by, I can honestly say getting "slimed" was worth it. Once.

The Vineyard House

It was at the request of a syndicated television show called *In Search Of* that I investigated a barrage of reported paranormal activity at an historic inn and restaurant called the Vineyard House where, it is proudly boasted, Ulysses S. Grant once made a speech.

The four-story Vineyard House, complete with ballroom, was first built in 1878 by Robert and Louise Chalmers as an homage to their brilliant vineyards, their equally brilliant wines, their financial wizardry, Robert's political talent that led him to the California state legislature, and Louise's self-proclaimed flair for all things elegant and cultural. For reasons that have never been clear, although a series of strokes and dementia might be a good guess, Robert suddenly suffered a complete mental breakdown, in response to which Louise kept him permanently chained in the cellar of their home, where he died three years later.

The vineyard and the Chalmers' financial holdings went straight downhill from there, and Louise was ultimately reduced to renting out rooms to boarders and leasing out Robert's former quarters in the cellar as a kind of spare jail when all the cells in the nearby town of Coloma, the capital of California's gold-rush territory, were filled. She finally died in 1913, alone and without a dime to her name.

After several decades of only mildly interested temporary owners and a lot of neglect, the well-intentioned old house was invested in by owners who had the patience and respect to appreciate its potential, and in 1956 it became the inn and restaurant that now exists.

From the moment the Vineyard House became a business, it's impossible to say whether it was the workers or the guests who were more aware of the unexplainable noises, activities, and even a rare sighting or two throughout the mansion. Invisible chains rattled throughout the night. Skirts rustled, footsteps echoed on wooden stairs, a woman wandered the halls talking quietly to herself, and no one who looked for the source of any of the virtual orchestra of sounds had ever found anyone to attach them to. A piano played by itself. One very drunken, noisy group came crashing through the front door late one night and went stumbling up the stairs toward their rooms, laughing loudly. A very disgruntled guest near the stairway, awakened out of a sound sleep and not happy about it, stuck his head out the door to his room to ask them to keep it down, only to see the three drunken, laughing men, all in clothing from some other era, slowly disappear into thin air before his eyes. Doorknobs turned, glasses slid from one end of the bar to the other, and beds went from made to unmade, all on their own power, with plenty of human eyewitnesses gaping in disbelief. One terrified couple fled the inn and immediately reported to the police that they'd heard a murder being committed in the room next to theirs. The police rushed to the room in question within minutes to find it not only completely peaceful but also completely unoccupied.

I try to go into haunting investigations with a completely open mind, but I have to admit, that wasn't easy on this one. Because I was doing this my way but on the timetable of *In Search Of*, I went in with far more information than I like to have, and the thought of a woman chaining her mentally ill husband in the basement to die frankly made me wish ghosts weren't already dead—if this woman really was around haunting the place, I was already having fantasies of chaining *her* in the basement for a while to see how she liked it. I'd already decided that if I had too much trouble with her, I wouldn't hesitate to summon my Spirit Guide, Francine, who at the very least can keep a cool head at moments when I'm ready to explode.

It was immediately apparent that Louise was very much around, and so was her husband, Robert. I'd caught a brief glimpse of a woman in a white chemise in an upstairs window as we arrived, and I couldn't be sure it was Louise. But their ghosts were in that house as surely as I was, hopeless and entrenched, with a feeling in the air that we were in *their* home, we could come and go as we pleased, but they weren't going anywhere, and nothing I could trot out of my nice neat bag of God/white light tricks was going to change their minds.

What caught my attention and fascinated me, though, was that this wasn't the usual ghostly stubbornness and confusion I'd run across so many times over the years, or a couple of Godless souls being defiant. Somewhere in the atmosphere of this house and the beings who refused to leave it, even if it cost them the sacred joy of Home they were entitled to, there was great love in this place, and, beyond that, I was shocked and curious to discover, there was kindness. As so often happens when you only have part of a story, I'd filled in a few too many logical, rational blanks on my own and come up with some wrong conclusions. It was time for me to wipe the emotional slate clean about what had gone on between Louise and Robert Chalmers and start over. And just to make sure I kept my own judgments out of it completely this time, I decided to go with my earlier instinct of letting Francine take over.

We went to an upstairs bedroom, where there was a brass bed and a window facing the entrance to the Vineyard House, the window where I'd seen the woman in the white chemise. As I've explained so often you're probably tired of hearing it by now, when I step aside to channel Francine, I'm absent and unaware of everything she says and everything that goes on. The excerpts that follow are from the tapes of her that were made by my Nirvana Foundation staff and a few newspaper reporters who were there as well. The tapes didn't air on *In Search Of*, nor would I for an instant want to mislead you into thinking they did. If I remember correctly, *In Search Of* was a half-hour show, and as I said, what I'll be giving you now are excerpts, not the full transcript. Francine had a lot to say that day, she doesn't edit herself, she should never have to edit herself, but it's Lindsay's and my job, and my publisher's job, to keep this from becoming a two- or three-volume book.

I think I settled in on or beside the brass bed near the window. I don't remember who all was in the room working cameras and sound and lights, but I do remember a reporter named Richard Winer being there. One of my staff who knows how to help me into a trance stepped up to me and put her hand on my shoulder. The tape will have to take over from there.

FRANCINE: Before the Chalmers came here, this ground was owned by a family named Bartlett. They gave refuge to people, slaves, who were running from plantation owners, escaping from the South to the North. When the Chalmers built their mansion, they kept that area in the cellar. It was never built to be a jail. It was a safe hiding place for these people escaping to the North. This house has a great history of many vibrations. Much of the laughter people hear is from the slaves who had finally made it to refuge. I know Sylvia thinks that it was just from Louise and Robert entertaining when times were good. Part of it is that. But part of it was the slaves, because they were so happy to be here. There is also a whistling sound that can be heard. That is from Mr. Chalmers, who had a horse who came to him when he whistled.

Louise still walks these premises. In fact, she is standing to my left right now. She's five feet four inches in height, wearing a white chemise, and her hair is down, although she usually wears it up. She can become very angry that someone has invaded her property, but she will not hurt anybody. She had a tremendous affliction with her stomach, a spastic colon that really bothered her through most of her life and did not put her in the best of humors, especially when the doctor used to come and bleed her. She also had a child who died at birth, and she and Robert shared that grief together. You may ask people who have been here if there are windows in this place that keep breaking. There is a splinter in one now. She used to get so frustrated that she would break furniture, and the sound of splintering wood can be heard, and sometimes a part of the furniture would go through a window. Her frustration was because of Robert, but not for the reasons people think.

When Robert's mind became ill, he also developed tremendous sores on his body that she tried to heal, herself, by using certain peppermint root plants that grow wild in this area, and lemons which she tried to put in a lime concoction with garlic. That's why at different times throughout this place, you will have a very strong, pungent odor of acidity and garlic. Because she tried to make poultices. She was terribly afraid to have a doctor come in, for fear the doctor would take him away. She took him to New York, around the turn of the century, to try to get some help for him. They wanted to incarcerate him. She kept saying, over and over again, "He will not be locked in a pesthole." She brought him home, and he had another spell, about five hundred yards outside this window. He fell off his horse and went into a seizure. She and four males took him down to the cellar room with bars on it, to keep him confined and safe, and she tried to give him as much comfort as she possibly could. It was the only way she knew to protect him from being locked away in filthy asylums full of madmen. It was a hard, lonely life for her, but she couldn't bear the thought of him living in chains among strangers who didn't care about him, frightened and abused until his death.

It was a tragic story of two people who were very much in love. He was very handsome, tall, and strong. She was very beautiful, with an hourglass figure, very white skin, jet black hair, and black eyes with heavy lashes. She was a very gifted woman. She wrote, she painted, and in the late hours she would play the piano.

There is nothing Sylvia or anyone else can do to neutralize this room, or this place. Many have tried. But you see, what you have here is what you people call a stalemate. Robert is still earthbound and therefore still in a state of derangement that prevents him from understanding his situation. So he won't go. And if Robert won't go, Louise won't go. It is as simple as that. It is as loving and kind and tragic and simple as that.

We're very aware of Robert and Louise on The Other Side. There are many of them, and we watch out for them. Someday, in God's wisdom and grace, we will get them and bring them back with us, where they will be healed and happy. Until then, this is where they choose to be, for the reasons I have explained, and this is where they will stay.

That was more than twenty years ago. As I was writing these pages I asked Francine about Robert and Louise. She tells me they're still at Vineyard House, but "it won't be much longer." What's frustrating is, to Francine, who's got a firm grip on the context of eternity, "it won't be much longer" could mean that it might be decades or even centuries before she and a legion of spirits find the opportunity to rescue Robert and Louise and bring them Home. As I point out to her fairly often, I'm still on earth, where if "it won't be much longer" goes on for more than about two weeks, we run out of patience. She listens, and then goes right on with her own timetable. Luckily, she lived one lifetime on earth. She remembers how flawed and silly and frantic it can get being human.

And I must say, my experience at the Vineyard House, and with Louise Chalmers in particular, was a good eye-opener for me. I marched in thinking, What kind of woman locks her poor mentally ill husband up in the cellar? I never dreamed the answer would turn out to be "An incredibly strong, loving woman who, knowing how the mentally ill were treated in most institutions at that time in history, was doing the only thing she knew to do to keep him safe."

It's literally true that I've read the Bible more times than I can count, and it very clearly says in that great book, no matter which version you read, "Judge not, lest ye be judged." (Matt. 7:1)

Which just goes to show that if you're going to read the Bible without *living* the Bible, you might as well not bother.

The Slaughter House

I know what you're picturing. It's exactly what I was picturing when I was asked to investigate a reported haunting at a place called the Slaughter House in the San Francisco Bay area, and it's exactly why I declined the invitation and promptly hung up. But the caller tried again, and hurriedly explained that the Slaughter House was just a nice, modest residence with an unfortunate nickname. The husband and wife who were living there were being terrorized by a presence they truly believed might harm them.

"Why don't they just move?" I asked.

"They can't afford it" was the reply.

Now, that I could relate to. If someone had suggested I move at that point in my life, I couldn't have afforded it either. It struck a sympathetic enough chord in me that I heard myself say, "I'll be there," before I had time to talk myself out of it.

For the record, I did ask where the name "Slaughter House" came from. I got a vague answer about a homicide in the house five or six owners ago, or a double homicide, or rumors of a homicide. I sat through fifteen or twenty seconds of stammering and guessing before I relieved the caller with a humane "Never mind."

The couple who owned the house were serious about getting to the bottom of whatever might be going on there. Almost as soon as I stepped out of my car in the driveway, I had a swarm of people strapping infrared cameras, heat sensors, and other equipment around my body. They started to explain what it all was. I politely assured them I didn't care. "You do your job," I told them, "and I'll do mine."

The house really was as modest and innocuous-looking as I'd been assured it was, and the owners, whom I'll call John and Mary, were as sweet, attractive, and "normal" as they could be. We sat in the front room for a few minutes so that they could give me some idea of what they'd been through. Besides the usual unexplainable noises, footsteps, and cold spots, and the occasional sighting of awful faces at the windows, their biggest complaint would have unnerved me too.

"We'll both wake up in the middle of the night to find a man standing over our bed," Mary told me. "He has this wild, insane look of pure hatred in his eyes, as if finding John and me together has outraged him. He even grabbed my arm once. I can still feel his hand on my skin, it was amazingly strong and ice cold."

"And I saw him do it and couldn't do a damned thing about it," John added. Then he looked at me for a long moment, almost studying me. "You know, you're very brave."

"What makes you say that?"

"Well, no offense," he said, "but we've had a few other psychics here trying to get rid of whatever this is, and none of them even stayed this long."

I wondered what I was missing. I hadn't sensed a single thing so far. "That surprises me. There's nothing in this room at all," I assured them. I stood, ready and eager to get to work now, and headed into the kitchen. Nothing there either. Into the small separate dining room. Still nothing. And on into the hallway, where, without feeling it coming for one second, I walked right into a cold spot. Not just any cold spot either. This one went right to the bone. I could see my breath, in an un-air-conditioned house in the middle of July. Apparently the machines strapped around me went berserk, because one of the technicians urgently stepped toward me, looking concerned. I waved him away and proceeded on down the hall until I arrived at the master bedroom.

In every haunting there's a "heart," a place from which all the paranormal activity emanates. In this haunting, that heart was the master bedroom. I could feel the highly concentrated energy like a force field the minute I stepped through the doorway. I walked to the bed and sat down, so focused on what I was doing that I was oblivious to all the people and equipment and noise around me. All I was aware of was my heart pounding, more from adrenaline than fear, and the growing awareness of a strong, deeply troubled presence approaching me.

I first saw him outside the window, looking in at me, not one bit sure if he wanted me there or not. He was very handsome, with thick dark hair. I made eye contact with him and held it to let him know that, yes, I could see him perfectly, and, no, he couldn't frighten me away. Then I simply said, "Come in."

Suddenly he was standing in front of me, taller and broader than I first thought. He was holding a scythe with a rough wooden handle, its long crescent blade looking old and used but still sharp enough to do damage. I deliberately didn't react to it, just continued making eye contact with him, and either he respected me for it or he was relieved that finally, after a long, long time, someone wasn't shrieking at him, frightened out of their wits. He gave a small, almost courtly nod.

"My name is Giovanni," he said. "What's yours?"

I told him, remarking to myself how rarely I meet a ghost with good manners. He kept staring at me, and I accurately guessed that he wanted me to keep talking to him. "What are you doing here?" I asked.

He spoke in a clear, quiet voice. "I'm sad because my wife is gone."

The instant those words came out of his mouth I was flooded with a rapid-fire montage of images in what seemed like less than a second. Another bed in this same room. A dark-haired man in the bed, not Giovanni but resembling him. A dark-haired woman in the bed with him. Both of them sleeping soundly. And then, Giovanni, eyes as cold and soulless as a shark's eyes, advancing silently toward the bed, the scythe in his hand, raised high above his head.

I'm sure I didn't seem to miss a beat, though, and I kept my face impassive, looking directly at him, "Giovanni, did you kill someone?"

He began to weep, speaking as best he could through wracking sobs. "It was wrong what my brother Anthony did. I brought Maria here from Italy to be my wife, and while I was out in the hot fields they were in here making love. I made them both sorry that they did this to Giovanni."

"After you killed them, what did you do next?" I asked, very quietly and without a trace of judgment.

"I ran away," he confessed. "I hid in the hills for a long time. Then I got very sick and felt very hot, and that's the last thing I remember."

In other words, he ran away with nothing but the blood-covered clothes on his back, disappeared into the cold, damp winter hills near the bay, and, without realizing it, died of pneumonia. I broke that news to him, explained to him that he'd trapped himself here on earth, and assured him that it was time for him to go on toward the light now so that he could be at peace.

He shook his head, ashamed and frightened. "I can't face God. He'll never forgive me."

"I don't know anything about a god who never forgives, Giovanni. My God is all loving, all knowing, all-forgiving, and embraces every one of us who holds out our arms to Him." He looked at me, taking this in. It wasn't the first time I'd met an earthbound spirit who was deliberately avoiding the tunnel and the light that would take them Home because they were sure they'd done something unforgivable in God's eyes. It wouldn't be the last, either, and few things break my heart more. There's no question that sooner or later, in some lifetime or other, we have to make things right in our own souls, to spiritually "balance the books" when we've intentionally wronged someone. But that's because our spirits are genetically programmed to ultimately seek their highest potential and their greatest good. God doesn't see to our eventually making things right. We see to it ourselves, with His guidance, His constant, patient, unwavering, unconditional love, and His powerful faith in us.

I spent almost two hours explaining all that and more to Giovanni. I reminded him that only by moving on could he free himself from the hell of guilt in which he'd imprisoned himself. At best, he'd join his wife and brother on The Other Side and learn firsthand that they'd long since forgiven him. In fact, in the perfection of The Other Side, there is no anger, there are no grudges, and everything is understood in the context of eternity. At worst, Giovanni would come right back to earth in utero and spend a lifetime making amends for the lives he took. Either way meant progress. Either way was a step toward liberating himself from the awful burden he was carrying. Either way there was hope, while the nonlife he was living now held no hope at all.

Finally, and with some reluctance, Giovanni agreed to go. He looked at me for one more nod of reassurance and then said, "You'd better be right." With that, he disappeared. And according to subsequent phone calls and letters from John and Mary, neither Giovanni nor any other earthbound spirit ever bothered them or set foot in the Slaughter House again.

As a postscript, I experienced another first that day. I was walking back to my car, exhausted and ready to go home, when a member of my staff said, "Sylvia, look at your arm." There on my upper right arm was a perfect trine, a very distinct equilateral triangle etched into my skin like scratch marks. Never before or since have I been marked or injured in any way during a haunting. I've investigated hauntings in which people claim to have received some fairly nasty wounds, but somehow, magically, the wounds seem to have healed by the time I got there. I know there was no mark on my arm before I entered that house, I know it was there when I left, I know that at no time during my hours with Giovanni did he touch me, I know it was nothing I did to myself, and I know it disappeared as quickly as it appeared.

So where did that perfect trine come from? Was it the manifestation of some kind of energy transfer from Giovanni to me, or from his dimension to mine? Was it a sign from the Holy Trinity that they were there protecting me, or supporting me in my efforts to convince Giovanni to move on? After all these years of research, study, and experience, I don't have a reliable explanation to offer.

Which means that there are still more questions to answer, still countless mysteries left to explore. And frankly, I wouldn't have it any other way.

IRELAND

If you're fascinated by ghosts and want to increase your chances of seeing one, I recommend a tour of Ireland, and the British Isles in general. I don't know of anywhere else on earth where ghosts are more plentiful. It may be the relatively damp atmosphere, which is as efficient as it gets for conducting spirit energy. It may be a rich, treasured history that makes spirits cling more fiercely to the earth when their bodies die. Or it may just be that ghosts are widely accepted, appreciated, and almost assumed to exist there, making them feel perfectly welcome to appear.

Whatever the reason, the ghosts pretty much upstaged the humans on my most recent trip to that enchanting, enchanted country. I was there on vacation, to rest, relax, and regroup after an especially busy year of readings, lectures, TV appearances, and tours. You'd think that sixty-six years of being psychic would have taught me by now that for me the words "time off" have limited meaning.

It started in Dublin, in the Merrian Hotel's cellar restaurant. I was studying the menu when, out of the corner of my eye, I noticed a woman with short dark hair, wearing a maid's uniform. When I looked directly at her she became downright perky and stepped up to me.

"My name is Maryann Sullivan, and I'm glad you can see me," she offered with a warm smile.

Before I could respond, a waiter arrived to take my order. I wasn't quite ready to discuss food yet. "You know, you have a ghost," I told him. "She moved here in 1772 and died several years later of tuberculosis."

"Yes, we've all seen her," he answered with complete nonchalance. "So tell me, what may I bring you for dinner?"

I can't begin to tell you how refreshing it was to see such an unruffled lack of either skepticism or astonishment at the news that we were in the presence of a ghost. And I heard that same tone of cool composure a few nights later at a dinner party at my friend Peter's house, when a woman named Edna informed me, "I have a ghost."

"Yes. A Franciscan monk," I replied.

The ghost didn't amaze her, but my knowing about him did. "How did you know?" she asked.

"Because I'm psychic."

"But you haven't even seen my house."

"True, Edna," I said, "but I still know who he is. He fell in love with a local girl, and he was so afraid he would renege on his vow of celibacy that he hung himself. Since he believes he'll go to hell if he moves on, he's decided he'll just stay here. His name is John Fitzgerald."

It turned out that Edna had already summoned the local vicar to send her ghost on his way, but the vicar wouldn't release him unless he knew his story. Now that she had her ghost's name and the relevant part of his history, Edna and the vicar could release John Fitzgerald into the pure white light of God's forgiving, unconditional love, a love John had never lost and never could.

A few days later I moved on to the west Ireland town of Cong, where I was honored to be staying in Ashford Castle, an exquisite ninth-century masterpiece that, it turns out, was featured in the classic John Wayne–Maureen O'Hara movie *The Quiet Man*. The instant I stepped through the massive entry doors and gazed out over the moat and the breathtaking grounds, I felt as if someone had waved a wand and whisked me back to some other lifetime in some other world.

I was shown to my room, with a view that took my breath away, and promptly decided that, even though I'm an inveterate coffee drinker, it would be terribly chic and sophisticated of me to order up a pot of tea instead. I called the front desk and came dangerously close to affecting an accent as I made my request.

"In fact, madam," replied a voice that sounded exactly like Sir John Gielgud, "we're serving high tea. Would you care to take it in the drawing room?"

High teatime. Who knew? So much for chic and sophisticated. But I was so charmed by the invitation to "take it in the drawing room" that I didn't care. Suddenly I was no longer Sylvia Browne in a pair of rumpled slacks, no makeup, and hair yanked into an unceremonious clump on the back of my head. Now I was Lady Sylvia, about to float gracefully through the castle to the drawing room in a gown Cinderella would have killed for.

I entered the wood-paneled drawing room, trying not to gape at the impossibly huge twinkling chandelier and the embroidered antique wingback chairs, took a seat by the window, and realized for the first time that I was the only guest there. I ordered tea and scones from a pretty waitress, then settled back to lose myself in the tranquil view of swans gliding on a glassy lake, and rolling hills that truly were the color of emeralds. Suddenly, inside the drawing room, in my peripheral vision, there was a quick flash of pink chiffon.

See what I mean about time off? Who was I kidding?

She was absolutely beautiful. Her hair was long and golden. The pink chiffon was her soft opaque nightdress. I knew her name was Lady Arlington Humphreys. She didn't look sad, just a little confused. She smiled slightly as she crossed through the room and out the door.

"Do you know you have a ghost here?" I asked the waitress when she returned with my order.

Once again, that refreshing nonchalance. "Yes, did you see her?"

"She just walked by," I said.

The waitress simply nodded and shrugged. "We see her almost every day, just around teatime."

I finished my tea and scones without incident and was standing to head back to my room when a strange wave of exhaustion hit me right between the eyes. I immediately recognized what it was. It had nothing to do with being tired. It's a feeling that's occasionally washed over me all my life, a signal that there's been a subtle change in the atmospheric energy, that something's about to happen and that I need to pay extra attention. I've long since learned to just go with it, let my instincts guide me, and stay out of my own way. So when I walked through the foyer, wanting nothing more than to go back to my room and collapse on the bed, and instead found my instincts aiming me straight toward one of the many doors that encircled this vast entryway, I didn't even bother to put up a fight.

I'm glad I didn't. I stepped through that door into one of the most magnificent libraries I've ever seen. The walls, from floor to ceiling, were gleaming wood shelves filled with countless books. Red leather chairs surrounded a seven-foot-tall fireplace. Persian rugs complemented the marble floors. I wondered in passing if anyone would mind if I quietly moved into this room and just stayed there for the next twenty or thirty years.

The lighting was dim, and it took my eyes a few moments to adjust. Only then did I noticed an old gentleman sitting in one of the overstuffed leather chairs. He wore a red smoking jacket and had white hair with a hint of red running through it. He was clearly very proud of his impeccably groomed muttonchops and waxed handlebar moustache. He held a book in one hand and a handkerchief in the other.

I tried to get his attention by clearing my throat, but he ignored me. Then he coughed harshly, covering his mouth with his handkerchief, and when he finished I could see spots of blood on the monogrammed white linen. He'd died of tuberculosis, I realized. I slowly walked toward him, hoping he might talk to me. He sat very still, getting my hopes up, but when I was only a couple of feet away, he disappeared.

I never got his name. It turned out I didn't need to. The castle staff knew exactly who he was. "We see him all the time," one of them told me. "He died here just before he had to forfeit his castle. We think that's why he doesn't want to leave."

Looking back, it's possible that I owe an apology to the dear ghosts I met in Ireland, because I didn't release a single one of them to The Other Side, nor did I even try. Intellectually, I know that there's a void, and a hopelessness, in being earthbound, a constant open wound that only embracing the sacred light at the end of the tunnel can heal. But there was something about the ghosts in Ireland— maybe just the fond, respectful acceptance of the humans who coinhabit the country with them—that made them seem almost content, to the point where I found myself thinking it would be presumptuous of me to disturb them. Instead, for better or worse, I left them to the spirits on The Other Side, far wiser and more powerful than I am, who can be counted on with absolute certainty to someday bring all the world's ghosts Home.

KENYA

I love Kenya. That's a fact about me that's as etched in stone as my height and the color of my eyes. I love the people. I love the animals. I love the smell of its air and the feel of its earth beneath my feet. I've loved it from first moment I stepped off a plane many years ago and saw it for the first time, that moment you've probably experienced, too, when you arrive in a brand-new place and know to the core of your soul that you've been there before, in some other life, and that somehow, against all logic, you've been homesick for it.

My first ghost in Kenya appeared while I was visiting there with my friends Dr. Ian Stewart and his wife, Robbie. I awoke one night out of a sound sleep to find a woman standing in front of me. Her eyes were wild with fear, and she was covered with blood. She was so real that I let out a loud gasp.

Alexander, the *iscari*, or guardian of the house, was sitting beneath my window. *"Mama, missouri-sana?"* he called out, asking me in Swahili if I was all right. At the same time Alexander's guard dogs started barking like crazy. The still air felt electrified, and I felt the hair on the back of my neck prickle as the woman abruptly vanished.

"Alexander!" I called back. "Something is terribly wrong!"

"I know, *Mama*," he answered. "The dead walk tonight."

There was no way in this world that I was going back to sleep that night, so I got out of bed, made tea for Alexander and myself, and went outside to sit with him until the sun came up.

"I saw a woman," I finally said.

He nodded and looked at me. "Me too. It happened too fast. She is not at rest."

My friend Ian called from his office that morning, very agitated. It seems there was a violent coup during the night. Among other atrocities, dissidents had stormed the home of one of the Moi dignitaries and killed his wife with a panga, a huge knife designed to cut through thick jungle brush.

Alexander and I looked at each other, stunned, knowing without a word passing between us that our night visitor had just been identified. When the phone call ended we prayed together that the poor woman wasn't trapped here, that we'd somehow just seen a glimpse of her on her way Home into God's arms.

I found myself watching Alexander while we prayed, by the way, so moved by him that the words of the prayer caught in my throat. This sweet man, my vigilant guardian, whose faith in God was as deep and sure as any saint's and whose interaction with the spirit world was as natural to him as breathing, would be looked at as "primitive" by the standards of any "civilized" society.

We should all be so primitive.

A few years later my then-husband and I were off to Kenya again to see Ian and Robbie. This time we headed to Tree Tops and Keekorok, a lodge off the Serengeti. Our first night there I was startled out of a sound sleep by someone bumping my bed. I sat bolt upright and found, standing at the foot of the bed, a beautiful, extremely upset East Indian man in a white turban and an orange Nehru-style jacket. He had materialized so solidly that for a moment I thought he might be part of the lodge staff. When I caught on that, no, this was indeed a ghost, I reached for my husband, wanting to include him in this experience. He either couldn't or wouldn't wake up. So I turned my full attention to the Indian man, who was almost in tears.

"Mem-sahib," he addressed me with impeccable courtesy, "please, you must help me, I am so afraid for my family. I know you can see me."

"Yes, I can see you, and of course I'll help you, if you'll tell me how," I said.

He was wringing his hands, trembling. "They're coming for us. We will all be dead by morning."

I decided against breaking it to him that it was too late, that he and his family were already dead. Instead, knowing that his family had safely made it to The Other Side, I opted for trying to panic him into looking for them, in the hope that in his frantic search he'd end up at Home before he knew what hit him.

"Then leave!" I yelled urgently. "Go! Find them and get out of here!"

With that, he instantly disappeared. My husband began to snore. As Montel says so often, "An ex is an ex for a reason."

The next morning at breakfast I was eager to tell Ian, Robbie, and my husband all about it. They listened politely and patiently, not disbelieving me but not completely convinced, either, until the maître d' stepped up to the table.

"Forgive me, mem-sahib," he said to me with a slight bow, "but I couldn't help overhearing your story. Are you aware of what happened on this very spot almost twenty-five years ago?"

I shook my head.

"A group of rebels from what was thought to be an offshoot of the Mau Mau descended on the town and brutally massacred the East Indian population. It was a great tragedy."

My breakfast companions were now gaping at me. One by one I gave them each a quick I-told-you-so glance, then gave the maître d' an incredibly generous tip. For sheer timing alone, it was worth every dime.

I never saw the man in the Nehru jacket again, but I still find myself thinking about him from time to time. I'm not sure why he had more of an impact on me than so many other ghosts. Maybe it's because it's rare to see a ghost as solid and distinct as he was. Maybe it's because he was so selfless, staying behind in search of his family instead of caring about nothing but saving his own skin. Or maybe it's because I can't begin to imagine what a raving lunatic I'd be if I couldn't find my family during some life-threatening crisis. In preparation for writing this chapter I asked my Spirit Guide, Francine, if she could locate him. She did. He's safe, healthy, and happy on The Other Side. Whoever "talked him over," I'm eternally grateful.

UPDATES

There are a few hauntings I've written about at length in previous books that have especially captured readers' hearts as well as my own. Since my editor, Brian Tart, hates it when I repeat myself, I won't go into as much detail about them as I have in the past. But because I have updates to give you about them, because I get asked so often about them, and because no chapter called Ghosts I've Known and Loved would be complete without them, I'll write the short versions of these stories so that all of you, even if you're new to my books, will know who I'm talking about when I fill you in on their latest news, or lack of it.

The Winchester Mystery House

In late 1884, Sarah Winchester, heiress to the Winchester weapons fortune, began building what is undoubtedly one of the most bizarre houses on this planet. A team of spirits she talked to every night in her blue séance room convinced her that a curse had been put on her, and that the only way she could escape the clutches of this horrible curse would be to build a house so huge and so insanely complicated that the evil spirits sent to inflict the curse would be unable to find her.

The result was a colossal monstrosity in San Jose, California, in which it's thought some 750 rooms were built, destroyed, moved, rebuilt, destroyed, and built again, 160 of them standing in architectural madness to this day. Hallways lead to dead ends. Staircases descend into brick walls. Secret passageways and hidden doors line miles of confused corridors, some of which are only two feet wide, others of which turn back into themselves like a self-defeating maze.

I suppose a case could be made that Sarah's plan to hide from this awful curse worked, since she died very unceremoniously of natural causes when she was eighty-five. But I think the Sarah Winchester story makes a far better case that the only person who can put a curse on you is *you*, by believing curses are possible in the first place. By spending her life trying to escape from a curse, she created a self-fulfilling prophecy, cursed by nothing but her own frantic paranoia and all the money in the world to indulge it.

Needless to say, when I was asked to investigate reported hauntings at the legendary Winchester Mystery House, I leapt at the opportunity. Off the top of my head, I would have bet that Sarah Winchester herself was still wandering the house in earthbound form, since all logic pointed to that probability—her terror of dying could easily have made her refuse to face it when she really did die, and her excessive attachment to that house had classic potential to trick her into thinking she'd rather be here than on The Other Side.

So much for logic.

Sarah Winchester is alive, well, and happy at Home, a thriving spirit who put in only one very brief appearance at a second-story window during a television show I filmed long after my initial introduction to the house.

Still visible, roaming the Winchester Mystery House, though, as diligent, loyal and protective as ever, are two of Sarah's employees. They showed up the night I did my first investigation there and identified themselves as the caretakers. It wasn't a friendly introduction. By all accounts, Sarah Winchester was very fair and kind to her staff, to the point where even death couldn't compromise their commitment to her. I was an intruder. They both glared at me, and the man growled, "Get out." But they never took a step toward me or posed any kind of physical threat, and they kept disappearing before I could free them from tending to a woman who was no longer there and tell them they have a wonderful reunion with her to look forward to on The Other Side if they'd just let it happen.

I've never given their names in print before, but I'm doing it now, in the hope that someone can validate the information. He was a large Nordic-looking man named Emile Hausen. She wore a white bandanna tied around her dark hair, and her name was Susan Hanna.

A niece of the Winchesters thinks she might remember someone named Emile working for the family, but she isn't sure enough to confirm it. That's the closest I've come to verifying that a Susan Hanna and an Emile Hausen were employed by Sarah Winchester in that impossible house. If you can come closer, I would love to hear about it. And whether or not you can help validate their identities, please include them in your prayers to help send them Home. They're still in that house, hard at work, eager for the approval of a woman who's long since moved on.

The Brown Lady

About a year ago I got a call from a lovely man at the BBC. It seems that the Brown Lady, one of the most famous and often-seen ghosts in England, had disappeared.

"No one's spotted her in months, Sylvia. It sounds silly to be worried about someone who's already dead, but we miss her and wondered if you can tell us what's happened to her."

The Brown Lady is generally thought to be the ghost of Lady Dorothy Walpole, sister of England's first prime minister, Sir Robert Walpole. The story goes that Dorothy's husband, a man named Viscount Townshend, discovered that before they were married, Dorothy had had an affair with a Lord Wharton, which Viscount Townshend found reprehensible and unforgivable. He promptly locked her in her suite of rooms at their home, Raynham Hall, where she died at the age of forty in 1726. Depending on which account you believe, she died of either smallpox, a broken heart, or a broken neck from her husband pushing her down the massive stairway in the Raynham Hall foyer. After her death she continued to walk the hallway and grand staircase at Raynham Hall, dressed in the long brown brocade gown that inspired her nickname, trying desperately to find her five children, whom she never saw again once her husband locked her away.

From commoners on tours of Raynham Hall to ranking officers in the British army to King George IV, who after one night vowed never to spend another hour in that "accursed house," people have been treated to the Brown Lady's unapologetic appearances since at least 1849, when sightings of her were first documented in writing. In 1936 a reputable photographer named Captain Provand and his assistant, Indre Shira, were hired to do a pictorial essay of the historic castle for *Country Life* magazine. Late one afternoon they were passing the grand stairway when they looked up to see what they described as a "misty form," in the shape of a woman, descending the stairs. Thinking fast, Provand raised his camera and managed to get a fascinating portrait of the Brown Lady's misty form that's often been called "the world's most famous ghost photo."

After becoming so familiar with her and genuinely fond of her since 1849 if not earlier, it's no wonder the British were concerned that no one had seen the Brown Lady of Raynham Hall for a suspiciously long time. As I told the gentleman from the BBC, I don't doubt that they'll miss her, but they have good reason to be thrilled for her. The Brown Lady is a perfect example of intervention from The Other Side. After almost three hundred years of being earthbound, despite a lot of earnest efforts to "talk her over" from here, the Brown Lady was rescued in late 2001 from her trapped, hopeless existence, as all ghosts will eventually be, by compassionate spirits, surrounding her with the full force of their loving, sacred power to take her Home.

The Toys"R"Us Ghost

There's no ghost my clients and readers ask about more often than Johnny Johnson, who's been haunting the Toys"R"Us store in Sunnyvale, California, since his death in 1884. He's a classic case of a ghost caught in a time warp—he's hard at work at his handyman job, tending to the Martin Murphy ranch that thrived on that same land a hundred years ago. He can't figure out for the life of him (excuse the expression) where all these loud, rambunctious children keep coming from who tear up his freshly planted vegetables, having no clue that the children are actually playing up and down the aisles of the toy store that sits there today. In fact, his complaints about children gave me one of my first opportunities to validate Johnny Johnson's existence for the Toys"R"Us store manager.

"Those twin boys who came through here a while ago were hellions," Johnny grumbled one afternoon. "Running around, screaming and yelling, like little animals, almost fell in the creek. I've never seen anything like it."

I casually asked the manager if by any chance a pair of twin boys had been in the store that day.

"Were they ever," he said, shaking his head. "Hell on wheels, those two, and their mother doesn't do a thing about it." He stopped suddenly, cocking his head a little. "Wait, that was hours before you got here. How did you know?"

"Your ghost told me," I smiled, and he was a believer from that moment on.

Johnny Johnson during his lifetime was a young itinerant Presbyterian minister who boarded at the Murphy ranch and was deeply in love with his employer's daughter Beth. Completely unaware of his feelings for her, Beth married another man and left the ranch to settle with her husband in Boston. The night I first met him in 1978, Johnny was still busying himself around "the ranch," believing with all his heart that someday Beth would come back to him. I started telling him all those years ago that Beth was dead, that he was dead, and that all he had to do to reunite with her was go to the light of God that was waiting for him. He got so tired of hearing it that one day he snapped at me and said, "If you don't stop telling me I'm dead, I'm never going to talk to you again." I decided that keeping the lines of communication open between us was better than nothing, so I've never mentioned it again.

A few weeks ago, so that I could write as recent an update as possible, I went back to the Toys"R"Us in Sunnyvale. I was so encouraged when I first arrived to find that Johnny was nowhere to be seen. I even felt my heartbeat speed up a little at the thrilling possibility that he'd finally taken my word for it and gone Home to find Beth and so many other loved ones who were waiting for him.

But a few minutes later I walked around the end of a far aisle and there, several feet away, near the back wall of the store, was Johnny Johnson. He was limping painfully as always from the wound to his leg that had killed him, raking an invisible pile of leaves beside a stream that no one else can even remember, let alone see. I asked him how he was, and he nodded without looking up, too busy earning his keep on the Martin Murphy ranch to take time out for idle chitchat. Out of respect, I decided not to bother him and left the store.

And so, until the spirits on The Other Side manage to retrieve him, I feel sad but safe in saying that if you've always wanted to see a ghost but haven't been sure where one is likely to appear, just go to the Sunnyvale Toys"R"Us and look for a tall, very slender man with a limp, dressed in work clothes, a lost, heartbroken look in his eyes. Say hello to him with an understanding smile on your way past, and above all, remember him in your prayers.

Chapter Four

THE GHOSTS WHO
HAUNT YOU

As I said in the Introduction to this book, I asked you to tell me about your experiences with ghosts, and I was grateful but not surprised at the hundreds upon hundreds of letters that flooded my office. I can sit on national television all day long and insist that ghosts are very real and very much among us, but I'm easy to dismiss—I'm psychic, after all, and therefore probably nuts. All of you who wrote to me, on the other hand, prove just by speaking up that good, decent, hardworking, God-fearing "normal" people are having ghost encounters on a fairly regular basis.

If you find yourself doubting that fact because none of your "normal" loved ones have ever mentioned anything to you about seeing a ghost, please ask yourself this: What would your response be if they did come to you with a story like that? Would you make them feel foolish, or perhaps shameful, for even suggesting such a thing? Sadly, that's not uncommon. I received letter after letter after letter thanking me for extending the invitation to talk about ghost experiences because either "no one else will take me seriously" or "I was raised to believe that ghosts and people who claim to see them are evil and in league with the devil." To be honest, when it's all said and done, I think not taking someone seriously when they're confiding in you, or judging an experience as evil for no other reason than that you don't understand it, is more foolish and shameful than any ghost story could ever be.

If you know me or my work, you know that I'm a firm believer in the value of open-minded skepticism, probably because I happen to be an open-minded skeptic myself. So as you read this wealth of experiences from the almost two thousand letters I received in the past few months, be as skeptical as you like about the stories as long as you're fair. But don't for a minute be skeptical about the sincerity of the people who wrote in. Not only did each of them mean every word, but the vast majority of them started or ended their letters with a phrase you might find yourself saying someday when you're hoping someone will take you seriously—"I would have bet any amount of money that never in my life would anything like this happen to me."

My husband and I didn't notice anything unusual when we first moved into our rented house. And when I started hearing noises, and thought I saw someone out of the corner of my eye even though I knew I was home alone, I convinced myself it was my imagination, until my husband confessed that he was hearing noises too. He also admitted to occasionally sensing a presence in our bedroom.

One night he swore he felt someone sit next to him on the bed, and it frightened him so much that to this day he insists on sleeping in the middle of the bed. I began having such intense feelings of being watched, and of a pressure at the foot of the bed, that it would wake me out of a sound sleep, and I would cover my head and pray to God to protect my family and me.

Not long after that incident with my husband, I woke up to what sounded exactly like a woman in high-heeled shoes walking around in my kitchen. I told my husband about it the next morning, being careful not to say anything at all when our little girl was in the room, because neither of us wanted to upset or frighten her. But later that day she asked me why I was up during the night walking around in the kitchen with my high-heeled shoes on.

Two weeks later I ran into a cousin I've been close to all my life. He told me about a dream he'd had in which he was at my house and there was a woman with black hair walking through the kitchen wearing high-heeled shoes, and then she flew into a hole in the floor.

He was laughing. I wasn't. I hadn't told him about the sounds my daughter and I had heard, nor had I told him about a hole that had recently appeared in the kitchen floor that we were having repaired.

The last straw was the day I went for a walk with my mother. I made a point of turning off the TV before we left the house, so I was shocked when we returned home, and before we'd reached the front door, we could hear music blaring from the living room stereo I hadn't even been listening to. Not only was the music almost deafening, but as we stepped inside I actually saw the stereo being turned off. My mother was afraid and quickly left, and I announced out loud to whoever or whatever was there that if there was a message I was supposed to be getting, I would listen to it in Jesus' name or not at all. I started talking to the presence whenever I heard or saw anything odd, and while the conversations were always one sided and I never did get a message that I know of, I must admit that I never felt threatened by the presence again.

We no longer live in that house. I heard recently that the current occupants are having some bizarre experiences surrounding the kitchen, and it made me wonder all over again who that presence was and what it wanted.——L.P.

The presence was a ghost, a woman named Clara Nugent, who was murdered in the kitchen of a previous version of that house many decades ago. She fit the description of the woman in your cousin's dream—black hair, tall, a long, pale, slender face, one of those people who perpetually looked as if they were almost under more stress than they could handle. Interestingly, she was wearing high heels when she was killed, running across the linoleum floor, when her heel caught in a hole in the linoleum, causing her to stumble and allowing her assailant to catch her and stab her to death.

Clara Nugent is a classic case of a ghost whose death was so violent and sudden that she had no idea she'd died. In her perception, she was still very much alive and going about her business, and she's been very confused about these intruders who were moving in and out of the house ever since, ignoring her, treating her as if she's not even there while refusing her pleas for protection from this man she's so justifiably frightened of. The good news is, Clara Nugent has very recently been embraced into the safe, eternal peace of Home by loved ones who've been watching her, so I would bet that the current occupants and everyone who lives in that house from now on will be sadly disappointed if they lie awake hoping to hear the ghostly sound of high-heeled footsteps crossing quickly across the kitchen floor in the middle of the night.

I once spent a night at the Miami International Airport waiting for a connecting flight to Argentina. It was deserted, around 2:30 or 3:00 A.M., not a soul in sight, and all the seats around me were empty. I was so immersed in the book I was reading that at first I didn't even notice the man who suddenly appeared and sat down next to me. When I did notice him I was immediately annoyed and uncomfortable, wondering why he'd insisted on sitting beside me when there were literally hundreds of vacant seats in plain sight. Then he asked me a question. I don't remember exactly what it was, but I do remember that it was personal, and I stood up to walk away and said, very sharply, "Why don't you leave me alone?"

His reply was "You know, I am the devil," and he let out a loud laugh that gave me a chill. After I'd walked about twenty steps from him I glanced back to make sure he wasn't following me and he was no longer there. I looked everywhere, but he was nowhere to be seen. That gave me even more of a chill—even running at superhuman speed, there was no place for him to hide or disappear to in those vast, empty, echoing, endless hallways.

Twenty-five years later I'm still uncomfortable about it. I've told my wife and my mother about it but no one else, until now, because I know I can count on you not to laugh. I've tried a thousand times to convince myself that I was asleep and dreaming, or so jet lagged that it was an hallucination, but the truth is, I know it happened, and I don't understand it. Do you? Thanks for your help.—B.F.

I do understand it, and it's fascinating. The ghost B.F. encountered was that of a man who, in the late 1950s, had been convicted of an unspeakable child murder and was being transported by federal agents to Rikers Island when, less than a mile from the Miami airport, he was killed in a traffic collision on the busy Florida highway. He died believing with all his heart that he was evil, and let's face it, a case could be made. What's especially fascinating is that, on some level, this man is aware that he's dead. But he's so convinced that he's evil and, in God's eyes, unforgivable, that he refuses to go on because he believes that for him, "going on" will mean condemnation to an eternity in the dark fires of hell. At the same time, he thinks he's just "alive" enough that he'll only appear in those few rare hours when the airport is virtually empty, to someone who's alone and seems unthreatening, because to this day he's consciously a fugitive, still trying to avoid being taken into custody again.

In other words, this ghost is typical of so many who create the hell they're living in and then cling to it, even more terrified of the hopeless, Godless future that lies ahead if they let go of this dismal earth. It's inevitable that this murderer will move on someday, not to The Other Side but through the Left Door and right back in vitro again for another incarnation. He can postpone it by refusing to acknowledge that he's dead, but he can't avoid it, and moving on through these dark cycles is the only way he'll ultimately be rescued and taken Home where God has always been waiting.

His story reminds me of a haunting I investigated in San Francisco many years ago. Employees and patrons of a magnificent museum there had been hearing sounds of movement, footsteps, and soft weeping, and getting occasional glimpses of a slender, fragile figure in what seemed to be a black dress or cloak, frightened, lost, hoping not to be noticed. The museum, it seems, was the site of a former convent, and still trapped there was the ghost of one of its residents, a fifteen-year-old novitiate whose life had been so tragic and full of despair that she'd killed herself. Convinced that suicide was a mortal sin for which God could never forgive her, she turned her back on the loving light of Home when the tunnel opened to her, too ashamed to face her Father, earthbound and desperately alone, in her own self-imposed hell with, she believed, no way out.

After spending several hours with her, I was finally able to "talk her Home," not by any superhuman magic on my part but by the simple act of reuniting her with her own powerful faith in a God whose love is so all knowing and all embracing that He could never turn away His own child, no matter how many times we might foolishly turn away from Him.

Shortly after my grandfather died, my mother and I were sitting in our living room talking about some disturbing things we'd discovered about him after his death, and about the fact that he'd openly disliked me. As the conversation progressed, a blur of color suddenly appeared, swept around the room, and then passed right through me, during which I became so overwhelmed by a wave of evil and hatred that I felt as if I'd gone into shock. My mother, in the meantime, was clearly alarmed and asked me what had just happened. She said that she saw my eyes follow something, then I jerked as if I'd been punched, a look of terror came over my face, and I became pale and visibly shaken.

I was convinced then and I'm convinced now, fifteen years later, that my grandfather's spirit assaulted me that day, wanting to harm me or even kill me if he'd been able to. Oddly, his wife, my grandmother, who died a few years after he did, also visited me. I was at the sink doing the dinner dishes when I smelled her perfume and then felt her hug me from behind. The sensation was so warm and comforting that I actually said out loud, "Thank you for the hug, Grandma. I miss you too."—D.M.

Fortunately, this is a fairly rare experience, but it does happen, and D.M.'s letter describes the sensations of it perfectly. It's important to point out that it wasn't the grandfather's spirit, it was the grandfather's *ghost* that assaulted D.M. that day. No spirit visiting from The Other Side could ever trigger emotions like "evil" and "hatred." And that ghost, as mean, dark, and sociopathic as the grandfather was in life, was simply taking one last cheap, unsuccessful shot at accomplishing something he'd failed miserably at when he was alive—like all entities from the Dark Side, he was trying to neutralize the power of her light, which is her faith in God and her love and her strength, because where there's light, darkness can't exist. Of course he didn't like her while he was living. Nothing is more irritating and even threatening to a dark entity than a light God-centered spirit who can see right through them and refuses to be manipulated by them.

As for the grandmother, that *was* a spirit visit from The Other

Side, not just to say hello but also to say, "I wasn't strong enough to protect you from your grandfather while I was alive, but I'm more than strong enough now, and he'll never hurt you again." During her lifetime, the grandmother was a classic case of a white entity whose power was completely diminished by the dark entity she kept trying to "save" and "change" and "love enough to bring out his greatest potential." She spent her decades with him taking his coldness and cruelty as her failure, not his, and his random moments of feigned warmth as encouragement, and it was only after her death, from the crystal clarity of Home, that she was able to recognize the common trap she'd fallen into. She's been an especially vigilant spiritual presence for her granddaughter since the day she died, to prove that ultimately, universally, God's light really does have more power than darkness, and that hug was nothing more and nothing less than a sign that she's never left her and never will.

For the record, there's another reason the ghost of the grandfather will never be a threat to his granddaughter again besides the grandmother's protection, and it's important to mention because it brings up a rule of the spirit world worth noting: for an entity that was both dark and earthbound, the grandfather's spirit made an unusually quick trip through the Left Door and back in utero again. That "horseshoe"-shaped journey can sometimes take decades, or even centuries. But the grandfather entered some poor unsuspecting woman's womb only months after that spiritual assault on his granddaughter, and once an entity has returned to a womb for another incarnation, it's just a fact that its ability to appear in either spirit or ghost form ends. If a spirit or ghost you've become accustomed to suddenly stops coming around, don't worry about them or feel rejected. One of any number of possibilities is that at the very moment you're thinking about them, they have no conscious memories of you at all, they're just a helpless, innocent fetus, waiting to be born.

My brother Mark was eighteen years old when he died. I was only six at the time. I'm twenty-two now, but it still feels as if it just happened yesterday, maybe because there were so many unanswered questions and it still feels like an unhealed wound to me. The cause of Mark's death was a single gunshot to the head, and it was officially ruled a suicide. But there was also evidence that he might have been murdered, including a lot of unidentified footprints around his body, that was never thoroughly investigated. To this day I'm caught between a need to find out what really happened and a sense of hopelessness, like I'll never uncover the truth no matter how hard I try.

Part of the reason for my determination is that I feel my brother tried to reach out to me. One night not long after he died I woke up to find him sitting on the edge of my bed, just looking at me. It was as if he was trying to tell me something, but I was too young to understand what was going on. My mother sensed his presence in her room at around that time, too, and even though she couldn't see him, she was sure it was him because she could very clearly smell him.

If you can tell me what happened, or at least tell me how I can help Mark find peace, I would really appreciate it.—N.S.

First things first—this death was not a suicide, it was the result of a completely random murder, a sad, simple case of the victim being in the wrong place at the wrong time. And while the killer technically got away with that particular crime, he's serving life in prison without parole for another murder he committed less than a year later that he was convicted of, so he's appropriately off the streets, behind bars, and miserable.

Even beyond that, though, this story illustrates beautifully why we have no business making any broad assumptions about the nature of ghosts and their motives for staying behind. For example, look at the contrast between the grandfather in the previous story and Mark in this one. The grandfather was earthbound for a very short time. While Mark's brother would have no way of knowing this, Mark was earthbound for a very short time as well. But the grandfather, being a dark entity, headed quickly on through the Left Door and back into another incarnation, while Mark, a white entity, soon recognized and embraced God's light and headed Home to The Other Side. The grandfather stayed behind out of cruelty and revenge. Mark stayed behind to comfort his mother and his little brother as the realization of his death washed over him and he began to understand what had happened.

Finally, this story echoes a plea I've heard so many thousands of times in my life it would literally be impossible to count, and the irony is, this very common concern is *one of the few things in all of God's creation that we never have to be concerned about.* Just as N.S. wants to know the truth about Mark's death "so that Mark can be at peace," client after client will ask for my help in making sure a deceased loved one is no longer angry with them about not visiting or calling often enough, or resentful about some ongoing feud, or hurt that they didn't make it to the hospital in time to say good-bye, or as depressed and unhappy as they were throughout their life. I've written about this and spoken about this at great length before, but since it still comes up all the time, I don't mind a bit repeating myself, and I'll even go so far as to ask that if you never believe another thing I tell you, believe this:

Guilt, anger, resentment, sorrow, hurt, turmoil, depression, unhappiness, even illness, injury, and all other forms of physical and emotional negativity are strictly and solely earthly experiences. *There is no such thing as negativity of any kind, in any form, on The Other Side.*

I really do understand how hard it is to imagine, when we're in the grip of our own grief and pain over the loss of someone we love, that they're not suffering too. But I promise you, it's our own pain, our own frustration and sense of "unfinished business," we're projecting onto them. They're whole, happy, healthy, and busy again back Home, looking forward to seeing us again when we get there but with plenty to do in the meantime, with the full perspective of eternity and probably thirty or forty other incarnations on earth to look back on and learn from. And since they themselves wrote their own detailed charts for every one of those incarnations, they're not left with any sense of unfinished business at all. They understand everything perfectly, just as we will when we join them there.

So please, next time you hear yourself saying, either to yourself or out loud, "I know my loved one made it to The Other Side, but are they okay? Are they happy? Are they at peace?" stop yourself and realize with absolute certainty and the same trust you put in God that with your very first comment alone, you've already answered all your other questions.

My thirteen-year-old daughter sees and hears ghosts, and apparently our house is full of them. I wish this were just her imagination, or an ongoing family joke, but the fact is, they terrify her to the point where she can barely stand to sleep in her own room. We've tried burning sage and sweet grass, we've tried praying for them to cross over, a friend of mine even performed a house blessing with holy oil, but the ghosts refuse to leave. According to my daughter, who knows all their names and how they died, the children don't want to go because they feel safe here, and the adults just plain refuse to leave. I've put in calls to the local priest, but he won't call me back. Maybe he's afraid he'll ruin his reputation or something if word gets around that he took me seriously, who knows? But things seem to be escalating. The other day one of the ghosts grabbed my daughter's arm because she wouldn't turn around to look at them, and neither my daughter nor my grandson, who also lives with us, will sleep anywhere but in the living room now because they're too afraid. Can you help us?—J.M.

Someone who doesn't know me or my work very well might not appreciate how rare it is for me to say this, but in a case like J.M.'s, if it's at all financially feasible, I suggest moving, as soon as possible.

It's not that J.M. or her daughter or her grandson are in any grave physical danger. But when the ghosts in the house outnumber the humans, when they start getting openly aggressive and when the children in the house are sensitive enough to be subjected to this much relentless taunting from a dimension beyond their own, it's time to assess whether or not the long-term strain on your family is worth the fight.

This particular assembly of ghosts is very unusual. A very long time ago the three adults who lived on that site—a woman, her son, and his wife—were involved in a kind of private foster care scam, making a fortune providing minimal room and board for as many children as they could squeeze into every corner of their house and indoctrinating the children to believe that their secret "family" was the only place they could count on being together and safe. Completely isolated, forbidden from attending public school or church or from having any other friends, the children had nothing else to compare their lives to, so it's not surprising that even in death they're clinging fiercely to the house, to each other, and to the three adults who are all the safety they've ever known or understood. The adults, Godless as they are, are in no hurry to move on. And since the children are afraid to go anywhere without the adults, they're trapped until the spirits from The Other Side rescue them and take them Home.

Again, no one believes more strongly than I do in the power of prayer, the cleansing brilliance of the white light of the Holy Spirit, and the spiritual compassion every ghost deserves for their desperate confusion about not even knowing they're dead. But the house doesn't exist that I consider worth living in if any ghosts in residence not only refuse to leave but also insist on frightening my family and disrupting our sense of security without even chipping in so much as a dime on the mortgage payment.

I've always had a love for older home furnishings and pieces of furniture. I don't even care if they're actual antiques that smart dealers and investors would love to get their hands on. As long as they appeal to me and bring me some kind of comfort that says "home," that's good enough for me. So imagine how excited I was when a friend of mine decided to relocate and had a huge going-out-of-business sale at her antique store. My favorite "steal" was a portrait of a Victorian woman in an oval frame. She wore a high collar and a tightly cinched waist. Her eyes were forlorn, and she looked as if a smile had never crossed her lips. I bought her for mere pennies, hurried home with her, and hung her in a perfect spot upstairs in my son Daniel's bedroom.

A couple of weeks later I heard my daughter's car pull into the driveway. She bounced into the kitchen, home from school, and froze at the sight of me, visibly shocked. I asked her what was wrong.

"How did you get down here so fast?" she finally managed.

"What are you talking about? I've been in the kitchen for the last hour," I told her.

"No you haven't. I just saw you in Daniel's room."

"You couldn't have."

"Mom," she said, exasperated, "you were looking down from Daniel's window as I drove up the driveway. You pulled back the curtains, held up your hand, and waved at me. Now, come on, stop kidding around, it's not funny."

She bounced on past me out of the room while I stood there dumbfounded, not having a clue what she was talking about. Any thoughts?—V.S.

This happens so often with things we buy, particularly used items and antiques, and believe me, no one loves antiques and charity thrift stores more than I do. I'm sure if V.S. hadn't been so excited with the charm and the amazing bargain of this Victorian portrait, she would have studied it, held it and "sensed" it long enough to notice that something felt a bit unsettling about it, as if it came with some unpleasant baggage. In this case the unpleasant baggage was the subject of the portrait herself. She was a very vain, unpleasant, self-centered woman who commissioned this painting, believing her beauty to be so rare and exquisite that it deserved the same timeless celebration as the Mona Lisa, the Venus de Milo, and other great works of art that transcended their subjects into legends. This spinster, too much of a narcissist to fall in love with anyone but herself, has stayed earthbound and attached to that painting, following it wherever it goes, waiting for the acclaim, adoration, and parade of suitors she's sure the portrait will help attract. Her wave to V.S.'s daughter from the upstairs window was no different than a wave from Queen Elizabeth to any anonymous loyal subject.

I would get rid of that portrait so fast its high-collared, tight-lipped head would spin, I don't care how big a bargain it was. Just as I would never stay in a house in which I felt my family and I were being spiritually threatened in any way, I would also never keep an object around that seems to carry its own problems, darkness, negativity, or confusion. I've heard all sorts of arguments against getting rid of an antique that makes someone or everyone in the family uneasy, from "It's so gorgeous!" to "It was so expensive!" to "It's going to be worth a fortune someday!" to "It's a family heirloom!" I'm sorry, but I'll give the same answer to every one of those arguments—"It's not worth it!" As far as I'm concerned it's no different than yelling, "Come in!" when the doorbell rings without checking to see who it is first because, after all, it *might* be Ed McMahon with a million-dollar check made out to you. True. But it's even more likely that it's a burglar, or your least favorite family member wanting to camp out on your couch for the next two or three months. When it comes to your home, your safety and peace of mind and the safety and peace of mind of your family are sacrosanct. Getting rid of unwanted intruders, both seen and unseen, no matter how attractive or valuable a package they come sneaking in on, is worth any illusion of sacrifice that might temporarily wash over you as you take that package to the nearest charity donation center or dump site.

> Since I was four years old I've been sensitive to spirits and ghosts. I've felt them around me and have gone from being afraid of them to having no fear of them at all. I'm now a forty-year-old woman with a great husband and six children, living in a house we love in the South Mountain area of Phoenix.
>
> Over the years I've known that various spirits and ghosts were following me from place to place, and I'm accustomed to odd things happening without ever feeling threatened. But in this house, we'll carefully lock all our doors at night before going to bed and wake up in the morning to find them not only unlocked but standing wide open. Obviously this leaves my family very vulnerable and unsafe.
>
> I've run out of things to try to make it stop. The few friends I've talked to refuse to take me seriously, so I can just imagine what the police would say if I tried to report it. But I'm really at a loss. Who's doing this, why are they trying to hurt me or us, and how can I get them to stop endangering the people I love?—D.L.

This is so interesting, a great example of how easy it is to jump to the most obvious, logical conclusion and be completely wrong. The ghost in this story isn't trying to hurt or endanger anyone. This is nothing more than a misunderstanding based on cultural differences.

The ghost's name is Little Bear. She's an Indian squaw, and her family and tribe occupied that land in the South Mountain area for countless generations. She had an infant son after a very difficult childbirth, and her mother was off with the other tribeswomen tending to the baby while Little Bear rested. A sudden, violent lightning storm triggered a fire that swept with tragic speed through the tiny village, trapping and killing all its residents, including Little Bear. Thick smoke suffocated her before the fire ever reached her.

In her reality, then, Little Bear is alive and well in the early 1800s, recovering from childbirth, waiting for her mother to return with her newborn boy. Like the other residents of her village, all of whom are trusted relatives and friends, Little Bear lives in a tepee. Doors make no sense to her, so locked doors are unimaginable, if not terrifying, with her on one side and her first child, only a few hours old, on the other.

Anytime you sense the presence of a ghost on or around your property whose behavior is consistent and seems to make no sense to you, it can't hurt to research the history of the land as far back as you possibly can—not just the structures themselves, or the structures you've heard about that used to exist, but the land itself—and see if there might be some cultural and/or historical explanation for what's happening. Remember, some ghosts are lucky and manage to get released, or rescued by spirits from The Other Side, in a fairly short time. But others, like Little Bear, her infant son due back in her arms "any minute now" and infused, by the way, with the Indians' innate reverence for the earth, might stick around for centuries, going about their business with no hint that they're potentially endangering anyone. As you pray for their release and encourage them toward God's magnificent white light, don't assume that you and they share the same race, lifestyle, or time frame, and certainly don't take this opportunity to give them a good scolding about their behavior. If they're frightening you or your family, or causing possible harm, it's fine to explain that as long as you assure them that you know it's not their intention. Mostly, keep reinforcing that the loved ones they're yearning to see, the peace and joy they're yearning for in their hearts, and the sacred arms of God who created them are within their reach, just beyond that beautiful light.

The ghost of a dark entity won't care, of course, and will keep right on going with their own selfish, obnoxious agenda, which we'll thankfully never relate to. But the ghost of a white entity, as Little Bear is, is ultimately no different than a white entity on earth or The Other Side—we simply want to love and be loved by God and each other, to keep learning how to be better at both, and then, someday, to go Home knowing we did the best we could.

It was 2:00 A.M. and I was on the Internet, researching the history of our beloved hundred-year-old home. I finally forced myself to lie down, my mind still moving a mile a minute but my body completely exhausted. I instantly fell into a very deep sleep and felt as if I had just closed my eyes when I began to hear music. I opened my eyes and looked at the clock. Three A.M. I was annoyed, even more exhausted after an hour's sleep than I had been when I went to bed.

I sat up, trying to pinpoint the source of the ongoing music, and finally decided it must be coming from my daughter's room upstairs. That annoyed me even more—playing music at that hour of the night is definitely out of the question. Then it began to dawn on me that this was ballroom music, hardly the kind of music she would listen to, and it wasn't coming from her room after all, it seemed to be coming from the ceiling area of my room.

I made a very conscious effort to ask myself if I was sure I was awake. Yes. I definitely was. I even pinched myself to make sure.

As the ballroom music continued I began to picture people in beautiful formal wear, dancing with such grace. Their voices began blending with the music, and the vision became more and more real, and more and more confusing, while I never doubted for a moment what I was seeing and hearing.

I looked over at my husband, in bed next to me. He was sound asleep. And then I saw two women, standing next to his side of the bed, teacups in hand. They were in elegant ball gowns, their finest jewelry, and expensively upswept hair. I couldn't make out their exact words, but I knew they were gossiping, and I had no patience for it. "Shut up, I'm trying to sleep!" I snapped, and then I rolled over, pulled my blankets over my head, and dozed off again.

The next morning I remembered the incident very clearly and I couldn't believe what I had done. I'd had this amazing, fantastic, wonderful experience, and what did I do? I told them to shut up! I've prayed every night since to be given another chance, with the promise that this time I'll give these visiting spirits the respect and appreciation they deserve, but it's never happened again.

It's worth adding that this vision, or whatever it was, had nothing to do with my research. Our home was originally built as a carriage/caretaker's house and most definitely didn't include a ballroom.

So who were those beautiful people, and why did they show up here?—K.M.

First, this story is another excellent reminder to be careful not to take the word "originally" too literally. It's so easy for us to forget that the land our houses are built on is far older than our most convenient memories and records, and there's even a limit to the written history of the land we live on. So to assume that with enough research we'll be experts on who if anyone "should" show up on or around our property from the spirit world is a nice thought but a little too optimistic to be practical.

Even more than that, though, it illustrates that ghosts aren't all that literal about the boundaries of the property they've chosen to inhabit. When you're trying to put yourself in their place, the best advice is to "think conceptually." Rather than think, Wait, this was the caretaker's house, there was no ballroom here; think, This house was once part of an estate where grand balls were held. It's the property, the expanse of land, that these ghosts are feeling an attachment to in this case, not a specific room, or a specific structure.

A perfect example is Johnny Johnson, the ghost who occupies the Toys"R"Us in Sunnyvale, California. I've written about him a hundred times, I think, in so many previous books that Brian Tart, my editor, is going to chase me up and down the halls with a bat if I tell the whole Johnny Johnson story again. But he's relevant here in that he can often be found kneeling near a back corner of the store. Why? Because while to us there's nothing there but a wall, to Johnny Johnson there's a creek there, running through the ranch where he thinks he still works for room and board, waiting for the woman he loves to come to her senses, realize she loves him, too, and leave her husband in Boston and come back to him. Again, it's their reality, their perspective, filtered through the enormous confusion of not even knowing they're dead, that we need to take into account when trying to understand them and their behavior, not the surface-level world we're often tempted to pretend is all that exists in our convenient present-tense lives.

I was ten years old and living in a two-story house in Jersey City. During the summer I loved sleeping on a sleeper sofa in the living room, which my mom occasionally allowed. One night I woke up—and I know I was fully awake—and saw a man and child of about eight or nine. They were both wearing black leather jackets and black pants, and they both had some kind of knapsacks over their shoulders. I saw them looking around touching things, but they certainly weren't stealing anything. They turned toward me as they were leaving, and I pretended to be yawning, but they didn't do a thing to me, either, and just kept going. After that, I occasionally heard them whistling and walking through the house. One night my mother slept on the sleeper sofa with me, and she heard someone taking their shoes off even though there was no one there. We never did ask the owner, who was in his seventies, if he knew anything about the history of this house or who these two might have been. Can you tell me?—P.D.

This is just a plain old classic ghost story, with a tragedy at its core. These two were actually brothers, the "man" a seventeen-year-old named Billy and the boy an eight-year-old named Henry. It was the early 1930s, and they had run away from the neglect and poverty of their home on a destitute farm some forty miles away in the hope of finding a better life somewhere, anywhere, else. But bad weather, bad luck, Billy's ill health, and missing their mother, whom they deeply loved, finally convinced them to turn around and head home again. A few nights into their journey, standing beside the dark highway in their black leather clothing trying to hitch a ride from one of the few passing cars, they were hit by a large cream-colored sedan whose driver hadn't seen them and who promptly sped away. They crawled to a small house near the road in search of help, not knowing it was abandoned, and died there together before they reached the door. By the time their bodies were found they were unrecognizable, and they were buried in unmarked graves in a pauper's cemetery several miles away.

The small abandoned house was soon torn down and replaced by the two-story structure that stands there today, but the brothers continue to seek refuge there, injured and exhausted but having no idea that their wounds were fatal, meaning no harm to anyone, simply wanting help and a place to rest as they perpetually make their way home to a place that no longer exists.

I gave my word to the actress who told me this story that if she'd write it out for me, I would never reveal her name, the name of any of the people involved, or the title of the film in question. She kept her end of the bargain, and so will I.

We were shooting outside of Paris, in a beautiful old château near Versailles. Almost from the first night, things seemed odd. The usually convivial group started having disagreements, quite heated at times. At first I tried chalking it up to the killer schedule we were keeping. Our first night there as I was soaking in the bath the lights went out. French electrics, I thought. I got out of the tub and turned them back on. As soon as I was back in the tub, off they went again. Early that morning there was a rush of air through the room, though the windows were tightly closed. The drapes billowed and flapped, even though they were nowhere near the heat register.

The next night the conversation at dinner was even more heated. My assistant and the makeup artist had a terrible argument. To keep peace, I asked him to go to her room and apologize. He agreed. She answered the door stark naked and chatted away to him the whole time as if she were fully dressed while rubbing cream all over her ample body. He quickly accomplished his apology and got out of there. Three days later she accused him of rape! (Please note, he "plays for the other team.") That same night my acting partner, after months of perfectly congenial professionalism, tried to shove his tongue down my throat! He was as surprised as I was and fell all over himself apologizing. Again, early that morning the same routine with the drapes, and this time my script decided to throw itself to the floor.

As we were leaving the château I really wanted the proprietors, a young couple, to know how much we appreciated their kindness, since none of these bizarre incidents were their fault, so I asked my driver Jean-Claude to go in and say it to them in his beautiful proper Real French. He came back to the car looking astonished. They had been not only grateful but shocked at the compliment and begged us to tell everyone that we'd enjoyed our stay. They were losing their shirts, it seems, because the place was so notoriously haunted that none of the locals would even come to eat there.——Nameless

I slipped this into the midst of ghost stories for a reason. I first wanted to point out that if you'd found yourself in the same situation this actress and the others were in, in which neither people nor inanimate objects were behaving in ways that made any sense at all, you could easily have assumed it was a haunting too. But I also wanted you to notice that at no time did anyone actually see a ghost or entity or energy form of any kind, including this actress, whom I happen to know is incredibly sensitive to the spirit world and spiritually gifted in general. She did tell me that she had a sense a couple of times that there was an "it" involved, and that the "it" was a little boy, but she never saw him, and because of the phenomenon that was really going on here, I have a feeling the idea of an "it" was just the result of a confusing, highly emotionally charged and very turbulent few days. Sometimes believing there's an "it" gives some tiny glimmer of comfort that if you can find "it," maybe you can chase "it" away or destroy "it." But with no "it" at all, you don't even know who or what your enemy is, you just know that something upsetting is going on all around you, you don't understand what it is, and you certainly don't know how to make it stop.

In this case, as you may have already recognized from our discussion of it in Chapter Two, the occupants and guests of this château were the victims of a classic imprint. Whenever there's a lack of any visible or audible entities, signs of "energy surges" like flickering lights and inanimate objects seemingly moving on their own, and most of all an overpowering, uncontrollable emotional response, positive or negative, that seems to permeate the whole atmosphere and everyone in it, it's a very safe bet that there's an imprint at work, and that the more tolerance and compassion you can offer each other when you're caught in the middle of a negative imprint like the château, the better friends you'll become once you're away from the influence of the imprint and back to normal again.

This château, it turns out, stands on the site of what was once a very exclusive, very expensive, very discreet brothel. The clientele were highly ranked officers in the French military, powerful men in government, and other gentlemen of influence with enormous amounts of money, and the women who lived and worked there were hand picked by the madame for their looks, discretion, and lack of family ties that might compete for their attention and loyalty to the brothel. Too much potential income and too much isolated proximity made the women hatefully jealous and vindictive toward each other, which their employer encouraged, feeling it added to an atmosphere that almost crackled with heightened emotions of every kind from the moment demanding clients of privilege from all over the world stepped through the brilliantly hidden private entrance. Everything from blackmail to desperately unsafe abortions to several "accidental deaths" of some of the less discreet, more ambitious women to suicides happened in that brothel in the explosive decades of its existence, and if involuntary anger and lewd behavior continues to overtake its guests to this day, it's fair to say it's not surprising and it's definitely not their fault.

I was getting a wonderful therapeutic massage from a masseur who's a big believer in the importance of energy flow for identifying and relieving areas of stress. I was lying on my back on the table, eyes closed, completely relaxed, when I heard a noise outside his apartment door. I then became aware of a presence inside his apartment door, even though I knew the door hadn't opened. My eyes were still closed, but I could "see" this presence in the apartment, and I finally asked, "Jimmy, is someone here?"

"You tell me," he replied, noncommittal.

This was a whole new experience for me. I was sure of what seemed to be happening, I just wasn't quite sure how easy it was going to be to say it out loud. "Well, there seems to be a man standing at your door."

"Inside, or outside?"

"He's inside the door," I told him.

I felt his hands hesitate on my shoulders, only for an instant, and then he proceeded again, strong as ever, and asked me to describe this man. I still hadn't opened my eyes, but I didn't need to. The man was standing with light behind him so that his face was in shadow. I knew he was tall, dark haired, and relatively young, maybe late thirties. I described his clothing and then added that his arms were full of rolled papers, like charts, or maps.

"Could they be drawings? Fashion drawings?" Jimmy asked.

"Yes," I said, feeling strongly that that's exactly what they were. "They're rolled like blueprints, and he's carrying them along with a grocery bag."

We lapsed into a long silence, during which I admit I felt pretty shaken. As I said, nothing like this had ever happened to me before, and I'm not some gullible adolescent, I'm an "old married woman" with two kids nearing college age. And then, just when I thought maybe I was coming to my senses again, the opposite happened instead—I realized this man was silently communicating with me.

"Jimmy," I managed after a minute or two, "I know what he wants. He didn't know I was going to be here, he knows I'm aware of him, and he wants to know if it's still okay for him to come in. He's really uncomfortable with me here."

Jimmy let out a long breath and said, almost to himself, "That's never stopped him before." Now I was *really* lost. And with that the massage was over. I opened my eyes and watched as Jimmy left the room, walking right through where the presence was standing. As he moved through it, it seemed to disappear.

I got dressed in Jimmy's absence, and when he returned a few minutes later he quietly offered, "I guess I owe you an explanation." And he proceeded to tell me about this young man, an old lover of his, who'd been a fashion designer. Two years after a bad, painful breakup, the young man called to tell Jimmy he was very sick and needed help. Jimmy brought him home and took care of him until he died, and he'd been visiting ever since, sometimes just harmlessly playing pranks like rearranging the bookshelves but other times deliberately bothering Jimmy during dates. I was the first person besides Jimmy he'd ever revealed himself to, so Jimmy had never talked to anyone about these visits before, and he hoped I wouldn't be scared away.

"Don't worry, I'll be back," I assured him. "But to be honest, I really would appreciate it if you'd keep your friends to yourself from now on."

I've been back many times. I've never sensed the young man again, although I did have an incredible experience with a white light that I both felt and saw with my eyes closed and Jimmy saw as well.—H.S.

I want to make it clear right up front that I know this woman. Not because I'm psychic but because she's a friend, I know what's been going on in her life in the past few years. Within a relatively short time, and with very little warning, H.S. lost both of her parents and was still reeling from those deaths when, I'll always believe, she began prophetically sensing the heartbreaking illness of her sister that would hit suddenly and irreversibly a handful of years later. So when I heard about H.S.'s experience in her masseur's apartment, I wanted it included in this book for the subtle spiritual reality it illustrates.

H.S. commented more than once that nothing like her encounter with this young man, this ghost completely unconnected to her, had ever happened to her before. Countless clients have told me similar stories of their first meeting with a visitor from the afterlife, or at the very least a dramatic growth in spirituality, happening in close proximity to the serious illness or death of a loved one, and I promise you, the timing is no coincidence. At first glance it might look like some connection to our predictable fear of death and a reminder to get our spiritual lives in order, which I guess could theoretically make us more conscious of the spirit world in a sort of knee-jerk obedience reaction. But the real explanation is far more interesting and far more comforting than that.

Never doubt for a moment that The Other Side isn't just the place the vast majority of us are going when we leave here, it's also the place we left to come here for this lifetime. It's our true Home, more familiar and beloved to us than earth could ever be, sacred and joyful and exquisite, and deep in our souls we yearn for it from the moment we enter a human body until we're released from that body again. In the course of our eternal existence, we spend infinitely more time in the spirit world on The Other Side than we spend in the human world on earth. You can argue with that premise all you want and swear that if that were true, you'd obviously remember it. But I'm willing to bet you don't remember being born, either, and I can't wait to hear you try to convince me that didn't happen.

When we find ourselves in the presence of a loved one who's gravely ill, or when a loved one leaves us for The Other Side or wherever else their spirit journey might take them next, our shortsighted, finite human minds are likely to react with some earthly twinges of fear, but the far more dramatic, turbulent, and far-reaching reaction will be a blurred, rushing flood of our own spirit memories. We may not even consciously realize it. In fact, we probably won't. But when our spirits recognize that someone close to us has gone to a Home we dearly miss, or that they may be going there soon, it wakes the spirit part of us, opens it, makes it vulnerable, and sensitizes it. We may be aware of seeing and hearing spirits and ghosts for the first time, as our own spirit becomes more exposed through its memories. Our dreams may contain more images of The Other Side than we ever recall their containing before, or we may astrally travel there during sleep more often than ever.

A practical analogy would be if a group of family and friends were taking a trip to your cherished, faraway hometown that you haven't seen in many, many years, but for some reason you weren't able to join them. What would be more natural than for your homesickness to intensify around their travel plans, for your images of home to intensify, for more memories than usual to come flooding back, for your heart to ache a little or a lot over the distance and the circumstance that has separated you from the familiarity that brought you such comfort? Magnify those feelings by thousands and it approximates what goes on in our spirit minds when someone we love either prepares to go Home or actually takes that sacred journey and we know it's not time for us to join them yet.

So while there's no doubt about it that the grave illness or death of a loved one is a terribly hard, emotionally unspeakable time, I do hope that in those rare moments when you're able to notice something besides the confining restraints of your pain and grief and the depth of your sense of loss, you'll become aware that your soul is continuously active, alert, and even more wide awake than usual, giving you clear, fascinating looks into other dimensions where confused ghosts linger on earth and spirits soar. Some scientists and psychiatrists call it "grief hysteria." Why H.S.'s grief hysteria would inspire her to sense and actually see the ghost of her masseur's deceased ex-lover, whom she'd never heard of until after she'd seen him and described him, I have no idea. I prefer my explanation: God promised us everlasting lives, and sometimes, especially when death is close by, He finds ways to grace us with reminders of that sacred promise.

My grandparents bought a small white house in the Maryland woods in the early 1950s. The family who lived in that house before them was tragic. The father was an alcoholic and very physically abusive to his wife and his children. According to the police and news reports after the fact, one day the father became particularly violent and was chasing his wife and two sons with some kind of weapon. The wife and one of the sons managed to escape from the house. The other son, Richard, wasn't so lucky and, in desperation, as his father hunted him down, climbed into the upstairs laundry chute to hide. Tragically, the flue for the chute was open, and eight-year-old Richard fell three stories, all the way to the basement, and died instantly when his head hit the concrete floor.

Richard has been haunting the house ever since, as my grandparents and our whole family will confirm. In fact, ever since I was a child, whenever we've sat down to Christmas dinner, we've bowed our heads to God and asked Him to bless Richard right along with the rest of us, as if he were one of our own. We've never doubted that Richard was around, and I think we all felt that maybe our family could more than make up for the love Richard deserved from his own family but didn't get.

Richard likes to make things around the house fall over for no reason at all, again and again and again, until we can't possibly not notice and there's no way we can come up with some "reasonable explanation" no matter how hard we try. He opens windows we know we've closed and has even let us sit and watch as he slowly eased open at least two inches a completely closed double-hung window. If there's a "normal" way for that to happen, we haven't been able to figure out what it is.

One day my mom was hanging curtains in the living room. No

matter how securely she'd get one end of the rod attached to the wall, she'd be right in the middle of attaching the other end when the first end would come crashing down. This went on for more than an hour until finally, in total frustration, she yelled, "Richard, cut it out!" The rod never fell again.

Some of the most dramatic Richard stories happened when I was a child. I used to play with him and spend hours talking to him, and because he had long hair I apparently thought he was a girl at first. Mom assumed it was an imaginary playmate until he told me he was a boy and his name was Richard, and then she started taking me more seriously. But she still wondered why no one else in the family could see him, especially my younger brother Erik. From what she tells me, my reply was "Richard doesn't like Erik." To this day I wish I could remember what Richard and I talked about.

Most memorable for other family members who witnessed it, though, was a day when some of my cousins were at the house, playing in the backyard. They looked over and thought they saw me standing in the back door watching them. They called to "me" to come join them, but "I" just smiled and waved. At that moment my uncle happened to come outside, walking through the back door and right through what they thought was me. They began screaming, terrified, and the figure they now realized was Richard instantly disappeared from the doorway while my uncle stood there staring at them, wondering what all the screaming was about.

I know how crazy all of this sounds, but we're a sane, normal, hardworking Christian family with nothing to gain from making up ghost stories. I'm not even sure why I wanted to write about it. It's not like we need to be reassured that Richard is real, because that's just a fact, he's as real as we are, and no one could convince us otherwise. I guess I just wanted to say to everyone who thinks that ghosts are imaginary, or that if they do exist they're evil, that the one who lives with us is a sweet, playful, harmless little boy who should never have died in the first place. We love him, we're glad he feels safe with us, and he's welcome to stay as long as he likes.—G.M.

This is a touching and heartbreaking story. And to give credit where it's due, it was actually sent by G.M.'s girlfriend, but it became a little confusing and I wanted the story to be as uncomplicated as the points it eloquently illustrates.

This is a case in which a combination of very sudden traumatic death and terror kept this child from having the first clue that he was dead. We've discussed cases in this chapter in which spirits remain earthbound because they're afraid they've done something for which God won't forgive them. Eight-year-old Richard, on the other hand, remained earthbound because he was afraid that if he came out of the shadows into the bright white light he saw ahead of him, his father would be able to see him and finish him off once and for all. So he hid and kept right on hiding, not really any lonelier or more frightened or unhappy than he'd been when he was alive. He ventured out a few times when the little house fell oddly silent for a while, but what captured his curiosity the most and eventually became irresistible to him were sounds he'd never heard within those walls before—sounds of laughter, and soft, loving voices and kind words and prayers and children playing unpunished. When he finally timidly revealed himself, he was pleasantly surprised to discover that one little boy seemed to notice him, accept him, and actually care about him. And as time went on a miracle happened and this amazing family who never hit or threw things or screamed at or terrified or mistreated or did anything else but love each other grew to love him and make him feel safe for the first time in his young life, and when he heard them include him in their thanks to God he forgot every bad thing that ever happened to him and felt like the luckiest boy who ever lived.

The situation between this kind, lovely family and Richard isn't an uncommon one between kind, lovely people and a harmless, even playful ghost they've become aware of and attached to. It's an odd two-sided coin. On one hand, showing compassion and tolerance for a ghost's confused, difficult situation is an admirable thing to do, especially if that ghost isn't being mean or aggressive or deliberately terrorizing the household, and most especially if that ghost is a child. The more consistent compassion a ghost gets from a person or family, the more trust the ghost feels toward them and ultimately the more likely the ghost might be of getting "talked over" toward the light.

On the other hand, though, if a ghost gets too comfortable right where they are, they might not feel motivated to leave the person or family to go toward the light or anywhere else, for that matter, and that can be particularly true in the case of a child around Richard's age. There's no hard-and-fast rule about this, but very often children who are around five years old or less have crystal-clear memories of their past lives and their lives on The Other Side, and they happily go Home in the blink of an eye when they die that young because they remember death and the joy of their sacred destination as familiar experiences they've been through many times before. They astrally travel to their past lives and The Other Side regularly while they sleep and have easy, conscious contact with their whole spirit consciousness when they're awake as well. Casually ask a child who's around five years old or younger a question like "Who were you before this?" or "How many other mothers have you had?" or "What kind of work do you do on The Other Side?" or even "How did your lifetime end the last time you were on earth?" The chances are that unless the child feels self-conscious about the answers or is afraid their answers might not be accepted as the truth, they'll offer some fascinating and surprisingly complex responses. Explore the details of their "imaginary playmates" and you could discover that they're actually ghosts, visiting spirits, or Spirit Guides. Ask very young children to tell you about their dreams and you could find yourself on the receiving end of some exquisitely simple descriptions of astral trips to the magnificent buildings, gardens, landscapes, and residents of Home.

Sadly and necessarily, though, as we grow older, our conscious memories of The Other Side and our past lives begin to fade, and we become less a part of that world and more a part of this one. We come to earth for the growth and increased wisdom of our spirits on their eternal journey, after all, and the more time we spend being preoccupied with the bliss we're missing back Home, the more time we're failing to take care of whatever it is we set out to accomplish here. So, as a general rule, by about the age of six or seven or Richard's age of eight, we start developing conscious amnesia of that sacred, perfect place we came from, where we'll go again as soon as this rough boot camp we mistakenly call "life" has ended, and we understandably start clinging to what we find here on earth as if it's all we've ever known and all we can rely on for our survival.

That's exactly why I'm both thrilled and sad for Richard that G.M.'s family came along. It's just wonderful for any child, even a ghost child, to experience unconditional love, to be embraced and wanted, to know what trust feels like, to see a home held together by kindness instead of threats and fear and violence. And yet it's all those same loving, positive qualities in G.M.'s family that are unwittingly holding Richard back from the true bliss that's waiting for him. Like every other ghost, he has no idea that he's dead, let alone that the happiness he's feeling with this dear family is only a hint of the eternal joy of The Other Side.

I'd say to G.M.'s family the same thing I'd say to all of you who have a ghost you've become attached to—and from the number of you who wrote me in that exact situation, I know there are a lot of you. You can use the same love and trust that's holding this ghost in place, in the comfort of your fond acceptance, to send them to the light and the far greater peace beyond than we on earth can ever hope to offer them. Precisely because you have a credibility with them that no one else has, you can tell them like no one else can that you have wonderful news for them—that they've left the bodies that stopped serving them well, and they're now free to step into the tunnel and let it take them to the light that stands at the open door to their real Home, where everyone they've ever loved is gathered, so excited, in the immediate presence of God, waiting to welcome them. You and they will miss each other, there's no doubt about that, but they've got work to do on The Other Side and you've still got work to do here. And in what will seem like the blink of an eye, with all of eternity to look forward to, you'll be together again at Home, and you'll be counting on them to be among the first to greet you when you get there.

They'll believe you, for two reasons. One is that you've earned their trust in the time you've spent together. The other is that you're telling them the truth, and the soul always knows the truth when it hears it. And even if it takes telling them a time or two to overcome their fear, they'll go, and you will have done the kindest, most self-less thing one spirit can do for another—sent them into God's arms with love, peace, joyful anticipation, and not one single regret or sense of unfinished business, as if by leaving they're letting someone down. God will thank you over and over again for helping one of His earthbound children find their way Home, you can count on it.

And by the way, for those of you who are wondering, I just can't stress this often or strongly enough: Don't spend one moment worrying that Richard's father might not have received the punishment he deserved for all those years of terrorizing his family and causing the death of that innocent little boy. It's a fact, a nonnegotiable universal truth, that anyone who deliberately harms a child, an animal, or an elderly person unable to defend themselves, or allows any of those defenseless beings to be harmed, will face consequences darker than any pain they ever dreamed of inflicting, in more lifetimes than they may think they've bargained for. I can't be more specific than that because the nature of their consequences aren't my choice, I'm sorry to say. Nor are they God's choice. Never forget that Godless people are never Godless because God has turned away from them, it's only and always because they've turned away from God, which deprives them of all His grace, forgiveness, and power. Just please don't get frustrated if it seems that someone got away with something as unspeakable as child, animal, or elder abuse. In this lifetime, or the next, or the next one after that, there's no such thing as "getting away with" anything. It simply can't be done.

Then, of course, there are those other visitors who aren't ghosts at all, not earthbound, not strangers, but instead so familiar that we're almost afraid to believe we really caught a glimpse of them, or a passing hint of their scent, because imagining such a thing would almost seem like a cruel trick. I could tell you over and over again, in chapter after chapter, that your loved ones and Spirit Guides visit you from The Other Side all the time in various ways, it's not just something that happens to us "wacky psychics." But since I probably couldn't put it nearly as eloquently as you yourselves put it in your letters to me, I'll just sit back and let you share these gorgeous stories with each other.

Chapter Five

THE SPIRITS WHO
VISIT YOU

My husband passed away in January of 2000. He died here at home at 4:00 A.M. A week after the funeral, strange things started happening in the house. At least once a week I began being awakened at 4:00 in the morning by what sounded exactly like him calling out my name. One night I swear someone was shaking my bed so hard that I actually got up to make it stop, and when I did I heard someone trying to break into the house through the back door. But they ran away when they realized I'd surprised them before they could surprise me. I felt as if my husband was there protecting me, shaking the bed to warn me.

Sometimes I wake up and actually see him standing in the bedroom doorway, and my daughter and I hear him walking around upstairs and on the stairway all the time. The living room will suddenly get cold and at that same moment I'll smell the aftershave he used to wear, or the hall light will be on in the middle of the night that I know perfectly well I turned off before I went to bed.

In some ways I love that my husband is still here with me, but I also want him to rest in peace. He was such a good man, I'm really hoping you can give me some idea why he hasn't moved on yet.—C.T.

I don't doubt for a moment that there are people who've been wondering throughout all these pages, Who cares what the differences are between a ghost and a spirit? Well, C.T. and a whole lot of others who are worried about their deceased loved ones care very much, and in C.T.'s case, she's worried for no reason at all. Her husband *has* moved on. He's a spirit, visiting her from The Other Side, not a ghost who's unable to rest in peace, and he *is* there to protect her, and to assure her that he's not only fine but very much alive, as eternal as God promised. The aftershave is a great clue—spirits love using familiar fragrances as a signal that they're around, while I've never heard of ghosts bothering with odors unless they're unpleasant ones. And waking C.T. up by speaking her name at 4:00 A.M. is also much more spiritlike than ghostlike. For one thing, it's a precise reference to C.T.'s husband's time of death, but for another thing, and more important, as I mentioned in the first chapter, it's the predawn hours that are prime time for spirit activity.

Mostly, though, there was the simple mention of C.T. waking to see her husband standing in the bedroom doorway. I hope you'll look back on the chapter of ghost stories and realize that no one mentioned recognizing the physical form of the person who was haunting them. Even the woman who had the horrible experience with the ghost of her grandfather passing through her never actually saw his ghost materialize. If you see a form materialize, and the form is that of a deceased loved one, I feel very safe in saying that 999 times out of 1,000 you're seeing a visiting spirit from The Other Side and not a ghost at all, and there's no need for you to put yourself through any needless concern and pain on their behalf. Count on it that they're simply doing their best to let you know that they're around keeping an eye on you and very probably planning one great reunion party for you when you're together again back Home. But until then, they're counting on you to be as busy and happy as they are in the lives they've resumed on The Other Side. Anything less and you'll be doing yourself and their memory a real disservice.

I'd been married to a man for eleven years and had become very suspicious of him. I can't even explain it beyond instinct and a gnawing, sick feeling in the pit of my stomach, but I knew something was very wrong between us. I had never followed my husband or gone through his personal belongings, but finally one day I went through everything I could find—dresser drawers, his vehicle, everything. It looked worse than I had anticipated. Not only did I find girls' phone numbers, but I also found drug paraphernalia, a gun, and even a stalking order. Now I was determined to find out the truth, so I set up a voice-activated tape recorder in the garage where he and his friends often hung out, hoping they would talk about whatever was going on with him. I put in a brand new tape, fresh from its shrink-wrapped package, and hid the recorder in a perfect place near his workbench.

When I finally checked the tape, I found nothing but the sound of tools on metal, when he was clearly working on something. I rewound the tape, ready to set it up to record again, when something prompted me to check it again. This time, clear as day, like a loud female whisper that faded in and out as if the woman whispering were moving toward and away from the tape recorder, I heard a voice saying over and over again, "Pornography, pornography, pornography." The hair stood straight up on my neck. Each time I listened to it the voice seemed to get louder. I looked up, feeling completely helpless, and said, "Okay, God, what do you want me to do with this?"

I didn't know where to turn. I called my sister. She couldn't even hear the voice over the phone. I showed it to my pastor, who had no idea what to tell me. Finally I decided I had to confront my husband with it. He was furious, as I probably would be, too, if someone tried to tape me without my knowledge. But when he heard that woman's voice and what she was saying, he completely lost control. He took a hammer to the tape recorder and started screaming, "I am not possessed!" (I never said he was—I have no idea why that word came out of him.) He threatened my life that night in front of our three children. That was July 2, 2001. I haven't spoken to him since that day.

I took my children and stayed in a shelter for three months, then summoned enough courage to call the police. They directed me to the detective who had been investigating my husband since 1998. I asked him if the investigation had something to do with drugs.

"No."

"Guns?"

"No."

"Pornography?" I finally said.

He glanced at another detective and then said, "It might have something to do with pornography."

My hair stood on end again.

The detective told me my husband was extremely dangerous. Later I learned that he had been drugging, beating, and raping young girls and women. He is still out there. The women involved are too afraid to testify against him.

I am so grateful to the "ghost voice" on that tape. God protects us in strange ways sometimes. Everything that happens has a purpose. I also believe that God never presents us with any burden we ultimately can't handle.—R.S.

Let's get something out of the way right up front: Within seven months of this book's publication, this man *will* be behind bars where he belongs, and I want to be among the first to hear about it when it happens.

There. Now. This is one of my new favorite stories, for a couple of reasons. The first is that this woman took a firm, nonnegotiable, no-second-chance position with her husband the instant he threatened in front of their children that he was going to kill her. I don't care that it was just a verbal threat. I don't care that it was during a heated argument and he was "probably just upset" or any of those other lame excuses. It's still abuse. It's still violence. No child should ever have to witness a parent being violent toward the other parent in any way, ever, let alone be given the message that violence in a relationship is acceptable. And see if this sounds familiar: "If I've told him/her once, I've told him/her a thousand times, that behavior is unacceptable, and I won't put up with it." Well, I'm sorry, but, duh, if you're still around to tell someone a thousand times that something is unacceptable, then clearly you're putting up with it, and if you think a child isn't bright enough to figure that out, guess again. R.S. did what I frankly wish more women would learn to do—she put being a parent ahead of being a spouse on her priority list and got her children to a place where she could guarantee their safety. I applaud her and all the rest of you, both women and men, who have the courage and selflessness to do the same, because I know there are a lot of you making that painful, difficult move every day. I also know firsthand that it's probably the most important thing you'll ever do in this life.

As for the "ghost voice" on the tape, repeating the word "pornography" over and over again, it wasn't a ghost at all, of course. It was R.S.'s Spirit Guide, whose name is Glenda, by the way. Glenda helped add to R.S.'s feelings that things weren't right, just as all Spirit Guides do to make sure we notice, and she certainly helped R.S. come up with the idea of setting up a tape recorder, which R.S. admitted herself was completely out of character for her. And I hope this story will remind you that setting up a tape recorder while you sleep, especially between the "prime spirit hours" of 3:30 and 6:00 A.M., is never a bad idea, because the spirit world really does find electronic devices and magnetic surfaces like audiotape helpful conductors for them to attach their energy to when trying to communicate in our dimension.

Every time I advise someone against setting up the tape recorder in their own bedroom, they look wildly intrigued, ask why, and then lean closer, as if I'm about to disclose some eerie secret of the supernatural, some weird effect that could be unleashed by the combination of a spirit, a tape recorder, and a sleeping person all in the same room together. I hate to disappoint them, and you, but the reason is that, for one thing, if you snore or talk in your sleep, you could drown out any spirit voices that might try to get through and end up with a tape neither you nor anyone else wants to listen to. For another thing, many people have a silly but not at all uncommon reaction to trying to go sleep with a running tape recorder in the room, where they feel compelled to get up every few minutes and check to make sure it's still on, still running, all the right buttons are still pressed, and on and on and on until they've driven themselves crazy and wasted a perfectly good night's sleep. For yet another thing, for some reason, when you're sound asleep and not accustomed to it, the sound of a tape recorder clicking off is almost guaranteed not just to wake you up but make you sit bolt upright in a panic for no reason, and why put yourself through it?

Set a tape recorder up in another room in the house, the quietest room you've got, a room in which you're least likely to record "spirit noises" and realize later that it was only the furnace kicking on or your Labrador puppy wrestling with a sofa cushion. There's no guarantee that you'll get results as dramatic as the experience R.S. had. There's no guarantee that you'll get any crystal clear results at all. But there is one way I can promise you'll never hear the sound of your Spirit Guide's voice on tape, or any other spirit who might be visiting you while you sleep, either, for that matter, and that is to not give them any way to tape themselves for you in the first place.

Just please do me and fairness a favor—if and when this subject happens to come up in conversation, remember, you've forfeited your right to say, "That's ridiculous." The farthest you can go and maintain your honesty is "I wouldn't know, I never bothered to try."

I was a teenager when I first saw my deceased grandfather in a mirror. I knew he was just there to acknowledge me and tell me he loved me, and I felt so comforted. Then, when I was in my thirties and having a difficult time in my marriage, my deceased grandmother appeared, sitting on the steps near me, and assured me my husband and I would work things out. We did, and our twenty-two-year marriage is stronger than ever.

I'm writing because I was adopted at birth and am desperate to find my biological mother. I recently had a dream in which the name Peggy Wilson came to me. The contact with my deceased grandparents makes me think maybe I should take this Peggy Wilson information seriously. On the other hand, I've heard you say many times that you're not psychic about yourself, so why should I be? My adoptive parents don't know the identity of my biological mother but think they vaguely remember the last name of "Simmon." If you can tell me a name or a place where I can start my search, I'd be so grateful. Thank you for your time.—G.V.

I admit it, the second paragraph of that letter is off the subject of spirits, and of this whole book, for that matter, but G.V.'s biological mother's name was Nancy Simmon, and she's no longer living. I was sure you'd all forgive me if I took a moment to pass that information along.

Now. That having been said, the first paragraph of G.V.'s letter is a good reminder that, whether or not we can see them or consciously hear and sense them, our Spirit Guides and deceased loved ones on The Other Side are particularly attentive to us when we're going through difficult times. That's just a fact, and hard as it can be to remember through depression or stress, you'll find it a comforting exercise to start with the assumption that you're surrounded by spirit help and then just jot down every sign you see of the spirit world's possible presence, even if you're unsure that that's what it is, even if you're skeptical, even if you feel downright idiotic and hide the list of those signs from everyone but yourself. Every time the phone rings and no one's on the other end, every time you find coins lying around where it makes no sense for them to be, every time you're sure you caught a glimpse of something behind you in a mirror but turned to find nothing there, every time you think you feel a gentle breath on the back of your neck but convince yourself you imagined it, every time your TV seems to change channels on its own or one of your clocks or appliances seems to have developed a mind of its own, every time an object disappears from a place you're absolutely sure you put it and then reappears again later in that very same place, every time you see an "imaginary" shadow or hear an "imaginary" voice whispering your name, simply write it down and put it in a drawer or some other out-of-the-way place. Later on, when the difficult time has passed and your anxiety has eased a bit, take out the list, or the collected scraps of paper, and see how many signs, or at least possible signs, you were given that the spirit world was trying to reassure you that not for a moment were you facing your hardship alone.

And by the way, don't get discouraged if you find yourself not writing down many of those possible spirit signs at first. It really isn't easy when you're preoccupied by depression or anxiety, and it's also a challenge when it's something you're not accustomed to. But you really will find that the more you simply remind yourself to keep your eyes, ears, and mind open, the more you'll notice; and the more you notice, the better you'll get at being sensitive to the signs that spirits really do give us all the time to convey the greatest message we could ever hope for: "God keeps His promises. We really are eternal, and there really is no such thing as death."

I was sitting in my room one day when I was about four years old and a female spirit came to me. She just floated a little above the ground, holding out her arms as if she had known me for years. I wasn't afraid. In fact, somehow I felt as if I had known her for years too.

She said her name was Jennifer and that she was my sister, but she died. She promised she would always be there to protect me. Oddly, I'd been having weird dreams the previous week, but this was my first real wide-awake encounter with a spirit, and I was amazed at how comfortable I felt talking to her.

Several days later my mother and I were taking a walk and I pointed toward the sky and said, "Mom, is this where my sister lives now?" She looked shocked and was holding back tears, and she asked me where on earth I had heard such a thing. I didn't answer her, and she never said another word about it.

Finally I told my father about the whole experience when I was four years old. He asked me what the spirit looked like. I said she looked like a teenaged girl, very pretty, with long hair. He asked a lot of questions without answering any of mine. I was getting more and more frustrated, because it was like I was onto something but no one would confirm that Jennifer, who had appeared in my room and held out her arms to me when I was a child, was real and not just one of those "grown-up" things that fell under the heading of none of my business.

Seven more years of silence about Jennifer went by, seven years in which I felt very alone and like an outsider in my own family. And then one day my father and I were together at his job and suddenly he just broke down and announced out of nowhere, "Son, you would have had a sister, but she was stillborn."

It was like the past, present, and future all falling into place with one simple statement. From that moment on I've known with complete certainty that it's not that I did have a sister, I *do* have a sister, who's watching out for me every minute. It's sad that others in my family refuse to talk about her or let her be real to them. They don't know what they're missing. And it's sad that so many people in general are afraid of the idea of visitors from The Other Side or refuse to believe those visitors are real, either, because they bring so much peace and comfort and protection if we'll just welcome them instead of turning our backs on them. Thanks for letting me tell my story.——W.B.

There are several points I want to make about W.B.'s experience, starting with his almost passing observation that the first time this spirit visited him she "just floated a little above the ground." If you'll remember, in Chapter One of this book, and in many other books before this one, I told you that The Other Side isn't some far and distant place beyond the moon and stars, but instead it's really only three feet above our ground level here on earth. One of the quickest and easiest ways to tell when we're seeing a spirit instead of a ghost is that a spirit will seem to be "floating a little above the ground," while a ghost will seem to be functioning on the same level we are. What's actually happening, as I explained earlier, is that the spirit is simply moving along on its own ground level, three feet above ours, which to our eyes looks like floating. W.B. was four years old when he saw the spirit of his sister and added that she was floating. There's no doubt about it that four-year-olds are young enough that, like all children, their senses are wide open to the spirit world and they haven't been taught yet that they're "not supposed to" see or hear anything that doesn't exist on this earth. Please tell me how a child that age would be well read or sophisticated enough to make up a sister appearing to him in the form of a spirit, let alone add a detail like the fact that she was floating.

And then there's the question of how else this child could possibly have come across the discovery that he had a sister except by hearing it from her. In some situations I'd suspect, as I'm sure you would, too, that it came from a lot of eavesdropping, snooping, and filling in blanks. But in this house, in this family, where the subject of this still-born baby sister is so clearly off limits, and it's a safe bet that any evidence she was ever a reality has probably been buried or destroyed? I don't believe that it would ever have happened, that any of the adults would have ever said a word if W.B. hadn't essentially said to both of his parents, "I know I had a sister, so let's start the conversation from there." So again, ruling out the other obvious possibilities, where else would a four-year-old have learned about this well-kept secret except from the secret herself?

The point I'm making, as you've probably caught on to by now, is that when you read or hear a story like this one, you can cheat yourself if you limit your reaction to simply deciding whether or not you believe it. When it comes to anything regarding your beliefs, *think*! Take it step by step, see what holds together and what doesn't, and what makes sense and what doesn't. And when, as in W.B.'s story, what makes the most sense appears to involve a spirit visitation, try to get your mind back to its glorious, sacred childhood openness and promise yourself and the spirits around you that no one's ever going to tell you again what you are and are not "supposed to" see and deprive you of the comfort, peace, and wisdom you might be missing.

I grew up in a farmhouse that's been in my family for over a hundred years. I was always especially close to my father's side of the family and particularly fascinated by stories about how my great-grandfather Henry had come from Denmark to create this Nebraska ranch.

One Fourth of July Eve (there's a reason I'm pointing that out) when I was eleven years old I had one of those nightmare falling dreams I know everyone's had. I came down fast, with a "hard landing" that jolted me awake. Flat on my back, breathing hard from being startled, I tried to calm myself by looking up at the ceiling that was glowing white from the full moon outside my open window. Finally, slowly, my eyes shifted toward my bedroom doorway. The last thing I expected was that someone would actually be standing there staring into my room! All I remember seeing in the shadowy moonlight was a man with small glasses, a high forehead, a distinctive jaw, a straw hat, and overalls, just looking at me. I was terrified. I yelled for my dad, at which point the man in the doorway turned in the direction of my dad's room and disintegrated into a million tiny pieces, so that by the time my dad got there the man was gone.

The next day when I described the man as best I could, especially the shape of his jaw and the high forehead, my father said, "That sounds a lot like Grandpa Henry. And, you know, the Fourth of July was always his favorite holiday." That was news to me. No one had ever told me that before.

Years later I actually saw a picture of my great-grandfather Henry. I was shocked at how identical the photograph was to the face I had seen in my bedroom doorway on that long-ago summer night. I might have only had a glimpse of him before he disappeared, but it was a glimpse I'll never forget and, more important, a glimpse I went "on the record" with when I talked to my dad about it the very next day, so it's not like my memory just got more convenient over the years. It was him. I don't need anyone to confirm that for me. I'm already sure of that.

What I am curious about is if there was any connection between the appearance of my great-grandfather Henry that night and the falling dream I had right before I saw him. And if there is a connection, what is it?—N.W.

There's absolutely a frequent connection between "falling dreams" and spirit visits, even when, as in N.W.'s case, the exact order of events is slightly confused. To understand the connection you need to understand what "falling dreams" really are, and rather than assume that each and every one of you has read my book *Sylvia Browne's Book of Dreams*, I'll give you the somewhat abbreviated explanation here.

Many of our "dreams" are actually astral trips, in which our spirits take advantage of the fact that our conscious minds are out of the way and leave our bodies for journeys to visit friends and places they miss on The Other Side or here on earth or even in past lives. These journeys are as real as any trips our conscious minds and bodies take when we're awake, they're just much quicker, much more efficient, and incredibly less expensive. Most of the time our conscious minds are completely unaware of our spirits' exits from and reentries back into our bodies, and we look back on the trips themselves as "flying dreams" and "dreams" about people, both alive and deceased, whom in reality we spent time with while these cumbersome vehicles that our spirits reside in here on earth snored and drooled their way through the night.

But every once in a while our conscious minds become just faintly awake as our spirits make their descent back into our bodies, and that's when that awful "falling dream" occurs. Left to its own natural instincts, the spirit knows exactly how to get into and out of a body as gracefully and smoothly as silk, having done it countless times in who knows how many years in who knows how many incarnations on earth. But let the conscious mind get involved and suddenly there's a moment of abrupt panic, a sense of danger that says, "Yikes, something's very wrong here, my body's here, my spirit's out there, I think that means I'm dead!" and the spirit has to make a much more unceremonious reentry, the difference between easing gently back in like a perfect dive that barely causes a ripple in the surface of the water or getting yanked back in like a loud, tsunami-causing belly flop. It's jarring, it's disorienting, and it's no wonder that we can wake up a bit frightened, confused, and unable to remember the exact order of the events that preceded it.

In this story, Henry and N.W. are old friends from past lives both here and on The Other Side, and N.W. was astrally visiting Henry during sleep when he was jarred awake, possibly even by some noise from his father's nearby bedroom or the bright moonlight pouring in through his window, since the moonlight and calling out for his father were kind of superimposed over the vision of Great-Grandfather Henry standing in the doorway and then disintegrating. In other words, the images N.W. remembered later make sense, they're just jumbled together and out of sequence as so often happens as a result of a "falling dream," actually just the spirit making a safe but quicker reentry into the body after astral travel than our conscious minds can adjust to.

I would like to tell you about my first encounter with a spirit. It was a male, and he kind of drifted on air, with his feet not touching the ground. I was thirteen years old, and I was alone a lot, since both my parents worked. This spirit came into our home several times, and when he did the radio or TV would go on, and I would always have that feeling of the hair standing up on the back of my neck.

The last time he appeared in our house was the day my sister was born. She was born with a hole in her heart. (She's fine now, and full of life, thank God.) I knew my parents were really worried, so I was in the kitchen, decorating the house and baking a cake, trying to cheer them up and let them know that I knew my sister was going to be okay. All of a sudden an old radio on the kitchen counter started playing. It was bad enough that it started playing without my even touching it, but what really scared me so much was that I looked at the wall outlet and saw that it wasn't even plugged in. It made my hair stand up, and I had to go outside for air.

A month later a letter arrived, telling us that our former neighbor of many years, a doctor who actually built our house and loved it and spent a lot of time reflecting on it during his long illness, had died.

He died the day my sister was born. And the radio that started playing that same day without being turned on or even plugged in was the last strange thing that ever happened in that house.

I find it hard to believe it was him, but I find it hard to believe it wasn't too. I guess I would just love to know one way or the other.—B.U.

In the 1960s my family was living in a house that was heated by a coal heater. One night it woke all of us up by suddenly sounding exactly like a blast furnace, like it was working overtime or something. I heard my dad get up, and I looked at the clock as I got up to go help him and noticed it was 3:01 A.M. Dad checked the coal hopper, and it was full just like it was supposed to be. He looked into the stove door, expecting to see a blazing inferno from the deafening roar that seemed to be coming from in there, but a normal, harmless fire was burning away. He checked the wiring and found no problems, he did everything he knew to do and that blast furnace sound just kept on coming from the same fire we'd had in that same heater, night after night, year after year, with nothing like this ever happening before.

We were still trying to make sense of it a few hours later when

my aunt called from Idaho. It seems that the sawmill where my uncle worked had burned to the ground, killing him and everyone
else in it. The first fire trucks on the scene arrived at 2:59 A.M.

I'll bet it won't surprise you that we never had another problem with that coal heater. God rest my uncle.——D.W.

I'm sure it's obvious why I put these two letters together, and I almost wish these two people would start writing to each other, because they were each on the receiving end of the same thrilling
phenomenon. And in both cases their experiences are made even
more credible by the fact that they obviously had no warning of these
impending deaths. Therefore they had no reason to start consciously
or unconsciously reading more into strange noises and odd occur-
rences than there really was and creating "weirdness" just because
they thought maybe there should be some under the circumstances.
Instead, they experienced things they couldn't possibly explain, got
through them as best they could, and then went on about their business. When news came that corresponded precisely with the timing
of their unexplainable experiences, each of them was spiritual, sensitive, open minded, and bright enough to consider the strong possibility that the spirit world just might be the connection.

And of course it was.

The energy released when the spirit leaves the body as the body
dies is a powerful force. That it would be able to affect devices that
are dependent on energy sources like electricity and heat in order to
function comes as no surprise at all. In fact, a newly liberated spirit
would seek out and delight in finding such easy ways to conduct itself
and make its presence so conspicuous.

But then comes the question that confuses most people, and
frankly, I'm not all that good at explaining the answer myself, because some of it involves physics, and just writing that word almost

makes me doze off. The question is some version of "So instead of leaving his body and going to The Other Side, that first man's spirit left his body and went to the house he built because he loved it so much?" Or "Let me get this straight, instead of going directly into the tunnel toward the light after it left his body, the uncle's spirit decided to stop off first and play with his relatives' coal heater? Doesn't that seem just the tiniest bit trivial?"

Even though I can't explain it to you with the brilliant scientific objectivity of a physicist, I can tell you what I know to be true and how I know it to be true. I know from almost sixty years of asking endless questions of my Spirit Guide, Francine, I know from my own experiences with astral travel and the astral experiences of thousands upon thousands of colleagues and clients and family members and staff, I know from reading literally thousands of books about the spirit world in all its aspects and variations, I know from studying every major work on every major religion in the world including twenty-six versions of the Bible, and I know from every spirit I've talked to in sixty-six years of being psychic: the instant the spirit is liberated from the body once and for all, our earthly laws/limits of time, space, physics, gravity, and all those other yardsticks we use to measure "possible" and "impossible" here cease to exist. In the spirit world, where eternity is a reality, there is no such thing as "past, present, and future," there is only "now." In the spirit world, you never hear that common earthly complaint, "I can't be in two places at once," because spirits can. They can absolutely bi-locate, or be any two places they want at the same time. And traveling to those places is neither cumbersome nor time consuming, since there are no bodies or luggage to drag around, and as for the trip itself, it's only a matter of thinking themselves there and voilà, they're there. It's exactly that incomprehensible and exactly that simple. And I'll tell you what else it is—it's as familiar to our spirits as the alphabet is to our conscious minds, we just have an impossible time remembering it, because part of our job while we're here on earth is to live by the constraints of the "house rules" and make the most of it. When we're spirits again, we'll be as free as the home builder in the first story or the uncle in the second—not *either* headed joyfully toward the light on our way Home *or* visiting earthly sites we're going to miss, but saying good-bye to beloved people and places on earth without for an instant interrupting our sacred journey to resume our lives on The Other Side.

For the past few years there has been a man following me around. Usually, he is just in my house, but he is around me a lot. At first I thought I was just seeing things until one of my friends saw him, too, and confirmed exactly what he looked like to me— not quite six feet tall, seemed to be in a black coat, maybe a trench coat, usually kept his hands in his pockets, and it was hard to make out his face and feet.

I can't honestly say he made me feel threatened, just uneasy at first. I got used to him after a while, and for a long time he stopped being so obvious. Then I moved in with a friend of mine who turned out to be someone I should have stayed away from. As soon as I moved in with this supposed friend, the man in the black coat began appearing again more and more often. Then one night I woke up too frightened to move or speak, somehow knowing the man was in the room with me. Finally I made myself look around and there he was, just sitting there in the chair next to the bed. I'm not quite sure how to explain my reaction, but somehow seeing him there actually startled me and calmed me at the same time, like I was getting a feeling that whoever he was, he was supposed to be there.

That week, my roommate and I had such a terrible argument that I ended up moving out. It turned out to be a good move and a relief to get away from that person who really wasn't a friend, I found out, and I haven't seen the man in the black coat ever since either.

Who was he? Is he gone? Was he somehow connected to my ex-roommate? Thanks for helping identify him for me.—D.H.

This is a good exercise for any of you who are able to see spirits. Ask yourself the following questions and see if you can't identify the spirit yourself without needing me at all:

When you first started noticing this spirit, did it seem to be most attached to you, or to someone around you?

If it seemed most attached to you, was it someone you recognized, like a deceased family member or loved one, or someone unfamiliar?

Looking past the general uneasiness of having a visible spirit around you, did this one seem to mean you harm, or did it seem well intentioned toward you?

When you found yourself in times of increased stress or potential danger, did this spirit seem to appear more often, or less often?

Likewise, when your life was calm and going smoothly, did this spirit seem to appear more often, or less often?

In D.H.'s case, and possibly in yours, the answers are that the spirit she began seeing was definitely attached to her, and it was someone who didn't look familiar to her, certainly not someone she'd been related to or met in this lifetime. He didn't seem to mean her any harm, she just felt uneasy because she wasn't used to having a visible spirit around her. As soon as she moved in with this roommate that she, by her own admission, should have stayed away from, this spirit, this "man in the black trench coat," started appearing more and more often, and as soon as she moved out, i.e., away from the stress/potential danger, he virtually disappeared.

Which is a fairly good description of a Spirit Guide and how they work. From now on, D.H., you might as well call him by his first name, which is Aaron.

I was twenty-one years old, probably older than many when they "play" with a Ouija board for the first time, but I was spending the weekend with my fiancé's sister and a group of her friends, someone brought it out of the game closet and I admit it, I was curious. Well, imagine my surprise when not only did a lovely spirit named Loren begin speaking to us through the Ouija board about the history of my parents' house in Rhode Island, some of which turned out to be true, but I think I even caught a glimpse of Loren herself, moving quickly past the French doors, with blond hair and a long dark red coat or cape of some kind. By the end of the session the Ouija board cursor was moving practically by itself, with my barely touching it, but Loren had started to become nasty and accused me of stealing a friend's bracelet, which was a lie and embarrassing in front of these people who didn't know me that well. It probably sounds silly to let something like this upset me, but I don't understand what happened and why this spirit who started out to be so sweet suddenly turned on me like that.——M.B.S.

This is one of probably thirty letters I got about Ouija boards, some people telling of amazing experiences with them, some telling of frightening experiences, and some being just confused and upset by them, as M.B.S. was.

Please listen to me about Ouija boards.

Get rid of them. Period.

It's not because they're evil.

It's not because they don't work. If you've ever used one, you know there's a good chance the cursor is going to start moving, words will probably be spelled out, yes and no questions will probably be answered, and all sorts of surprising responses will probably come spilling out.

I want you to get rid of every Ouija board in your home for the simple reason that using a Ouija board is no different than throwing open your front door to anyone and everyone who happens to show up there. Without bothering to find out who they are, where they came from, what they want, why they're there, whether or not they are dangerous, whether or not they're psychologically stable, how long they intend to stay, etc., etc., etc., etc. You just say, "Come right on in," and then you're surprised when it doesn't always go well?

So now you're wondering why it wouldn't always go well if all spirits from The Other Side whom you're trying to contact are happy, loving, and peaceful. That's exactly the problem—that's true of all spirits from The Other Side, who as I've said are opportunistic and look for energy to attach themselves to, including ours, so that they can communicate. But of course ghosts, confused and some-times deranged as they can be, are opportunistic, too, with their own agenda, and often look for ways to frighten or bully us intruders away. Dark entities headed for the Left Door or even astrally travel-ing around right here on earth can spot an opportunity a mile away and stop by for a good time, too, for that matter. And your energy, conveniently localized on a piece of plastic, poised to move it around on a piece of wood with letters on it, is like an indiscriminate wel-come mat for all of the above, a microphone for all of those voices with no guarantee that you'll always know the light from the dark, a message delivered in love or simply a message delivered in a sweet, melodic voice that really means you harm.

So to all of you who wrote about Ouija-board experiences, I don't doubt for a moment that you were sincere and it's not that I'm not taking you seriously, but addressing the specifics is like trying to carefully analyze the thoughts and behavior of an entity who may or may not have been a pathological liar and/or a psychopath.

It's worth repeating, with emphasis:

Get rid of your Ouija boards.

Ever since my daughter was about two years old she had what doctors and specialists called night terrors. She would appear to be awake, yet would be having a complete conversation with someone or something, in a dreamlike state. Some of her "dreams" would terrify, and I would be unable to wake her. She would call out for me and scream to make "them" leave. These episodes would last anywhere from a few seconds to fifteen minutes to all night long.

One morning, after a particularly awful night, I called both my church and a psychiatrist, not sure which if either of them to turn to. The church recommended the psychiatrist, and the psychiatrist felt she was perfectly fine, just having "night terrors." I had her tested to make sure she didn't have schizophrenia or bipolarism or any of those chemically caused mental illnesses, but her test results came back normal. The tests seemed to frighten her as much as the "dreams," which made me feel even more desperate to find answers.

When she was four years old she would hear voices and cry and tell me to make them stop. I would ask her what the voices were saying, and she would reply that she couldn't tell me or didn't want to talk about it. Again, the psychiatrists all said she was normal, and the voices she was hearing were just her own thoughts that she either didn't understand or didn't have the vocabulary to convey.

She's now seven, and yesterday she asked me if it was okay to fly in her dreams. I asked her if she's been flying in her dreams, and she said no, she just wanted to know if it would be okay if she did. I told her that dreams are normal, and that some people fly in their dreams and others swim or do other things that they normally can't do when they're awake.

She thought about that and then finally said, "Mommy, I do fly in my dreams a lot, and I really like it. It makes me happy, and I wish I could really fly."

I'm convinced that my daughter is experiencing something that I can't understand, but I believe maybe you can.—J.L.

This letter is so loaded with issues it's hard to know where to start. I'm sure that one of the many reasons I reacted so strongly to it is that if I'd been the first psychic in my family, if I hadn't had three hundred years' worth of psychic ancestors and a psychic grand-mother right there in the house to calmly explain things to me from the time I was born, the childhood described here could easily have been mine.

It's as natural for children to be psychic, to be tuned in to the spirit world, as it is for them to breathe. The spirit world of The Other Side (or, on rare occasions, through the Left Door) is where they've just come from. They're still making the transition from that dimension to this one, so seeing and hearing both worlds is a matter of course and something that doesn't occur to them as odd or un-natural unless they're made to feel self-conscious about it. I can't urge you strongly enough never to do that to a child. If your child tells you they're talking to someone you don't happen to see or hear, please don't assume you're right and they're wrong and begin scold-ing them about making things up. Take it from me, being told you're making something up when you know perfectly well you're not is about as confusing and discouraging a message as you can get, even if you're "only a child." As I said, I was lucky—I had Grandma Ada right there, who not only knew I wasn't making things up but could see and hear the same things I could and explain them to me. But every once in a while when she didn't happen to be around, my mother was only too happy to do her best to make me wish more than life itself that I could just be a normal kid, whatever "normal" was.

Very young children have any number of issues to deal with, and it's more difficult for some than for others. The transition from the freedom of spirit life to the confinement of living in a human body again can be scary and/or infuriating. The realization that you've left countless friends in the perfect, exquisite beauty of The Other Side to live among these strangers in this flawed place called earth, even though it was your choice, can be jarring.

And when you're as young as the girl in the story, your most recent past life on earth, i.e., the last time your spirit resided in a human body, is going to be a very fresh memory and, depending on what that past life was like, not necessarily a happy, safe or secure memory either. Lindsay and I wrote a book entitled *Past Lives, Future Healing*, which deals with a phenomenon called cell memory. To grossly oversimplify the basics of cell memory, when the spirit chooses to incarnate for another lifetime on earth, it invariably has a reaction to finding itself human again that permeates every cell of this new body with emotionally charged responses that begin with the words "Last time I was in a body I . . ." As a result the body reacts to whatever the rest of that sentence is: Last time I was in a body I . . . *became paralyzed when I was three years old*, or I . . . *fell off a bridge and died at the age of forty*, or I . . . *had chronic asthma from the time I was an infant*. Healing that "cell memory" from the past life can heal any number of chronic "mystery" fears and illnesses in this life, and countless "night terrors" in children can be "cured" by quietly reminding them over and over while they sleep that "What you're remembering is a whole other time and a whole other place. It's all taken care of, it's over, you're in a brand-new body and a brand-new life now, and you never have to go through that last life again." Surround them in your mind with the white light of the Holy Spirit, keep reminding them that the past life that's scaring them is over and they're safe now, and don't worry that they're too young to understand what you're saying. Even the tiniest of babies have spirits as old as eternity itself, and it's those spirits who will hear you and find peace in the God-centered truth of your words.

Being free of these silly human bodies is more natural to very young children than being confined to them, so they rack up millions of "frequent flyer" miles in astral trips while they sleep, as their spirits visit The Other Side, friends from past lives, and anywhere else they can go that feels safer and more familiar than this strange place they've found themselves now.

And then there's a pet peeve of mine, that makes my hair stand on end. I happen to believe that if there's anywhere you should be able to go where the subject of interaction with the spirit world should at least come up in a positive, loving way, it's your church. Unless your particular religion embraces the belief that when you're dead, you're dead, I so wish many religions would give more thought to opening their minds a little and embracing some of the joy, power, and comfort that would be consistent with their own belief systems.

God, the messiahs, the saints, and all our departed loved ones, according to most religions, are very real and very much alive, they simply exist in spirit as opposed to human form.

We can and should talk to them on a regular basis. That's called prayer.

They cannot and should not talk back to us. If they do, and we hear them, that's called nuts.

I will never understand that, and I will never, ever agree with it.

But I will continue to hope that churches keep exploring, keep thinking, keep stretching, and keep demanding more and more of themselves until they can do better for worried parents and children who hear voices than give them a choice between an exorcism and a psychiatrist.

> Two days before my mom died, while she was on the respirator in the hospital after suffering a stroke and a heart attack, she came to me during the night. I was sitting on the couch, unable to sleep because of the stress of worrying about her, and suddenly there she was beside me. She was somewhat transparent, but I could see her clearly, and I was ecstatic because she was speaking to me, even though she wasn't really using her voice. I could feel her deep love and her presence. I asked her what she wanted, and she smiled.
>
> She reassured me that all was well and that she would be going Home two days later. She wanted me to help my brothers with her departure, and she gave me messages for them. Ten years later she still comes to visit us from time to time, and I can feel her warmth and see her smile before she leaves.—A.L.

This short, sweet story is a reminder of an area of confusion in far more letters than I expected. It's either something people aren't aware of or something they forget, but it's so important that I'll keep right on saying it as often as I need to until it's a fact that's made its way into everyone's heart:

The spirits of loved ones who are ill or even comatose can visit us just as surely and just as strongly as the spirits of loved ones who have died.

I can't begin to describe the confusion and occasional pain not knowing that simple fact seems to cause. Some letters told of spirit visits from loved ones who were ill and the panic at the assumption that they must have passed away. Others told of spirit visits from loved ones who were ill that were dismissed or ignored completely because those who were visited knew the loved one was still alive.

I wish I could make promises when all I can offer is the small flame of a "maybe," but I will tell you that I've worked with clients who've had very real spirit visits from spouses and loved ones suffering with everything from Alzheimer's to severe Parkinson's disease to Lou Gehrig's disease to an irreversible coma. The condition of the mind and body has nothing whatsoever to do with the perpetually healthy, joyful, loving spirit, so the visits are invariably as comforting and reassuring as they can be. If you have a loved one who's gravely ill and their spirit hasn't visited you, please don't let it enter your mind that they don't love you enough or they don't care. I know that my own worry and grief has blocked loved ones' spirits from visiting me when they were ill, and if anyone should know better, it should be me, let's face it, and it's also not at all uncommon for spirits of the gravely ill to visit The Other Side every chance they get, and how could we possibly begrudge them that?

If your answer to that question was "But we've got so little time left together," you're forgetting yet another thing the gravely ill are already beginning to remember quite clearly again—"so little time left together" is just an earthly illusion. The truth, God's truth, is that we have eternity.

As a child, my grandfather and I were very close, and one of my clearest memories was the clean, distinctive smell of the shaving talc he used every single day. It was a smell I associated with him and him alone for as far back as I can remember until the day he died when I was twenty-one.

Years later I gave birth to a son, and he was still a newborn when the big controversy about the DPT shot exploded on the scene. (The DPT shot was to immunize against diphtheria, whooping cough, and tetanus, but it was also rumored to cause catastrophic fevers, potential brain damage, and an increased threat of Sudden Infant Death Syndrome.) All new mothers were nervous about the adverse affects the vaccine could have on their baby, but I admit, I took nervous to a whole new level. I was absolutely frightened out of my mind on the night before my baby was to have his first baby shots. I was sitting alone in the dark in my living room, well past midnight, almost in tears I was so scared, when suddenly a long-forgotten but instantly recognizable scent began floating into and filling the room. It was my grandfather's talc! I couldn't believe it. I looked around for some possible source, some logical explanation for the smell. But of course I saw nothing, heard nothing, there seemed to be no one there but me.

And yet for me to deny a scent as strong and as distinctive as this one would be to deny my own senses and the overwhelming feeling of comfort that was settling over me. I knew then as I know now that somehow my grandfather came to me in my living room that night, when I was afraid, to tell me not to worry, that my baby boy would be just fine.

I had never known before that one of the ways a ghost can communicate with the living is through smell. It has never happened again, but there's no doubt that I received a visit that night, and my grandfather was right, my baby boy got his shots and everything really was just fine.—C.P.

I'm sure you're way ahead of me—this was a visit from the grandfather's spirit, not the grandfather's ghost. On the rare occasions when ghosts emit an odor, it's invariably a really unpleasant one. "Scent" is not one of the words that would leap to mind.

What's really worth paying attention to in this story is that C.P., instead of focusing on the bizarre phenomenon of her grandfather's presence and either her fear or amazement over that, was able to cut to the core of that phenomenon and figure out what he was doing there and why he had come. It was about her, yes. But it was to reassure her and calm her *about her son*. It wasn't just to temporarily dis-tract her until she remembered what she had to do the next day and let the anxiety of it get a grip on her all over again.

Messages from spirits really aren't that complicated. You know, if you've seen my lectures or TV appearances and/or read my other books, how often people seem sure that a deceased loved one is trying to tell them something, they just can't figure out what it is, and they're so disappointed when I say, "They're trying to tell you that they're fine, they're with you, and they love you." Sorry, but 99.9 times out of a hundred that's the message—your deceased loved one isn't deceased at all. There is no such thing as death. Which I happen to think is the most incredibly powerful message we can get, but I've actually had clients, upon hearing that, look almost disgusted and say, "So not a word about who's supposed to get the Lexus, huh?" And when spirits visit during times of anxiety, particularly spirits who visit rarely or who have never visited before, as in the case of C.P.'s grandfather, you can bet there's something very deliberate about the timing and purpose of that visit.

When any transcended spirit makes its presence known to you in any way, if the rest of your mind goes blank with shock at that moment, hold on to this one truth—that loved one, whoever they are, has come to you from a busy, joyful life, in a place of unspeakably exquisite beauty where they live among the messiahs and the Angels, and where the very air they breathe sparkles with the tangible presence of God. Any visit from them, no matter how subtle it is or in what form, is a blessing and an honor and proof of the eternity we have to look forward to as well. They are absolutely there to promise that we're going to be fine, and that our children are going to be fine, and that in the end there's no need for any of us to be afraid, because while we're all doing the best we can at taking care of each other, God, who created us all, is taking care of us.

My father died a year ago from cancer. He was fifty-six. He hadn't been able to spend much time with my daughters and had never met my youngest until my mother and stepdad took them on a cross-country trip to visit him one last time. Sadly, he was so sick by then, and my girls were still so young, that I'm afraid they didn't remember much about him, but I know it meant a lot to him.

Months later all of my daughters were sleeping in my oldest daughter's room when they all began yelling for me, very upset. I ran in to find them terrified and asked them what was wrong. They said they heard doors opening and closing in the hallway, and someone with "heavy feet" and "swishy pants" walking up and down outside their door. The more they described the sounds and tried to duplicate them, the more I found myself starting to smile.

All his life my father walked with an unmistakable heavy, lumbering gait. He also, God bless him, and I say this with all the respect and fondness in the world, had the flattest "bottom" I've ever seen and never wore a belt, so his pants always sagged and you could hear the loose fabric of his pantlegs swishing against each other when he walked. I explained this to my girls, and from then on they knew not to be afraid and whenever they heard those noises, they just said, "Hi, Grandpa!" and felt proud, knowing he'd come all the way from The Other Side to check on them because he didn't get enough time with them while he was here.—J.J.M.

When my father was very young, he had a great aunt who lived with his family. One day his older sister was baby-sitting him while their parents were out for the afternoon. He walked past his great-aunt's room and noticed that she was packing up all her belongings. He asked her where she was going. She told him she was going to be gone for a very long time and that she loved him, and then she walked out the front door with her bag in her hand.

As soon as his parents got home my father told them about his great aunt leaving. They apparently stared silently at each other for several moments, and then finally, a little awkwardly, my dad's mother asked, "Do you remember what she was wearing?"

My father described as best he could the dark blue high-collared jacket and long skirt his great aunt was wearing when she walked out the door. There was another silence, and then my father's parents led him into the parlor, sat down with him, and told him why they were acting so oddly. They believed every word he was telling them, because they'd kept from him where they'd been so he wouldn't be upset, but they'd spent the afternoon at that same great-aunt's funeral. And the outfit my father described her wearing when she left was exactly what she was wearing in her casket.

I've talked to everyone who was there that day—my father, my grandparents, and my father's older sister—and they have identical memories of it, they assure me it hasn't been embellished or exaggerated over the years, and they each become kind of quiet and preoccupied when they talk about it. It happened, there's no doubt about that, it's just that to this day they still can't quite understand it.—E.W.

These stories are beautiful examples of spirits at their most opportunistic, in the most complimentary sense of the word. How brilliant of the spirits in both of these stories to demonstrate their presence to children, who share the distinction with animals of being the most psychic creatures on earth, and let those children and the innocent accuracy of their descriptions provide proof the adults might have either ignored, dismissed, or tried to explain away.

Think about it. You've been a spirit before. You'll be a spirit again. When you decide to visit a loved one on earth, aren't you going to do everything in your power to maximize the odds of that loved one knowing you were there? I am. And children are wonderful messengers for the spirit world, as long as they're taught from the time they're born, while their memories of The Other Side are still fresh anyway, who spirits are, where they come from, why we on earth are so blessed by their presence and especially why there's no need to be frightened of them.

Good for the spirits in these stories for being so smart, and good for the children for doing such excellent jobs of reporting what they saw and heard. It's incalculable how much richer their parents' lives are because of it.

I was in my early teens when I was awakened one night by the feeling of not being alone, like the weight of a person on the edge of my bed. With my eyes still closed I tried to dismiss it as probably just being my cat Cleo, but it slowly dawned on me that this was far too much weight for Cleo. So finally I pried my eyes open and saw a young girl sitting on my bed. She had long dark hair, and she was wearing a dark dress, and she was just sitting there looking at me. It was a very peaceful, loving feeling, not at all scary. But as soon as I started to wake up fully, I felt the weight lift off my bed and she was gone. I quickly decided I'd just been dreaming about the girl, it had been my cat after all, and Cleo had simply jumped off the bed. But as I looked around I realized that Cleo wasn't in the room, and my bedroom door was locked, so obviously no one had been there at all. It really was a dream. Odd that the weight on the edge of the bed was so real in a dream, though. That was a first for me.

The next morning I was telling my sister about it and found her staring back at me with her eyes wide open, amazed and a little scared. I asked her what was wrong.

"I woke up last night to the feeling of someone rubbing my back," she said. "It didn't scare me at first because I thought it was you. But then when it stopped and I looked around, there was nobody in my room with me. You didn't come in and rub my back last night?"

I assured her it wasn't me, and we decided we should tell our mom, because she's a real practical, down-to-earth person and we knew she could make sense out of what happened.

To our surprise, she said that *she* had been awakened during the night too. She wasn't sure exactly what noise or feeling of movement or sense of a presence woke her up, she was just sure that one of us kids was in her bedroom, and she sat up in bed to see what the problem was. When she saw that neither one of us was in there, she got up and went to look for us and saw each of us sound asleep in our own rooms. It confused her and kept her awake for a while before she was finally able to get back to sleep.

All three of us are convinced we were visited by a ghost. I've always wondered if it could have been my baby sister who died at birth. But from everything I've heard and read, ghosts do not age. Do you think it could have been her checking in on us? This happened in 1970, and we've never seen her since. If it was her, we wish she would come back.—M. W.

There's no doubt about it, it was her—her spirit, not her ghost, and she's been back many, many times, she's just been more subtle about it, playing with clocks and phones and electrical devices and moving things from one place to another so that you occasionally wonder if you're getting a little absentminded.

But what's really fascinating about this story is the lengths to which spirits will go to be recognized by the people on earth they come to visit.

M. W. is correct in her belief that ghosts don't age. Trapped as they are, they're also frozen in the time warp in which they died—or, in their case, in which they refuse to believe they died—and that's the age they remain until they finally and inevitably move on.

On The Other Side, though, all the residents who've ever been incarnated are thirty years old. Everyone, including me, inevitably asks, "Why thirty?" My Spirit Guide, Francine, answers, "Because they are." But we wouldn't necessarily recognize a visiting spirit if they came to us in the form of a thirty-year-old unless we knew them best when they were around that age here on earth. Spirits want their visits with us to be joyful and comforting, not confusing guessing games. And what else is a child going to be but confused if their beloved frail, gray-haired eighty-year-old deceased grandfather comes to visit in the form of a muscular, athletic, raven-haired thirty-year-old? How comforted would a young twenty-year-old grief-stricken mother be if the six-month-old baby daughter she lost to SIDS showed up in spirit form to introduce herself as a lovely thirty-year-old woman?

We're able to understand all these things perfectly and without explanation when we reunite on The Other Side. But the Spirit World, knowing our limitations and literal minds here on earth, makes whatever physical adjustments will help us catch on to their identity, and M.W.'s story illustrates that fact nicely, even though M.W. was the only one to actually see their deceased sister in spirit form. There would have been no clues at all for M.W. in the sight of a thirty-year-old young woman sitting on the end of her bed. And the sight of an infant, as M.W.'s sister was when she died, lying helplessly on the bed, might have startled M.W. or upset her more than it comforted her. But the sight of a girl that M.W. perceived as young, i.e., younger than M.W., and a spirit as well, capable of disappearing into thin air in a locked room, gave her a couple of good hints. Then there were the feelings of peace and comfort she got from her brief contact with the spirit, feelings she could equate with love and family and safety and security. Add the news that this spirit apparently visited her sister and her mother on the same night, not visibly but with the same gentle, loving effort to say hello but not disturb, and, led by the description M.W. was able to offer, this family was able to identify exactly who their visitor was.

For a period of more than six years of my life, I spent a lot of time with a man who was very special to me. We frequently talked about marriage. What kept stopping me from going through with it was his excessive drinking.

In case you think I'm being judgmental when I use the word "excessive," I should add that when we broke up, he was exhibiting severe symptoms of alcoholism and experiencing hallucinations. That was in the 1980s, and he was about forty years old.

I saw him rarely after that, even though we lived in the same area and had mutual friends. The next time we spoke was in the spring of 1997. He'd married and was getting divorced by then, and he wanted to see me. I was surprised at how easy and natural our conversation was, as though no time had passed, but even after all those years I realized I was still angry at him for the excessive drinking he'd allowed to destroy the wonderful life we could have had together. He gave me his number, but I knew I wouldn't call him.

Another year passed. I moved to Florida. In August of 1998, I went through a terrible period of dark depression after losing a job and being betrayed by someone I thought was a trusted friend. One night in particular I remember lying in bed believing it was possible that I really wouldn't ever find another job and that my elderly parents, as if they hadn't already done more than enough for me in their lives, would find themselves having to support me yet again, which would be unbearable to me. I prayed very hard for help that night, asking God for any hope he could offer and for me to please not feel so useless, weak, and alone.

I don't remember falling asleep that night, but I do remember that the minute I did I was dreaming, and in my dream that long-ago special man was there. He said, "You can lean on me," and he told me to put my head on his chest. I did, and I felt an amazing sense of relief. The next thing I knew, we were walking on the beach. He was to my left, with the ocean beyond him. He'd always had a terrific sense of humor and I associated him with lots of laughter, but in my dream he was very serious and determined. All of a sudden he stopped and turned to me.

I'm not sure what he said or how I knew this, but he wanted to pull something from me. I resisted, still resenting him, I guess. It wasn't my heart he wanted, it was more like my essence, my drive, my inspiration, for lack of a better word. He insisted, and there, with our just facing each other, the next thing I knew I had this incredible feeling of sparkling unity that seemed to rise up like a pilot light being reignited, and then the intensity and he were gone.

When I woke up the next morning I had the warmest, most grateful feelings toward him, and I wanted to contact him. Suddenly, for just a few moments, I was able to cherish all the things I'd loved about him, with no interference. But then, inevitably, those other ugly memories came flooding back in too and once again, I didn't call.

Less than a month later, in November 1998, I landed a terrific job. Maybe two weeks after that at most, just after Thanksgiving, an old mutual friend of his and mine called whom I hadn't talked to in ages. After a few minutes of general catching up I finally asked how "he" was doing.

"I thought you knew," she said. "He passed away. Very suddenly. In the spring of '97. Come to think of it, I saw him the morning he died, and he said he'd just spoken to you the day before."

Now that I know he was gone when I had that "dream" about him, I no longer believe it was a "dream" at all. I believe with all my heart that I went to visit him on The Other Side. When I thought he wanted to pull something from me, I was wrong. What he really wanted was to give me something he wasn't healthy enough to give me in life, much as he would have liked to—hope and strength and a sense of direction and all those things I prayed for that night.

I must have complained to him a thousand times during our relationship that he was never there for me when I needed him. That thought will never cross my mind again. I treasure the honor of meeting his spirit on that beautiful beach, seeing the amazing man he truly was, and knowing that I can now always remember him with no anger and with all the gratitude and respect he deserves.

And finally, I have to say, I've always been skeptical about the idea that we all come from The Other Side and we'll all go there when we die. I thought if there really were a place that perfect and that spectacular, we'd remember it or know about it somehow. Since we don't, it must not exist, right?

Wrong.

I was there, with my friend, I know I was.

And it's this simple. The only reason we don't know about The Other Side is that if we did, we wouldn't want to be here anymore.—T.H.

I don't have a single thing to add to that but "Amen."

Chapter Six

HAUNTINGS, VOICES, AND SECRETS OF THE RICH AND FAMOUS

During the writing of this book I got a phone call from a documentary film producer on behalf of a prestigious, highly respected internationally syndicated television network. The producer's proposal went like this:

For an enormous paycheck, they would fly me first class to the site of the tragic, controversial death of a famous celebrity. I would be given five-star accommodations during my stay, and all I had to do in exchange was stand as close as possible to the exact spot where the celebrity had died, trance my Spirit Guide, Francine, and let her tell the cameras and a worldwide audience of countless millions what had really happened.

I already knew what Francine had to say. She'd told me what had really happened on the day of the tragedy. And there are two things I know about Francine that are indisputable: She never lies, and she considers it a moral breach of her oath to God as a Spirit Guide to edit the information she's given. Bearing those two things in mind, I gave the producer the only answer I could possibly have given him under the circumstances.

I said no.

So much for "everyone has their price." Honestly, it wouldn't have mattered if he'd doubled it, or tripled it, or started adding zeroes until he'd run out of paper. There were and are some confidences I'll never betray and secrets I'll always keep, because to do anything else would hurt too many people, because I've made my own promises to God, because if people can't trust me with their secrets I'd be in the horribly lonely position of never being able to trust anyone with mine, and because at the end of the day, I have to live with myself, and without integrity, I'm not sure I could.

Don't get me wrong, I've made some mistakes along the way—and I mean some real whoppers—that if you don't know the whole story could make it look as if my integrity was a little blurry from time to time. Again, ask me and I'll tell you exactly how stupid I've been, how naive and inappropriately trusting of the wrong people I can be, and just how incredibly unpsychic I am about myself. But accuse me of ever being deliberately dishonest, or indiscreet, or greedy and ambitious at someone else's expense, or careless about the issue of integrity, and you'll have a fight on your hands, and that includes the subject of celebrities, both past and present. I don't solicit them as clients, I don't reveal their names or discuss them when they are clients, and I never, ever indulge in "ambulance chasing." In other words, when there's a famous missing-person or murder case making headlines, if I come up with relevant information, I'll contact my friends in law enforcement, but I will absolutely not approach the families. I'll return their calls and make time for them in a heartbeat if they ask, which they often do, but I won't intrude on their private tragedy, and if you ever read about my involvement with them, that information will never come from me or my office.

You're probably wondering about now if I'm setting you up for a chapter in which I bring up several well-known people and then proceed to tell you that they were all nice and I don't care what the tabloids said, they all really died of natural causes. And, no, that's not what I'm doing. You'll find some interesting surprises and some secrets in these pages, you have my word, and you know I wouldn't bother writing a whitewash chapter where I'm just going to lie my way through it as if my credibility with you means nothing to me. But I would never write a celebrity smear chapter, either, and I'll tell you why. As silly as I feel saying this, I guess in my own way, as far as being widely and frequently recognized is concerned, I qualify as a celebrity. And I have no complaints about that. The vast majority of people who spot me on the street, or in a store or a restaurant, and come over to say hello are just as lovely as they can be. Every once in a while, though, someone apparently gets it in their head that "celebrity" means "public property" and/or "deserves no courtesy," walks up to me with a sense of absolute entitlement, and nails me with some brief, scathing insult before walking away again as if they've just checked an important item off their to-do list. Mind you, they would never behave like this toward a total stranger, but because they recognize me I no longer fall under the category of "stranger," and I've honestly learned over all these years to laugh it off, with one exception—it still offends me beyond words when it happens in front of any of my grandchildren. It hurts them, it makes them cry, and I don't appreciate trying to come up with a good answer to "Why would someone be mean to you when they don't even know you?" when there *is* no good answer to that.

If I don't like it when someone does it to me, I'm not about to deliberately do it to anyone else, and there's no question that everyone I write about in this chapter still has living family members and/or friends whose feelings matter very much to me. In fact, a few words to those family members and/or friends: I hope you can read the genuine underlying respect in the pages that follow, and please accept my heartfelt apologies if anything I say inadvertently offends you. If you have questions, or information you'd like to explore further with me in private, please don't hesitate to get in touch with me through my office and I'll be happy to help in any way I can. Just explain to my staff which of the people in this chapter you're calling about and your connection to them, and they'll discreetly take it from there, you can count on it. They haven't been with me for thirty years or more without learning a thing or two about discretion, after all.

The Bela Lugosi House

You might think that any psychic researcher interested in hauntings would have leapt at the opportunity to explore the house of "Dracula" himself, Bela Lugosi. In my case, you'd be wrong. For one thing, believe it or not, he was before my time. The film for which he was best known was shot five years before I was born. For another thing, meaning no disrespect to Mr. Lugosi and his many fans, but I've never made it all the way through *Dracula* without either suffering brief spurts of involuntary laughter or falling sound asleep. For yet another thing, when the opportunity did present itself, I was in the midst of an insane schedule of readings, a lecture tour, and a stack of pro bono criminal cases. So touring the Hollywood home of an actor who'd been dead for decades, whom I knew nothing about except that he'd starred in a film I didn't care for, frankly sounded like a waste of time I couldn't afford.

There was one reason and only one reason I finally agreed. His name is Nick Nocerino. He's a vastly experienced paranormal investigator I'd worked with, liked, and respected enormously. He and noted paranormal photographer Chuck Pelton, with whom I'd also worked, had already committed to exploring the Bela Lugosi house, and it was their involvement that made the invitation irresistible. I trusted Nick and Chuck. I knew their integrity, their objectivity, and their rock-solid commitment to absolute authenticity, for better or worse, ghosts, spirits, or nothing at all. If they thought Bela Lugosi's house might be worth looking into, who was I to pass it up?

And so off the three of us went, Nick, Chuck, and me, in a van loaded with countless pieces of high-tech equipment, having no clue what, if anything, we were about to uncover. Nick, who'd done his homework and knew almost everything there was to know about Bela Lugosi and the house itself, asked if I had any questions, or if there was anything about the man's life I wanted to be briefed about. My answer was an almost urgent "Absolutely not." I insist on walking into haunting investigations with as little factual information and as few predispositions as possible, so that whatever I experience is fresh, spontaneous, and as completely unbiased as any worthwhile investigation on any subject should be.

We arrived late in the evening, and Nick promptly began strapping equipment to me, as he always does when we work together. I would love to detail all that equipment for you and dazzle you with my technological expertise, but the truth is, I don't have any technological expertise to dazzle you with. I know that some of the equipment measures energy patterns and my heart rate and body temperature. I know that Chuck uses infrared film, which registers heat and electrical variations in the atmosphere. I know that Nick carries an EME box that works like a Geiger counter to measure electromagnetic energy. In general, though, as far as I'm concerned, the electronics are Nick and Chuck's problem, not mine. I have my own priorities and more than enough on my mind during a haunting exploration without worrying about knobs, gauges, and dials.

The property hadn't been inhabited for several years and looked sadly run down, and its layout seemed odd. The buildings formed a square, wrapped around a courtyard with a central fountain I imagined was once lovely. To the right was the main house with big heavy entry doors. To the left were stairs leading to other rooms, with a narrow balcony in front of them that reminded me of a drab, deserted motel. Strange, I thought, that those rooms were separate, not connected to the other living quarters.

We stepped through the massive doors into the main house. It felt oppressive and depressing, as if there had been a lot of unhappiness within its walls, a terrible unrest bordering on hysteria. But these were purely psychic impressions, impressions I'm sure you've had, too, when you've walked into a room that looks orderly enough but seems charged with an energy all its own, that either comforts you and draws you into it or makes you want to race straight back to your car as quickly as possible. The more Nick and Chuck and I explored the main house, the more apparent it became that there were no ghosts there, no lingering spirits, no haunting to alert their electronic gauges or my psychic ones. We finally emerged back into the courtyard, and as we pulled those heavy doors closed again, I remember wondering if anyone had ever heard laughter, or joy, or playfulness, or prayers echoing behind them.

It was time to head up the stairs to those oddly separate rooms beyond the fountain. I don't know about Nick and Chuck—I didn't ask them—but after finding the main house so "clean" and free of ghosts, I wasn't expecting anything other than the same musty, depressing gloom we'd just left.

So I felt almost blindsided by the sudden realization that the more we climbed those stairs, the more my whole body felt as if it were made of lead and the harder it was becoming for me to breathe. A rush of panic charged through me, and I'm not ashamed to admit that if Nick and Chuck hadn't been with me, I would have run away as fast as I could rather than face whatever was waiting at the top of those stairs. Nick has the tape recording to prove that I was keeping

up a running commentary the entire time, describing this flood of
sheer dread, but I don't remember saying a word or even experiencing anything as normal and familiar as the sound of my own voice. I
finally regrouped enough to stop and provide the three of us with the
best protection I had in my arsenal—I surrounded us with the white
light of the Holy Spirit, and after a few long, deep breaths of the
warm night air we pressed on up those steps, crossed the narrow balcony, and opened the first door.

I was immediately overwhelmed, almost assaulted, by some of the
most horrifying images I've ever witnessed. I was gaping at a room-
ful of people dressed as vampires, very gothic long before it came
into vogue. Chalk-white, blank faces. Hollow kohl-lined eyes. Lips
dark, red as blood. They were all talking unintelligibly, in a low,
droning monotone. Three of them were standing and flailing around
in what seemed to be some insane drugged frenzy. Four others were
lying on the floor, crumpled and limp like discarded rag dolls. One of
the men was holding a glass, and he slowly and deliberately cut his
arm and let his blood drain into it. He then passed the glass around
the room, and everyone drank from it. As they drank they slipped
into a sick, dark euphoria, as if they'd just shared a kind of terrible
communion.

The effect was nightmarish and completely hypnotic. I couldn't
move, couldn't speak, couldn't even turn away, as desperately as I
wanted to. It was several moments before I realized that, for I don't
know how long, Nick had been frantically screaming my name, begging me to get out of there. According to the gauges strapped to my
body, I was burning up in that ice cold room, I was being hit with so
much electromagnetic energy that I was about to overload, and my
pulse rate was racing off the chart. I knew it wasn't the sights themselves that had held me captive, it was my certainty that these poor
earthbound souls were trapped in a ritual that kept repeating itself

over and over and over again, despair and futility consecrated in a perpetual, Godless haze of drugs, blood, and darkness.

Once I'd managed to back out of the room, Nick slammed the door shut and he and Chuck headed for the stairs, eager to leave. Part of me was ready to race them back to the van. But the rest of me knew we couldn't go yet. We weren't quite finished.

"Where are you going?" Nick asked in a voice edged with tension.

I'd moved to the other door at the top of the stairs. "We need to look in here before we go. I promise, I'll make it quick. Do you mind?"

I was already reaching for the doorknob, making it clear that I was going in with or without permission. I can't stress enough that Nick and Chuck weren't frightened of anything we'd confronted or might be about to confront, they were just desperately concerned for my safety. So I understood their hesitation, but I wasn't a bit surprised when I found them right behind me as I slowly swung open that second door and stepped inside.

It took my eyes a moment to adjust to the pitch blackness in the room. At first all I could see was a large, thick shadow that I thought might be an oversized couch, or maybe a bed. My breath grew short again when I realized that what I was looking at was a gleaming, highly polished wooden coffin. Open. And from within its satin folds, Bela Lugosi himself, wrapped in a cape, dark hair slicked back, slowly sat up and looked coldly and directly into my eyes.

"You weren't invited," he said.

"No, I wasn't," I answered quietly. "I'm sorry for the intrusion."

I stepped out onto the balcony again and closed the door, joining Nick and Chuck, who were visibly shaken. They hadn't seen what I saw, or heard Bela Lugosi's hollow voice, but they'd heard my response to it and sensed the overwhelming hopelessness and the lifeless life inside that room. None of us spoke as we headed back down

the steps into the courtyard, which was surprisingly peaceful considering its proximity to such horror. We sat there in silence for a while,
each of us privately processing what we'd experienced at the top of
those stairs. Chuck poured us each a cup of coffee from his thermos.
It was such a normal, mundane gesture that I think it helped us all
back to the luxury of plain old ordinary reality.

"Okay, Nick," I eventually said, "now you can tell me about Bela
Lugosi."

It was a long, often heartbreaking story. Bela Lugosi was born in
Hungary in the late 1800s. He left home at the age of eleven and, a
few years later, found his way into theater work, which led him to
the United States. His career reached its pinnacle in the early 1930s
with *Dracula*, *Murders in the Rue Morgue*, *The Black Cat*, and scores of
other films that buried him in typecasting from which he never es-
caped. From the late 1930s until he died in 1956, his work was spo-
radic and often humiliating as he struggled to make enough of a
living to support himself, his third wife, and his only child, Bela Lugosi, Jr., who was born in 1938. Somewhere along the line he became addicted to the morphine he'd been given for chronic pain in
his legs, and there were legendary secret parties in the separate
building on the Lugosi property where drug-induced blood rituals
were practiced and Bela himself, clinging desperately to the one
identity that had brought him any semblance of fame or success,
would often sleep in a coffin.

Tragically, the more Nick told me, the more the grotesque images
in those rooms at the top of the stairs made sense, and the more horrified I was for the poor, lost earthbound souls whose emptiness I'd
glimpsed that night, so buried in their darkness that they couldn't see
the light of God that was waiting to guide them Home. I thought
long and hard about going back up the steps and trying to release
those ghosts from their awful, endless, joyless time warp, but I felt

much too depleted and temporarily overpowered. Don't misunderstand, I never have a doubt in the world about the omnipotence of God under any circumstances. But in the face of that much deep, desperate negativity, I occasionally doubt myself, and when self-doubt creeps in, no matter how much white light I can summon, I find that discretion is almost always the better part of valor.

And so, instead, Nick and Chuck and I held hands and prayed with all our hearts for God, the Christ Consciousness, the Holy Spirit, and the Principalities, the most powerful of the legions of Angels, to please send someone to lead these confused, bewildered earthbounds to the loving eternity of The Other Side where they belonged.

I can usually shake off even the most overwhelming negativity quickly and easily. After a long lifetime in this business, I'd be insane by now if I couldn't. But the leaden feeling, the futility, the rushes of panic, and the sheer despondency of that house and its stranded inhabitants stayed with me for days. Years later, I still pray for Bela Lugosi, that actor I first thought I could barely be bothered with, and for those others who got lost in the same dark vortex that pulled him under. I hope you'll pray for them too.

The Hitchcock House

My trip to the former home of the late, great director Alfred Hitchcock began as nothing more than a mundane favor. My friend Lavona had friends who were thinking of buying the house, they were feeling a little apprehensive about it, and they wondered if I'd be willing to check it out for them. I was sure their apprehension had to do with Hitchcock's legendary film credits, brilliantly terrifying thrillers that they were, and I assured Lavona that there's no reliable connection between a house and what its former owners did for a living. But I also quickly agreed to visit the house and see if I sensed any good reason for Lavona's friends to pass it up——not because I was worried about them but because frankly I wasn't about to pass up a chance to tour Alfred Hitchcock's estate myself.

It seemed fitting that the house was set into the gorgeous, mystical Santa Cruz Mountains in northern California, which are rumored to be filled with everything from witches' covens to burial grounds cursed for centuries by the angry spirits of the Native Americans who had died there. After driving along a winding road in a heavily wooded area, I arrived at a stone entrance with a statue of St. Francis of Assisi prominent in a niche in the wall. Adoring animals as I do, and "adoring" is an understatement, it made me smile to be greeted by their patron saint.

It also made the next sight I saw all the more horrifying. Lying on the ground near the statue were two huge, gorgeous dogs either dying or dead, with foam coming out of their mouths. If I hadn't known they were a vision, not reality, I would have pulled them into my car and set land speed records getting them to the nearest veterinary emergency room without another thought to the Hitchcock house or anything else. As it was, I simply started up the path toward the house, deeply shaken, my eyes filled with tears, repeating over and over, "Oh, my God, oh, my God, those poor beautiful dogs."

Lavona came out to meet me, took one look at my face, and said, "Sylvia, what on earth is it? What's wrong?"

"Lavona," I demanded, "who poisoned those dogs?"

She was shocked. "How did you know about that?"

"I saw them. I'm psychic, remember?" I was straining to remain calm and just barely succeeding.

It didn't improve my mood one bit when she casually informed me of a rumor years earlier about witches in the area who didn't like the dogs barking at them and decided to put a permanent stop to it. I even started wondering which of us to smack first——her for being so nonchalant about animals being poisoned, let alone at the feet of a St. Francis statue of all places, no matter how long ago it had happened, or myself for letting my curiosity get me into this. I was debating those options when our hostess, a woman Lavona had arranged to show us around, emerged from the house to greet me and introduce herself. I hope I was polite. The truth is, I was still so upset that I really don't remember.

As we followed our hostess inside I was in the midst of muttering to Lavona, "Let's make this quick, I'm already done in," when I stopped cold to gape at my surroundings. I couldn't tell you a thing about the size of the rooms, the furnishings, or any of the other details of the house I'd been so looking forward to exploring. All I could see were walls covered with bloody handprints, and cowled figures standing everywhere, watching us, like cloaked and hooded monks with nothing but darkness where their faces should have been.

Lavona gently touched my arm. "What now?" she whispered, concerned but not wanting to alarm our hostess.

I didn't have the voice, let alone the energy, to describe what was surrounding us. I was silently trying to explain it away as some projection on my part, maybe my own imagery from all those years of watching Hitchcock movies. But I'd never associated Hitchcock with blood and gore, or with shadowy figures in cloaks and hoods, and I was far too experienced to believe that those images were coming from me. They'd been there in that house before I arrived. Long, long before I arrived. Finally I whispered back, "Tell your friends they can't buy this place. It's not just weird, it's horrifying."

I was taking a quick, perfunctory look around the kitchen, wanting nothing more than to be back in my car, pulling into my own boring, ordinary driveway, when I suddenly blurted out, "What was Mrs. Hitchcock so afraid of?"

Our hostess stared at me, shocked at my presumption. "Why in the world would you think such a thing?" she asked.

"I don't think such a thing, I *know*. Mrs. Hitchcock was terrified here," I assured her. "Show me her room."

"Right this way." She sounded a little smug, as if she were about to prove to me how wrong I was.

She led the way through a private courtyard to a small separate building made of stone. There were bars on the windows and double-bolt locks on the impenetrably heavy front door. We stepped inside this totally secluded bedroom and then our hostess proudly displayed a special hidden feature of Mrs. Hitchcock's private quarters: at the push of a button, a red emergency phone appeared from a drawer. Let's see. A separate room completely isolated from the main house. Bars on the windows. Double-bolt locks on a door so thick a Sherman tank couldn't have blasted through it. And last but not least, a secret crisis phone. It didn't take a psychic, or a rocket scientist, either, to piece this puzzle together.

"No," I said to Lavona and our hostess, rolling my eyes, "Mrs. Hitchcock wasn't afraid of a thing."

The two women shrugged sheepishly, and Lavona offered a weak "We just felt she was a little eccentric."

Please, God, I thought to myself, don't ever let my loved ones see me in abject fear and dismiss it as eccentricity. But out loud I simply repeated to Lavona, "Under no circumstances should your friends buy this house. Period." Then I sat back, leaning against the wall, wanting desperately to get out of there and just trying to summon the courage to make it past the cowled figures and those beautiful dogs lying dead at the entrance, when some movement outside the barred window beside me caught my eye. I looked to see a small, thin, gray-haired woman in a black dress with white cuffs, a white collar, and a white apron. A very dapper man in a black suit was standing beside her.

"Who's the elderly couple?" I asked, assuming our hostess or Lavona had hired a maid and butler for our day together and flattered that they went to the trouble. Flattered too soon, as it turned out.

"There's no one here but us," Lavona replied.

"Oh, yes, there is," I told them both, and I went on to describe the couple, who were still standing outside the window. The two women simply glanced at each other, shrugged, and muttered something about "probably the shadows." It didn't seem worth the trouble to try to convince them I wasn't hallucinating, so finally, more exhausted than I could remember being in a long, long time, I stood, managed a thank-you of some kind, and left. I'm grateful to this day that no cowled figures stood in my way and the dogs were gone from the entrance as I rushed to my car and drove away, completely drained. "That's it," I promised myself. "No more hauntings. I'm not ever putting myself through this again." For the record, I didn't even believe it as I said it.

Three weeks later my secretary walked into my office with an envelope from that day's mail. Inside was a black-and-white photograph of the Hitchcock family. Beside them stood an elderly man and woman—the exact couple I'd seen through the barred windows of Mrs. Hitchcock's bedroom. I sat quietly praying for them to be released, to understand that their devoted caretaking of the Hitchcocks and their deeply troubled property was over, they'd done it well and they could follow God's light to the joy of Home now.

As for the rest of the images that so horribly upset me that day and, I'm willing to bet, so frightened Mrs. Hitchcock that she slept behind double-locked doors with a crisis phone readily at hand, I don't believe they were directly connected to the Hitchcock family. I'm psychically certain that they were too deeply entrenched and far too doomed to have such recent origins. Instead, as we discussed in Chapter Two, I'm convinced that the land the house is built on is holding imprints of centuries of Godless evil, darkness that could take centuries more to be completely neutralized. The cowled figures were imprints of a long-ago cult who, hidden among the thick forests in those beautiful, mystical mountains, considered themselves Druids and used that Celtic pagan philosophy as an excuse to act out self-devised rituals that included human sacrifices. The bloody handprints on the walls of the Hitchcock house are the only traces these sadistic pseudo-Druids' victims left behind.

One of the clearest tip-offs to the fact that this was an imprint rather than a haunting was the presence of the heartbreaking wounded dogs at the entrance to the property. Remember, spirits from The Other Side never appear with injuries or illnesses or any form of physical disability. And since dogs, like all other animals, take an instantaneous trip Home when their bodies die because of the perfection of their souls, they couldn't have been ghosts. So if I hadn't already psychically known that I was dealing with an imprint, the dogs would have been all the proof I needed. As with most imprints, though, clear-headed logic wasn't strong enough to have much of an impact on the overwhelming emotional power of so much concentrated darkness.

I still get a lost, empty feeling when I think of the Hitchcock house and the land around it, all that spectacular beauty masking so much negativity. Whoever is living there now, I would love to hear from you. But whether I do or not, please know that you're in my prayers.

The White Horse Tavern

There were rumors of a haunting at the White Horse Tavern on Hudson Street in New York City, and Montel Williams asked me to check it out on camera for his show. All I knew about this alleged haunting going in was that workers would put all the chairs on all the tables at the end of the night and come back into the room to find two chairs on the floor again, pulled up to one of the tables with two freshly poured shots of whiskey waiting there that no one among the living had poured.

I knew a little more about the White Horse Tavern, but not that much. I knew it was more than a hundred years old, and I knew it had reportedly entertained a wide variety of patrons in its long history, from Norman Mailer to Dylan Thomas to William Styron to Theodore Bikel to such folk artists as the Clancy Brothers and Bob Dylan, while Steve McQueen tended bar. I found myself being sorry I'd missed it.

It didn't take a psychic to sense that this wood-framed building carries a deep appreciation of its past. There's old wood and glass everywhere, an embossed tin wall, and a carved horse's head on a post in the middle of the room. A wealth of framed photographs and the expanse of well-worn wooden floors lend a sense of informal comfort, so that it was easy to understand why such a wide variety of people, from the anonymous to the noteworthy, have felt at home here for over a century.

There were no patrons in the White Horse Tavern when I arrived, only the pub's owner, along with Montel's producers and camera crew. So there was no immediately apparent source of the loud, rich, liltingly accented male voice, reading poetry I couldn't quite make out, that I heard from the moment I stepped in the door.

"Is someone else here?" I asked the owner.

He assured me no one was.

It was then that I saw an overweight, unhealthy-looking man with deep-set eyes sitting at a table drinking. It was his voice I was hearing, sure and compelling, and I was certain that the man had once captivated this room with his recitations and stories, with a rapt, appreciative crowd hanging on his every word and even taking notes. I was also certain that he'd started drinking a very long time ago and wasn't thinking of stopping anytime soon. I described him to the owner.

"That sounds like Dylan," he told me.

Dylan Thomas. Just my luck. You'd think with a degree in English literature, I would have been brilliantly informed on Dylan Thomas's life and works. But the truth is, except for a passing reference to him here and there, my professors focused our attention on Chaucer, Homer, Shakespeare, and *Beowulf*. The closest we came to "contemporary" writers was probably James Joyce, who was born in 1882. So it's an understatement to say I hadn't found myself in the presence of one of my idols, or even someone I was conversant about. As his voice continued to fill the room, I got a sense that his self-destruction was deliberate, and that his liver was at least partly involved in his death.

"Dylan Thomas was only thirty-nine when he died of alcoholism," the owner informed me, "but, God, did he look older."

He certainly did. I would have guessed that the man I was looking at was at least twenty years older than that, bloated and dissipated as he was. Another impression came over me, and I couldn't resist asking the owner about it. "He liked to tease the waiters and waitresses, didn't he? Especially by poking them." The owner nodded. Not a significant detail, but I always appreciate validation.

And then, oddly bragging, Dylan Thomas announced, "I once drank nineteen straight whiskeys in a row, you know."

I don't know, which made me sadder—the idea of anyone putting their body through that much abuse, or the fact that he was misguided enough to be proud of it. But before I could respond to him, something or someone else nearby unexpectedly caught my eye, and I turned to see what or who it was.

Her hair was as raven-black as her dress, a harsh contrast with pale skin that she exaggerated with an unflattering dusting of white powder. Her lips were bloodred, and her eyes were small, almost beady, the overall effect being one of a woman who was trying to draw attention away from the fact that she never had been and never would be a beauty.

I knew instantly that her name was Marian Lee and that she was deeply in love with Dylan Thomas. Her greatest joy was hanging around the White Horse Tavern night after night when he was in New York, listening to him for hours on end and hoping that he would finally notice her and return her feelings. Sadly, it never happened. But that hope, and the devotion of that unrequited love, keeps her wandering among the tables of the White Horse Tavern, still trying to catch more than an occasional passing glance from Dylan Thomas.

Neither Dylan Thomas nor Marian Lee was with me long enough for me to "talk them over," or send them Home. I'll keep praying for them until their loved ones from The Other Side come for them and bring them peace. Until then, I'll remember meeting them, and noticing an odd little image from that day that struck me at the time and has stayed with me ever since. As I said, the White Horse Tavern is decorated by a lot of framed photographs. After my brief encounter with Dylan Thomas, I recognized that many of them are of him. Directly opposite one of those photographs of him is a photograph of an elderly woman. I asked the owner who she was. He didn't know. I do. It's Marian Lee, much later in her life. Her eyes are fixed on his across the room. And at least in still-life form, he's finally looking back.

Several days after my trip to the White Horse Tavern, I read a few accounts of the brief, gifted, often tortured life of Dylan Thomas. Those accounts claimed that he died on November 9, 1953, five days after claiming to have drunk eighteen whiskeys in a row. It was nineteen. Take my word for it. If you'll pardon the expression, I got it straight from the horse's mouth.

Elvis Presley

It wouldn't be accurate to say I either liked or disliked Elvis Presley during his career. I think my position on the subject of Elvis could best be described as nonexistent. I wasn't informed enough about him to *have* a position. I knew he was a rock-and-roll star. I knew he was very handsome. And I knew he had a beautiful voice when he sang ballads. Other than that, I was too busy with my children and my own career to pay much attention to his, let alone try to figure out what all the fuss was about.

To this day, then, I have no explanation for the sense of significant loss I felt along with countless others around the world at the news on August 16, 1977, that Elvis Presley was dead at the impossibly unfair age of forty-two. I still remember that I was at my desk in my office when I heard about it, and that everything seemed "off" for the rest of the day, and I scolded myself more than once for my reaction. After all, it wasn't as if we'd just lost a great humanitarian, or a Nobel Peace Prize winner. This was just a great-looking guy who'd made a lot of records I didn't own and a ton of movies I'd never seen, so my sadness didn't make much sense. And yet, entitled to it or not, I felt it, and I cried.

I couldn't have been more shocked when, within hours of Elvis's death, the press was calling, asking for anything I could give them on his passing, ideally some kind of actual contact with him on The Other Side. Of course, I was hardly the only psychic whose phone was ringing that day, but you have to bear in mind that in 1977 my "fame" was still in its growing stages, and I wasn't exactly a renowned Elvis Presley expert for obvious reasons. I said I'd be glad to do what I could and offered to trance Francine, my Spirit Guide, to try to get in touch with Elvis, which is never guaranteed to be successful.

Even back then it wasn't unusual to find articles about psychics in the tabloids. But it may have been a front-page first for the *San Francisco Chronicle*, which announced that a psychic named Sylvia Browne, through "her spiritual guide, an Inca spirit named Francine who died in 1519," had successfully contacted and talked with the late, great Elvis Presley less than twenty-four hours after his death.

Sometimes it frustrates me that in order for Francine to borrow my body and voice for trances, I have to excuse myself for the duration. This is one of those times. I would love to have witnessed this and had these conversations with Elvis myself. As it is, all I can do is share the information I heard on tape after the fact, with some editorializing on my part—like, for example, the impressive speed with which Elvis made it to The Other Side, for Francine to be able to talk with him so clearly and so soon after he died. It was a quick, easy trip Home for him, sped along by a faith in God that was always alive and well at the core of his soul.

He was in a very, very small room when he died, he told Francine, and was immediately conscious of the fact that he had passed over. He'd had a headache earlier that day, didn't feel well, and his back hurt, and he went into this small room with a book. He died very quickly in that room, without struggling or suffering. He'd had problems with his lower intestine for the previous two and a half years, which he'd mentioned to a few friends—particularly a John and a Charlie—and he was on medication and steroids, but his death was unintentional and accidental.

Elvis was immediately met on The Other Side by his adored mother, Gladys, for whom he'd designated the pet name "Gladiola" here on earth. Waiting for him with her were his twin brother Jesse and a friend named Chuck. His life at Home is blissful, filled with music, his voice even richer and more heavenly than we can imagine, and he and countless other transcended musicians give magnificent, celebrated concerts.

Looking back on his life as Elvis Presley, his real passion and inspiration were rooted not in rock and roll but in gospel music. It's interesting that his focus on rock and roll was the result of something called "infusion," which in this case means he was spiritually tuned in enough to know what will make people happy. It's not a form of selling out. It's a form of communicating joy, the sweet, divine, God-centered joy Elvis was capable of and intended even when he fell short of accomplishing it. And ironically, although his passion was gospel music, his favorite of all the songs he ever recorded was "Heartbreak Hotel."

He always wished he'd been as skilled at loving individual people as he was at loving large, more anonymous groups of them. No one was more precious to him than his daughter, Lisa Marie, and there's no question that he loved Priscilla, he just felt their marriage was doomed because they had so little quiet, private, "normal" time together. He hoped Priscilla would remember that at one point they planned on having many children, just to validate that this was really him talking, offering information that no one else could possibly have.

Elvis was aware of sixteen separate attempts on his life, which understandably made him paranoid, fearful, and anxious. Relaxation and sleep did not come easily to him without medication. He had a premonition of his death six months before it happened, and for those last six months he came to think of the song "My Way" as his farewell message to his fans.

To further confirm that this really was Elvis talking, he passed along a few personal messages to his father, Vernon. One was simply the name "Ruta May." Another was that Vernon's concerns about his chest area weren't as serious as he might think. Yet another was a game they played when Elvis was a boy, in which one of them would start a nursery rhyme and the other one would finish it.

Francine took it as a matter of course, but I don't mind telling you that I was blown away when, within a few short weeks of the *San Francisco Chronicle* article's appearance, both Vernon Presley and a very close friend of Elvis's named Charlie Hodge called to validate the information Elvis had passed along through Francine. I'll always be grateful to both men, not only for the validation but also for the time and trouble they took in the midst of their grief to let me know that Elvis's words from Home, so clearly and unquestionably his, had brought them some comfort.

Oh, and one more thing. It seemed too far off in 1977 to be of much interest, but I certainly did a double take when I reread it in preparation for writing this book: Elvis distinctly told Francine that he'd already planned his next incarnation. He'll be a singer again, this time with light hair and light eyes.

He'll be born in the year 2004.

Marilyn Monroe

It was another case of "I didn't know I cared." If you'd asked me when I woke up on the morning of August 5, 1962, how I felt about Marilyn Monroe, I'm sure I would have come up with the titles of a couple of movies she was in that I liked, and to be honest I imagine I would have gone on to say that while she was obviously pretty, I didn't take her very seriously and I wasn't sure why anyone else did either.

And then that day the news hit that she'd died all alone, at the age of thirty-six, in some little house in Los Angeles, and suddenly you would have thought I was her biggest fan. I'm not sure if it was the idea of a young life so abruptly and sadly taken or if it was an unsettling sense that something about the news story was wrong, but I was shaken by the reported suicide of Marilyn Monroe and found myself preoccupied with her lovely, troubled face and the little I knew of her turbulent life for the rest of that day and for a very long time after that.

So I wasn't about to turn down an invitation from a nationally syndicated television show to visit the house where Marilyn Monroe died to see what, if anything, I could find out from Marilyn herself, if she chose to communicate with me at all. It was made clear to the producers and everyone else right up front that we weren't going to be let into the house itself, or even very close to it. We'd be let inside the gate, but that was it.

"Will that be a problem?" one of the producers asked me.

"We'll find out when we get there" was all I could tell her. I can make all the promises in the world about myself. But about ghosts and spirits? I've learned the hard way never to try to second-guess them, and I hadn't even explored yet whether or not Marilyn had made it to The Other Side.

The day of filming arrived, and we pulled up to a house—more like a bungalow, really—so small and ordinary that it seemed as if it couldn't possibly have contained a star as big or a woman as complicated as the one who had lived and died inside it. I knew the moment I stepped out of the car that she wasn't earthbound, that she was safe in the sacred peace of Home, and I was so relieved for her. I also knew I wouldn't be needing Francine. Marilyn Monroe was accessible and willing to talk to me.

One of the first people I was introduced to at the house was a sweet older gentleman named James Dougherty, who turned out to have been Marilyn's first husband. News to me, of course—I thought her first marriage was to Joe DiMaggio, but I wasn't exactly an expert on her life story, and I only knew about her various marriages and rumored affairs because I watched the same TV shows everyone else did. Jim Dougherty was quick to clarify that he'd never married Marilyn Monroe, he'd actually married Norma Jean Baker, Marilyn Monroe's given name, on June 9, 1942, when they were both too young to know how far apart their dreams were destined to take them. But he still spoke of her with fondness and respect, and her death had obviously touched him deeply.

We stepped inside the gate, as close to the house as we'd be allowed to get, and I heard myself haltingly pronouncing a brief Latin phrase. Jim stared at me as I repeated it.

"It's in the tiles above the entrance to the house," I explained to him. "It means 'All are welcome here,' or 'Everyone is welcome here.' "

He was gaping by now. "Have you been here before?"

I shook my head.

"Then you're for real," Jim said, "because that's never appeared in print or anywhere else. How did you know it's there?"

"Marilyn's telling me about it," I told him.

He became very quiet—or if he didn't, I wouldn't have known the difference, because Marilyn was talking, and I didn't want to miss a word. I feel as if I should emphasize that I knew almost nothing about Marilyn Monroe's life then and still know almost nothing about it, so I can report what she told me but I certainly can't judge it or comment on its accuracy. I'll leave that to those of you who are experts on the life and death of this fascinating woman.

The one point she was adamant about and repeated over and over again was that she knew people were saying she committed suicide, and it simply wasn't true. She said she had a red book, a journal or diary, in which she kept her most confidential thoughts and information. A few people were aware of its existence, including Bobby Kennedy and Joe DiMaggio. She had told Bobby that she was planning to reveal the contents of the red book to the authorities. She didn't believe that Bobby felt threatened by that or that he was in any way directly involved with what happened to her on the night of August 5, 1962. What she did believe was that he had possibly told "the wrong people" about it and that "they" decided the only way to eliminate the threat of her revealing the information she might have in that book or in her head would be to eliminate her. She described being alone in her bedroom that night, taking too many pills, no doubt about it, and making some very confused, blurry phone calls. But her memory was very clear of a man she would only refer to as "Dr. L." coming into her bedroom and sticking a needle directly into her heart, a lethal dose of what she believed to be Nembutol.

She was increasingly worried in her final years that Joe DiMaggio might have known too much from her confiding in him, and that the information she had given him might have compromised his safety. There was no question that she loved him throughout her life, and it was a frequent source of the depression that plagued her that loving her had probably caused him more pain and potential danger than joy. She was visiting him often from The Other Side, especially while he slept, and she'd be the first to greet him when he came Home.

Before her voice faded away, she repeated for probably the tenth time during our conversation that her death was not a suicide. And then, with many things to tend to in her busy, happy life on The Other Side, I'm sure, she was gone.

I liked her. She sounded like someone who meant well and wrongly assumed that other people always did too. I was glad she made it Home so quickly and that I hadn't had to step aside and let Francine have the pleasure of meeting her while I missed the whole thing.

* * *

A few weeks later I walked into a restaurant in New York and saw Joe DiMaggio having dinner by himself at an out-of-the-way table. The instant I spotted him I had this odd feeling of closeness to him, as if I'd recently spoken to a dear mutual friend of his and mine I knew he'd want to hear from. I had no idea that there was this unwritten rule throughout the city that no matter where DiMaggio, aka Joltin' Joe, aka the Yankee Clipper, possibly the greatest baseball player ever to wear the much revered pinstripes of the much revered New York Yankees, chose to show up with his quiet, graceful presence, he wasn't to be approached. (It's a tribute to his brilliant career that my apathy about baseball, and sports in general, couldn't run deeper, and even I knew who Joe DiMaggio played for and what his nicknames were.)

So, armed with the courage of the ignorant and ill informed, I marched right up to DiMaggio's table, extended my hand, and introduced myself. "Mr. DiMaggio, my name is Sylvia Browne," I said. "I'm a psychic, and I recently did a documentary on Marilyn Monroe. I was sure you'd want to know that she's very happy and at peace, that she visits you often, and that she loved you very much."

That lovely, courtly gentleman stood, gently shook my hand, and held the empty chair at his table, inviting me to sit with him. He wanted to hear everything Marilyn had had to say and seemed comforted by it, although he kept his thoughts to himself. I didn't need him to tell me that he had rock-solid faith in the eternity of the spirit and a deep love of God. It radiated from him. So I knew he didn't doubt a word I was saying. It didn't matter that he didn't know me. It only mattered that he knew and loved Marilyn, and he could recognize her voice when he heard it, even if it was being translated through the deep, raspy paraphrasing of a total stranger.

I heard much, much later that Joe DiMaggio never, ever gave

autographs. He gave me one, without my asking, and I'll always treasure it.

Joe DiMaggio died on March 8, 1999, at the age of eighty-four. His passage to The Other Side was almost instantaneous, and Francine told me that, true to her word, Norma Jean Baker, aka Marilyn Monroe, was the very first to joyfully welcome him Home.

Jimi Hendrix

It was the mid-1970s. I had just finished a day of readings when the producer of a nationally syndicated radio show called to invite me to do his show later that week. I liked him, said yes as I always did when he called, and asked if he had anything specific in mind for that particular show.

"It's the fifth anniversary of Jimi Hendrix's death," he said. "I'm hoping you can get in touch with him. You think you can do it?"

"Well, you know how those things go," I reminded him. "No guarantees. But I'll be happy to try."

As we hung up the phone a few minutes later I thought back to that day five years earlier—September 19, 1970, to be exact—when the news hit that Jimi Hendrix had died. A younger, "music crowd" friend from L.A. happened to be staying with me for a few days, and when I got home from a day of readings at the office I innocently asked, "Who's Jimi Hendrix?"

She gaped at me, incredulous, as if I'd just asked, "Who's John F. Kennedy?" or "Have you ever heard of a cartoon character named Mickey Mouse?"

"Jimi Hendrix?" She enunciated his name as if she were talking to someone who didn't speak English fluently. "You know, brilliant rock-and-roll guitarist?"

"Yeah," I said, rolling my eyes, "there's something I really care about."

" 'Purple Haze'?" she added.

I shrugged. Never heard of it.

"Set his guitar on fire at the Monterey Pop Festival?" she went on.

"Deliberately?" I asked, thinking that sounded pretty stupid.

She shook her head. My hopelessness was starting to get on her nerves. "Played 'The Star Spangled Banner' at Woodstock? Oh, look. There he is."

She was pointing at the TV, where the news was covering the young guitarist's death and showing footage of his Woodstock performance of our national anthem. I was prepared to find it as incomprehensible as I found most rock and roll. Instead, it was mesmerizing, and Jimi Hendrix himself was so intensely charismatic that I couldn't believe I'd been unaware of him until then. Just as you don't have to know a thing about basketball to appreciate Michael Jordan's talent, or know a thing about golf to understand how gifted Tiger Woods is, or know a thing about ballet to be in awe of Baryshnikov, you didn't have to know a thing about rock and roll or even particularly like it to figure out that there was something pretty extraordinary about Jimi Hendrix. He'd died of a drug overdose in London, the newscaster went on to say, two months short of his twenty-eighth birthday. In a few short minutes, I'd gone from "Who's Jimi Hendrix?" to being sorry I'd missed him.

Now, five years later, I settled in at the microphone for what my host and I hoped would be a chat with the late, great guitarist, and within moments, to our mutual relief, there he was, happy to talk, fascinated, I think, that someone on earth could finally hear and understand him.

It was interesting how eager he was to clarify that the overdose that caused his death was accidental. Like Marilyn Monroe, he was adamant about erasing any lingering misimpressions that he might have committed suicide. Jimi Hendrix didn't mean to cause fatal harm to himself. His one joy, his true genius, was his music. He knew that drugs were going to destroy that joy if he didn't put up an immediate, dramatic fight, and at the time of his death he was making plans to check himself into a private rehabilitation clinic.

I don't know if it existed on paper or not, but I guarantee that someone who knew him at the time was aware of a song he was in the midst of writing about a girl he'd loved and lost, a song he thought might be his best work ever but never got to finish. And by the way, Jimi Hendrix's personal life was proof that quantity never takes the place of quality. Women all over the world wanted him, for the most superficial reasons, but the few women he let himself imagine a future with weren't about to tolerate the months and months of absences, the groupies, the drugs, and the restlessness that seemed as inevitable to him as breathing. He longed to find a woman who could offer him stability, just as surely as he knew he would always try to escape from that stability in the long run, and he agonized over that self-destructive conflict throughout his brief adulthood.

I asked him to describe what happened when he died, and he told me about going to a place that seemed dark and full of sad, silent people with downcast eyes who were just moving aimlessly around, never looking at each other, hopeless, full of despair. He felt he was there for a very, very long time until finally a brilliant light appeared, seemingly just for him, and he followed it Home, where he found the sacred joy of loved ones from all the lives he'd ever lived and the embrace of God Himself welcoming him back to his birthright of eternity.

Not until a terrifying astral trip of my own twenty years later, followed by a lot of research and a lot of information from Francine, did I understand where he'd gone. It's called the Holding Place, and it's where those spirits go when they die who are neither committed enough to the light to go straight to The Other Side nor dark enough to be sent through the Left Door and horseshoed right back into the womb again. They're confused, not at all sure where they belong or where they fit in. They're like lost children in search of an identity, still capable of being won over by white entities or dark ones, and therefore best described as gray, trying to figure out whether becoming dark or light will win them more approval and affection. They're the criminals who were absolutely capable of being rehabilitated, the white entities who were so defeated time and time again that they were ultimately overtaken by their anger and frustration, the mentally ill and chemically imbalanced who created chaos during their lifetimes with no way to stop themselves, and, in Jimi Hendrix's case, the victims of substance abuse who were desperately searching for the strength to get help.

When I found myself in that awful expanse of despair that I later learned was the Holding Place, my instincts were impelling me to frantically run up to one hopeless shell of a person after another, begging, "Please say you love God! You've got to say you love God! Just say you love God and you can get out of here!" Ultimately, it turns out to be the choice of each spirit in the Holding Place whether they'll move on from there to the pitch-black Godless abyss beyond the Left Door or step into God's waiting arms on The Other Side, where there is a Home for them, and for all of us, eternally prepared.

I read a lot of quotes from a lot of Jimi Hendrix's friends after he died, and I know that he was very much loved by those closest to him and that the joy of his music touched countless people all around the world. I wouldn't even be a bit surprised if each one of those five hundred thousand pacifists who had gathered in upstate New York in August of 1969 for three days of that peaceful miracle known as

Woodstock said a prayer or a simple thank you for the magic Hendrix performance they witnessed when they heard the news of his overdose. But it's a safe bet that all that love and all that joy and all those prayers and all those thanks and Jimi Hendrix's own innate goodness were the forces that gathered into that brilliant light he described, powerful enough to pierce the despair of the Holding Place and lead him safely to The Other Side.

Where Are They Now?

In no particular order, not because I asked for these specific names but because they were given to me:

John Candy, the gifted comedic actor who died of a heart attack on March 4, 1994, at the age of forty-three, made an instantaneous transition to The Other Side.

The equally gifted comedian **Phil Hartman** was the tragic victim of a murder-suicide on May 28, 1998. He was only forty-nine years old when he died, and he's currently earthbound. That surprised me until I heard the reason—his children lost both of their parents on that horrible night, and he's stayed behind to comfort and protect them. Within the next few years he'll feel secure enough about his children's well-being to let them go, and there's a vast team of loving spirits on The Other Side already preparing for that moment when they'll rescue him and bring him Home. His wife, **Brynn**, in the meantime, who murdered him before taking her own life, went to The Other Side immediately. I have to admit, that surprised me too—not exactly the destination I expected, I guess, for the perpetrator of a murder-suicide, but who are any of us to second-guess God? There's no question that she'd been propelled quite literally out of her mind that night by a combination of ingested substances; but the destructive monster those substances created was left behind when the faithful, loving, well-meaning spirit of Brynn Hartman asked for God's forgiveness and was welcomed to The Other Side.

Four of my all-time favorite actors made it to The Other Side before many in the room with them even realized they were gone: **Richard Harris**, who died of cancer on October 25, 2002, at the age of seventy-two; **Rock Hudson**, whom we lost to AIDS at the age of fifty-nine on October 2, 1985; **Jimmy Stewart**, whose great heart gave out on July 2, 1997, when he was eighty-nine years old; and **James Coburn**, whose heart failed him as well at the age of seventy-four on November 18, 2002.

Others I admired weren't quite so lucky. **Spencer Tracy** remained earthbound for several years after he died of a heart attack on June 10, 1967, at the age of sixty-seven. He was frankly just too stubborn to leave Katharine Hepburn and too unsure of where he might end up to take any chances. I'd be shocked if she didn't sense his presence very often and very strongly during those years, and he finally did go Home when it turned out that his faith was even more powerful than his stubbornness. No one, though, could top **Katharine Hepburn** when it came to both stubbornness and dignity. If she did sense Spencer Tracy's presence around her after his death, she would never have believed it or acknowledged it, because her Yankee pragmatism simply didn't allow for intangible concepts like life after death. Alive is alive, she was sure, and dead is dead, which had a lot to do with her great reluctance to let go of this particular lifetime. Convinced that this was it, the end, all there was and all there ever would be, she held on until the age of ninety-six. But on June 29, 2003, her fragile body gave in to the inevitable complications of old age and quietly took its last breath. I would love to have seen the look on her face when this proud, self-assured, "dead-is-dead" spirit exited its body to find none other than her beloved

Spencer Tracy right there waiting for her to take her hand and personally escort her Home.

Natalie Wood, only forty-three when she drowned on November 29, 1981, didn't make an immediate trip to The Other Side, either, a classic case of a spirit so shocked by the suddenness of what happened that for a few years she truly had no idea she was dead. She's long since made the transition, though, and is leading an ecstatically happy, busy life at Home.

Frank Sinatra, whose eighty-two-year-old heart gave out on May 14, 1998, went to The Other Side in an instant, while his dear friend **Dean Martin** had a much harder trip. Dean was seventy-eight years old when he died on Christmas Day, 1995, of acute respiratory failure. He'd actually never stopped grieving the death of his beloved son Dean Paul Martin in 1987, and even after he died Dean's grief kept him earthbound. In a gorgeous example of how love and eternity work in God's ultimate perfection, it was Dean Paul who came from The Other Side to bring his father Home.

Another of my heartthrobs, the brilliant Welsh actor **Richard Burton**, died on August 5, 1984, of a stroke at the age of fifty-eight and, while not particularly lacking faith in God or the afterlife, made a deliberate choice to remain earthbound simply because he was and is, for lack of a better description, a sensualist who essentially prefers it here and has yet to fully grasp the idea that he's no longer alive. He has no intention of leaving in the near future, either, and I'd be shocked if Elizabeth Taylor weren't aware of amazingly real "visits" from him during her more serious illnesses, since he continues to consider her to be very much his business.

Bob Crane of *Hogan's Heroes* fame and **Sal Mineo** of *Rebel Without A Cause* fame, both murdered (Bob Crane on June 29, 1978, at the age of forty-nine, and Sal Mineo on February 12, 1976, when he was only thirty-seven), are still earthbound to this day. While no one has ever been successfully convicted of the murder of Bob Crane, a man named Lionel Ray Williams was convicted and sentenced to life in prison in 1979 for the stabbing death of Sal Mineo.

The exquisite **Eva Gabor** left right on time for her chart, of course, but much too soon for my taste when she died of pneumonia on July 4, 1995, at the age of seventy-four. She had a joyful, devout faith in God, and I have personal, firsthand knowledge that every single day of her adult life she made a point of performing some act of kindness for someone, most often anonymously. Needless to say, the parties to welcome her Home are still going on to this day.

Similarly, **Nicole Brown** and **Ron Goldman**, both murdered on June 12, 1994 (Nicole was thirty-five, Ron was twenty-five), were on The Other Side within seconds, before their killer had even exited her property. (I will not flatter that man by including his name in this book. I've never seen anyone in my life who's more addicted to seeing his name in print, and it's not going to happen here.)

John Lennon, murdered at the age of forty on December 8, 1980, went Home in an instant, too, as did the brilliant comedian **John Belushi**, who died of an accidental overdose on March 5, 1982, at the age of thirty-three. **Timothy Leary**, Harvard professor and LSD guru of an entire generation, even made it straight to The Other Side when he died of cancer on May 31, 1996, at the age of seventy-five.

Genius author **Truman Capote** and the tragic **Dr. Sam Sheppard**, who was wrongly convicted of murdering his wife, shared the sad fate of dying of complications of alcoholism—Capote on August 25, 1984, at the age of fifty-nine and Dr. Sheppard on April 6, 1970, at the age of forty-six. They also shared the same joyful ending of immediate journeys to The Other Side.

And then there were those two other young, beautiful people we lost so suddenly—**Diana, Princess of Wales,** in a limo accident on August 31, 1997, when she was only thirty-six, and **John Kennedy, Jr.**, who, with his beautiful wife and her sister, died in the crash of his small plane off the coast of Martha's Vineyard on July 16, 1999. He was thirty-eight. I'm not being flippant, just literally accurate when I say that both Princess Diana and John were at Home, John in his mother's arms, before they knew what hit them.

Finally—and I'm going to maintain my professionalism all the way through this one, no matter what it takes—there's the most outspokenly devout atheist of the American talk show circuit herself, **Madalyn Murray O'Hair**, who was abducted in 1995 and whose murdered body wasn't found until 2001, along with the bodies of her son and granddaughter. You know how I've said time and time again that God never turns away from us, but He gives us all the free will in the world to turn away from Him? Well, she certainly did just that, she did it at the top of her lungs, and she meant it. So when she died, she went straight through the Left Door and right back in utero again. Which means that somewhere on this earth at this very moment some lucky couple are the proud parents of a child who less than ten short years ago was the world's loudest, most foul-mouthed, most obnoxious atheist.

Good luck with it.

Chapter Seven

TO FIND A GHOST AND
PROVE A GHOST:
THE PENINSULA SCHOOL

I love being right. I don't know anyone who doesn't. My career depends on my being right a lot more often than I'm wrong, and I've been tested at somewhere between 85- and 90-percent accuracy as a psychic. Averaging, let's say, twenty clients a day for fifty years, plus another forty years of lectures, print interviews, radio and television appearances, added to several decades of very private pro bono work with the medical and psychiatric communities and various law enforcement agencies, and my own extensive research and writing, I wouldn't have the strength, the skill, or the courage to try to calculate the number of hours of information I've transmitted in my sixty-six years on earth this time around, and I'd be ecstatic to find out that 85 to 90 percent of that information has been accurate and give all the credit to God where it belongs.

There's no doubt about it, either, that when I miss something, I miss it, and when I'm wrong, I'll be the first to point it out. The terrorist attacks of September 11? Not one inkling. The sniper killings that held the Washington, D.C., area hostage in the fall of 2002? I called Lindsay and recorded detailed descriptions of the two suspects several days before any arrests were made. They turned out to be very accurate descriptions of the two alleged suspects who were mistakenly surrounded by the authorities at a gas station and completely exonerated several hours later. I've been thrilled to hear it when I turned out to be wrong about the outcome of a missing-persons case or two, and heartbroken on more occasions when I turned out to be right.

All of which is bound up somehow, I'm sure, in my lifelong rabid pursuit of follow-ups and validation. Not that every psychic doesn't like a client to nod or have their face light up and say, "That's uncanny! You got it exactly!" But I almost don't know when to quit. Once I sink my teeth into an investigation—and I admit it, particularly a haunting investigation—I'm like a pit bull if there's even a hint of paranormal activity going on.

And if there's not, it might amuse you to know, I don't care how many television cameras are rolling or how good a story it might make, there's not a chance in this world I would ever fake a haunting and claim something's there when I don't feel a thing. I promise you there's film of me in editing room wastebaskets around the world, walking from room to room saying, "Sorry, guys, but if this house is haunted, I'm Princess Caroline of Monaco," and, "Yes, there's a terrible cold spot in this room. You know why? Because it's the dead of winter and someone's blocked the heating vent in here." There are things I can be accused of that I'm sure I need to work on. Fraud is not one of them. I point that out not to pat myself on the back and say, "See what a terrific, moral person I am?" I point it out because I happen to believe in some of the basic, inevitable laws of God's universe, including "You reap what you sow." I don't even want to think about what kind of dark payback I'd have ahead of me if I'd spent all these years deliberately and knowingly tricking people out of money I'm not entitled to.

Maybe if I were just a psychic I wouldn't care quite so much about validation. But I'm also a researcher, with my own Nirvana Foundation created for that specific and very active purpose. And above all, I'm the spiritual head of a nondenominational ministry called Novus Spiritus and as passionate about my relationship with God and my faith as anyone you'll ever meet. So when I investigate a haunting and then feel a genuine need to find out how much of the information I got was accurate, that need has very little to do with my ego. A much larger part of it is about lending still more credibility to the psychic research of the Nirvana Foundation and psychic research in general. According to my logic, if I perform impeccably accurate, monitored investigations and follow-ups that are conducted with integrity from beginning to end, maybe I can make a dent in balancing out the outrageous number of rip-off artists in this "business" of mine that I happen to consider an ironclad contract between me and God.

But most of all, if I can walk into a strange place I know nothing about and begin getting, seemingly out of nowhere, a wealth of information about that place, its history, and previous residents, including names, physical descriptions, and significant events, *and that information turns out to be true,* where did the information come from? We can rule me out, and we can rule out the staff and crew I brought with me, who do no prior research on the place or they'll be on their last investigation with me. That leaves no one but the "resident experts," any ghosts who are lingering there to give me details I'd have no other way of knowing.

Now, if ghosts can give me information I can validate, that means those ghosts are very likely to be legitimate. Which means that, even though they happen to be ghosts for the time being, their bodies may have died but their spirits survived death.

That reason alone for wanting to validate whatever haunting information I possibly can makes the other reasons pale in comparison.

If you think I'll ever pass up a chance to add one more shred of evidence to the mounting proof of God's eternity, guess again.

If you've seen the 1975 Disney movie *Escape to Witch Mountain*, you've seen a San Francisco landmark called the Peninsula School, previously known as the Coleman Mansion. If you've never seen the movie, just imagine the house you'd expect to see in a film with the words "witch mountain" in the title and you'll have a good idea what the Peninsula School looks like. It's a huge, hulking gothic mansion with a wraparound front porch lined with slender columns. The facade of the balconied second story is a row of tall arched windows enhanced by an abundance of decorative trim. The first time I saw it, it reminded me of an aging spinster, too big-boned and awkward to have her dance card filled, wearing an outdated gown and all the expensive jewelry she owns at the same time as if to say, "You see? I really do have a lot to offer."

I was summoned to the Peninsula School, along with my Nirvana Foundation staff, to get to the bottom of some specific and longstanding observations by both the students and the staff. For as long as anyone could remember, footsteps could be distinctly heard echoing from what would turn out to be empty rooms and hallways, and the ghost of a woman has been seen by virtually everyone who's ever attended or taught at this private, prestigious school. Some said she was dressed entirely in green. Others said that she herself was green. Entire classrooms of children, as many as twenty at once, had group sightings of the green woman, and, when asked to draw what they saw as best they could, came up with remarkably similar sketches, including their best renditions of the fact that to each child she seemed to be transparent and that she also seemed to glisten with moving, shimmering lights. Teachers routinely corroborated the children's sightings of the green woman throughout the school, and one teacher in particular had a face-to-face confrontation with her one night, alone in a dark hallway, that went on for several moments, even after the teacher turned on a light, until the green lady, at her own convenience, vanished before his eyes.

Because I insisted that all my Nirvana Foundation work be documented, my staff had tape recorders running from the moment I first set foot inside the Peninsula School until I finally walked out the door again, however long that took. They followed me around, upstairs and down, occasionally muttering an explanation into the microphone of where we were and even more often offering no explanation at all. I complained about that once, and they patiently reminded me how jarring it is for me to hear "nonsense noise" when I'm tuned into a haunting, a reading, a trance, you name it. They were right. I was wrong. I apologized for complaining. In my own brief but loving way.

Rather than walk you through a narrative, descriptive version of my investigative tour of the Peninsula School, what follows is a transcript of the tape recording of that tour. When you find yourself unsure of quite where we are in the house itself, don't blame my staff, they were just being careful not to disturb me. After the transcript you'll see why I was so eager to include it. And again, all my staff and I knew as we entered the school was that it had previously been known as the Coleman Mansion and that a woman in green was said to be haunting the place.

The Transcript

This house is very, very old. I'd say this house is a hundred years old, but there were other buildings 120, 130 years ago. For some reason I get the feeling that this house was never used for what it was meant to be used for.

I'm picking up something about a John, something, Coleman.

There's one place upstairs that I really want to get to because it's really energy packed.

(STAFF VOICE: "As Sylvia walks up the stairs") There's an awful lot of pressure right in this area. I'm getting three different impressions. I don't know if they're nuns, or if they're men in black robes walking around. There's another impression of a man with dark hair and dark eyes. It looks like he's bearded. And there's someone getting some kind of trauma in the chest area, like something entered the chest. Something sharp entered the chest.

I'm getting the name Kathryn. I'm also getting the name Marie, and Carmen. I also get the name Coleman, but I know that this is the Coleman place. I get the name John. John, and I also get the names Joseph and George.

In this room right here, that we can't get into, I seem to get a lot of pressure and energy, and I get a sense of falling.

I know this is a school, but I don't get a sense of a school. I don't think it's been a school for very long when you look at its whole history.

I keep getting this man and this woman and three other couples. A dark man, a light female, and something about the stairs. The steps, uh, I think we had a woman falling down the steps. And for some reason, I see nuns or monks walking around.

The sharp pain I get in the chest—I get the feeling she left after the sharp pain and is just walking around. Light hair, light eyes. She looks really young, maybe nineteen or twenty, something like that. A sharp pain and falling, falling frontward over a box. It was so useless. Just so useless.

The dark, bearded man with nice teeth and a square jaw, I get the feeling that he's hopeless, that he feels a sense of futility. Once he was very much in love, though.

And there's something about a bird, a, a parrot, yes, it's a parrot.

This was never meant to be a school. I think a lot of laughing, dancing, and music have come through here.

I'm also getting something about milk. Cow's milk, in those old tins with the handles, that were put on a flatbed truck of some kind.

(STAFF'S VOICE: "In the pantry") The dark-haired man seems to be very prominent here. There are two older people—short man, short woman. They're older, and they almost look alike, they look like they could be brother and sister. Glasses. And they both have real rounded faces. Nettles, nuttles, or something nettles. Seemed like a name. I'm also getting the name Alcott, something Alcott. The old couple, I think, came in and rejuvenated the house, brought it back to life. This seems like a house that traveled right down through the family, but everyone who started something in this house, it never really lasted that long. It seems to have been four or five different things. Some places are homes forever, and I don't think this was a home forever.

There seems like there was a period when the house was empty. Closed. Then there was a dark-haired, dark-eyed woman who was here, very severe looking, hair pulled back, severe, big brown eyes. Seemed to walk around with an older, kind of shuffling light-haired woman. I think she got the house.

(STAFF VOICE: "Moving to the study") Now, that's really funny, because when I walked in I saw a monk right over there looking out the window. Cowled, you know, with a hooded robe. I don't know if the family had people come in who had a religious background, because they're just fleeting. At first I thought they were nuns, but, no, that's wrong, it was too harsh a garment. This room was like a study, and the land extends way, way back. Just huge. Acres and acres and acres."

The Research Begins

Now that I'd gone on record (or tape) with my impressions at the Peninsula School, it was time for my staff and me to start learning everything we could about the building, the land, and the people whose lives and spirits had impacted it during its history. I'm sure you're thinking, Big deal. Ten minutes on Google.com. How hard is that?

Today? Not hard at all. But in 1977, when this particular haunting investigation happened? Not only was there no such thing as Google.com, but there was no such thing as a personal computer to explore it on. So instead, we spent countless hours in a brilliant San Francisco research facility called the San Bruno Archives, tracing every deed, tract map, and public record we could find about that specific property. We left the tape recordings from my hours inside the house in a drawer at the office. This was a search for general information. The specifics could come later. And I encourage you not to bother glancing back through the transcript, either, on this chronology of the transfers of ownership in the life of the Coleman Mansion/Peninsula School. I'll be taking care of that for you myself before you know it.

Chronological History of the Coleman Tract

pre-1850	unknown
1850s–80s	Woodside Dairy, owned by Isaiah Woods and Alvin Adams, managed by John Murray
1870s	Martha/Marie Coleman's first connection to the property, details not specified in public records
1880	James V. Coleman builds Coleman Mansion for $100,000, reportedly for his wife Carmelita
1882	Colemans reportedly "tired" of their mansion without ever moving in, willing to sell at a loss
1885	Carmelita Coleman died (death notices dramatically inconsistent)
1898	Harry P. Moore and family rented mansion to breed race-

	horses; references that mansion had been occupied in intervening years
1903	Coleman heirs hire D. Bromfield to subdivide the land; Shainwald, Buckbee & Co. to handle sale of property after subdivision
1905	Attorney Jenks of San Francisco purchased tract for $110,000
1906–07	Seminary students from St. Patrick's Seminary temporarily housed at the Coleman Mansion after their seminary was destroyed by earthquake
1907	Attorney James W. Cochrane of San Francisco purchased 165 acres for $100,000
1912	Rumor that a military academy was to be opened at the mansion; not confirmed, but the property was sold to an unnamed party
1913	Rupert T. Hooper family purchased mansion and nine acres surrounding it
1915	Edward S. Munford family purchased and remodeled mansion and renamed it "Tenacre"
1918	Mansion sold to Hibernia Bank for $851 "on foreclosure of a mechanic's lien"
1923	Roman Catholic bishop of San Francisco purchased mansion from Hibernia Bank for $10; mansion may have been used again as seminary
1925	Frank and Josephine Duveneck of Palo Alto rented mansion from the Archbishop for $100 per year and founded the Peninsula School
1929	Archbishop sold the mansion to the Duvenecks for $26,000

The Research Continues: Getting Specific

Now that we had an overview of what was beginning to sound like the Mansion Everyone Wanted to Buy but Nobody Wanted to

Keep, it was time to start filling in the details as best we could. We read newspaper articles. We talked to any descendants and friends and neighbors of descendants who would talk to us. We read countless obituaries and proud leather-bound family biographical sketches with proud, sternly posed professional portraits, and we heard the same enthusiastic gossip from sources who had no way of knowing each other. We verified what we could, made note of what we couldn't, and spent months putting it in some kind of order we could work with.

And not until then did we finally pull the original tapes of that day inside the Peninsula School out of their drawer and start going through them point by point, comparing them with the spiral notebooks full of information we'd gathered and organized.

What follows are quotes from the tape transcript, organized into recurring subjects to keep this from getting annoyingly repetitious, and the corresponding historical material we uncovered about those subjects, which you'll see immediately beneath each quote. I'll give you all the results—the hits, the misses, and the question marks— and let you be the judge of whether or not voices from the afterlife were talking to me that day.

The Transcript Quote:

"This house is very, very old. I'd say this house is a hundred years old, but there were other buildings 120, 130 years ago. . . . I'm also getting something about milk. Cow's milk, in those old tins with the handles, that were put on a flatbed truck of some kind."

The Historical Information:

My tape of the Peninsula School was made in 1977. The Coleman Mansion that houses the school was built in 1880. Prior to that, starting in about 1850, or 127 years before I arrived there, the property was the home of the Woodside Dairy.

The Transcript Quotes:

"For some reason I get the feeling that this house was never used for what it was meant to be used for. . . . This was never meant to be a school. . . . Everyone who started something in this house, it never really lasted that long. It seems to have been four or five different things. Some places are homes forever, and I don't think this was a home forever."

The Historical Information:

There's no question that the Coleman Mansion was originally built in 1880 to be a grand private home. By all accounts, though, it was never actually lived in until 1906, when the seminary students used it as temporary quarters until their permanent home could be rebuilt after the earthquake. From the 1890s on the house was rented and bought by any number of families and investors, all of whom had great plans for it, not one of which was ever carried out until the Duvenecks bought it in 1925. They were the first to use it consistently, as the Peninsula School, but even they never lived in it, so, no, not once was it ever used as the private home it was originally intended to be.

The Transcript Quotes:

"I'm picking up something about a John, something, Coleman. . . . I get the name John, and I also get the names Joseph and George."

The Historical Information:

We were never able to find a single Coleman whose name was John. There was a John Murray who managed the Woodside Dairy. As

for Joseph and George, the closest we came was a Joseph McDo-
nough, who was the uncle of the man who built the Coleman mansion (James V. Coleman), and a George H. Irving, whose company
purchased the Coleman tract in 1910. If you're not turning hand-
springs over those connections, it's okay, neither did I.

The Transcript Quotes:

"I don't know if they're nuns, or if they're men in black robes
walking around. . . . Now, that's really funny, because when I
walked in I saw a monk right over there looking out the window.
Cowled, you know, with a hooded robe. I don't know if the family
had people come in who had a religious background, because they're
just fleeting. At first I thought they were nuns, but no, that's wrong, it
was too harsh a garment."

The Historical Information:

As we learned, not once but possibly twice—both in 1906 and
again in 1923—the mansion provided temporary housing for seminary students. The first time was due to the tragic San Francisco
earthquake, and the second time was as a result of its $10 purchase
by a Roman Catholic bishop. "Fleeting" is an apt description, though,
since even in 1923 the arrangement only lasted two years before the
Duvenecks rented the mansion for $100 a year and founded the
Peninsula School.

The Transcript Quote:

"I think a lot of laughing, dancing, and music have come through
here."

The Historical Information:

According to Josephine Duveneck, there was a decades-old tradition among the students of nearby Stanford University to hold dances on the moonlit terraces of the mansion. In later years Stanford students also began appearing at the mansion every Halloween hoping for an appearance by the ghostly woman in green.

The Transcript Quote:

"There seems like there was a period when the house was empty. Closed."

The Historical Information:

The mansion was closed from 1885 to 1898. In 1898 it was actually rented but never lived in, so technically it was closed from 1885 to 1906, and then closed again from 1907 to 1925.

The Transcript Quote:

". . . the land extends way, way back. Just huge. Acres and acres and acres."

The Historical Information:

While the mansion site was considered to be one acre by 1977 after being subdivided time after time after time, the original tract of land on which it was built went on for a vast 166 acres.

The Transcript Quotes:

"There's another impression of a man with dark hair and dark eyes. It looks like he's bearded. . . . A dark man . . . The dark bearded man with nice teeth and a square jaw, I get the feeling that he's hopeless, that he feels a sense of futility. Once he was very much in love, though. . . . The dark-haired man seems to be very prominent here."

The Historical Information:

The Coleman Mansion was built in 1880 by James V. Coleman, a San Mateo County assemblyman. Family portraits and descriptions show an extremely handsome dark-haired, dark-eyed man with a perpetual moustache and a strong, firm jaw. His reputation was that of a powerful, hard-driving man. The hopelessness and sense of futility I felt from him can undoubtedly be explained by the next set of quotes and corresponding historical information, which is when the plot really began to thicken.

Transcript Quotes:

"And there's someone getting some kind of trauma in the chest area, like something entered the chest. Something sharp entered the chest . . . I'm getting the name Carmen . . . The sharp pain I get in the chest—I get the feeling she left after the sharp pain and is just walking around. Light hair, light eyes. She looks really young, maybe nineteen or twenty, something like that. A sharp pain and falling frontward over a box. It was so useless. Just so useless . . . Nettles, nuttles, or something nettles. Seemed like a name."

Historical Information:

We found no one associated with the history of this house whose name was Carmen, or whose last name was either Nettles or Nuttles. Carmelita Nuttall seemed pretty close, though, and she definitely had a connection to the Coleman Mansion. In fact, she inspired it. Carmelita Nuttall was her maiden name. Her married name was Carmelita Coleman, and her husband, James, was building the mansion for her. Light haired and light eyed, she was described by local society columns as being "peerless in beauty and accomplishments," and in 1880 when construction on the mansion began, she was twenty years old. There are several versions of this story, but the most widely agreed upon and certainly the most enduring goes like this: While waiting for their lavish new $100,000 mansion to be completed, James and Carmelita Coleman were living in a suite at a posh San Francisco hotel. Early one morning James returned from a business trip and Carmelita, lovingly helping him unpack, accidentally dropped the gun he always carried in his valise. Just as she reached to retrieve it, it hit the floor and discharged, firing into her chest at almost point-blank range and killing her instantly. She was twenty-four when she died. Carmelita never spent a single night in the mansion that was to be a monument to her husband's love for her, and James was too distraught to ever set foot on the grounds of the Coleman Mansion again, despite the ironic fact that it had just been completed. If that wouldn't make a man feel a hopeless sense of futility, I don't know what would. There's not a doubt in the mind of anyone who's seen or heard of the green woman who haunts the Peninsula School that she's Carmelita Coleman, claiming her rightful place as hostess and lady of her mansion, graciously entertaining her guests while waiting for James to come home.

The Transcript Quote:

"And there's something about a bird, a, a parrot, yes, it's a parrot."

The Historical Information:

Carmelita Nuttall Coleman's only listed surviving relative, according to her obituary, even though there were others who weren't listed, was an extremely wealthy San Francisco financier uncle named John Parrott.

The Transcript Quote:

"I'm getting the name Kathryn. I'm also getting the name Marie."

The Historical Information:

Marie Coleman was James Coleman's mother. Her sister's name was Kathryn, called Kate in this very close family.

The Transcript Quotes:

"There are two older people—short man, short woman. They're older, and they almost look alike, they look like they could be brother and sister. Glasses . . . The old couple, I think, came in and rejuvenated the house, brought it back to life."

The Historical Information:

Marie Coleman was very close to her brother William O'Brien, James's uncle, and it's considered very likely but unverifiable that they consulted with him regularly on the construction of the mansion. They certainly weren't around to "rejuvenate" it, though. The E. S. Munfords remodeled it in 1915, and Frank and Josephine Duveneck transformed it into a school in 1925, but there's no indication of the Munfords' age and family relationships, and Frank and Josephine were in their thirties and husband and wife, not brother and sister.

The Transcript Quote:

"I'm also getting the name Alcott, something Alcott."

The Historical Information:

We never found anyone associated with the Coleman Mansion, the Peninsula School, or the many transactions involving the land whose name was Alcott or even resembled Alcott.

The Transcript Quotes:

"There's one place upstairs that I really want to get to because it's really energy packed. . . . (UPSTAIRS) In this room right here, that we can't get into, I seem to get a lot of pressure and energy, and I get a sense of falling. . . . Something about the stairs. The steps, uh, I think we had a woman falling down the steps."

The Historical Information:

There were two fascinating but completely unsubstantiated rumors that we kept hearing over and over again about the Coleman Mansion. Both of them involved falling, both of them were presented to us by at least one person as "absolutely true," and both of them showed no hint of traceable clues in any of the local newspapers that we could uncover at the time of the alleged incidents. As a psychic, I don't dispute that there was a tragedy in the mansion that involved falling. But I can't and won't verify either or both of these stories as accurate.

The first story focused on a room near the head of the mansion's main stairway. The door to that room was missing a doorknob, so I wasn't able to go inside, but it was part of a much larger upstairs assembly room that I was able to explore, where the sense of falling was unavoidable. I found out much later that the floor of the whole assembly room area, including the room with the missing doorknob, was only added in the 1940s by the Peninsula School. From 1880 until 1940, the main stairway led to an area called "the gallery," open from the ground floor to a skylight and entirely encircled by an ornate wooden railing, creating a breathtaking sense of space, light, and openness. The rumor goes that one day in the 1880s, when the mansion was unoccupied but owned by the Coleman family, a "Coleman relative" (a variety of names were mentioned) summoned "a certain man" (another variety of names were mentioned, along with alleged connections to the Coleman relative in question) to the vacant mansion "for some business that demanded the utmost privacy and discretion, shall we say," according to one marginally reliable source.

This "certain man" was subsequently carried out of the mansion in a body bag, the story goes, having fallen to his death over the polished wooden railing of the gallery to the marble floor far, far below.

The second story is even sketchier than the first. It simply states that an uncommonly beautiful but disturbed young woman, driven to despair when the man she loved rejected her, threw herself down one of the mansion's many stairways, killing herself instantly. This theoretically happened in 1906. Now, what we know about the mansion in 1906 is that the St. Patrick's Seminary students moved there temporarily when their own quarters were damaged in the great earthquake. But the great San Francisco earthquake happened in April of 1906. If this young woman was in the mansion before April, when it was supposedly vacant, who was she and what was she doing there? If she was there after April of 1906, had she been rejected by one of the seminary students and committed suicide in a fully occupied building? If that's the case, there's no guarantee that there would be a record of it, but I keep clinging to the hope that nine out of ten people and institutions are decent and honest and wouldn't cover up a death. And then there's the most obvious question of all—did this young woman exist at all? Again, I do think there was a tragedy in the mansion that involved a falling death, but I don't believe either of these stories included enough accuracy to even hint at whatever the true, heartbreaking story really was. I never explored it. If I ever go back to the Peninsula School, that will be the next investigation on my list.

There's a mention in the transcript of "a dark-haired, dark-eyed woman" who was "very severe looking, hair pulled back, severe, big brown eyes. Seemed to walk around with an older, kind of shuffling light-haired woman. I think she got the house." I have no idea who those women were, or *if* they were. My staff and I put together a list of all the families whose names were even slightly involved with the mansion or the property—all branches of the Coleman family, including William and Kate O'Brien and their children, the John Parrott family, the Harry P. Moore family, the James W. Cochrane family, the George H. Irving family, the Rupert T. Hooper family, the Edward S. Munford family, and so on, and so on, and so on. We then gathered as many family photos of each of them as we could and I studied them until I went cross eyed. Needless to say, there were plenty of dark-haired, dark-eyed women and just as many light-haired women, and I didn't get a "hit" on any of them. That's not to say they weren't in those photographs, that's simply to say that if they were, I didn't recognize them.

Or, I might have been wrong that those two women were ever there.

The Conclusions

As I said earlier, I'm not going to go back and count up my totals and tell you how I did. I'll leave it up to you to keep score if you want.

What I'd much prefer you focus on is those things about which I was right, so that you can ask yourself where the information came from. I suppose in a really goofy, insane world, which it sometimes seems to be, I could come up with the image of a parrot out of thin air when the name Parrott was an issue, or start saying "nettles" for no apparent reason and have it be a coincidence that a key player in the history of the Coleman Mansion had the last name of Nuttall. Or my Nirvana Foundation staff and I could have cheated and, the instant we found out we were going to the Peninsula School, floored it to the San Bruno Archives, done months' worth of research in the two weeks' notice we were given, and I could have gone in already knowing all the right answers, in which case my accuracy should really have been 100 percent, shouldn't it?

Then there's that other possibility, also known as the truth, which is that the information was given to me by those who possessed it. And those who possessed it were the spirits and ghosts, all of them as capable of transmitting thoughts and images as we are, who joined me in that giant old mansion that day in 1977 to tell me their stories and give me glimpses into their lives and their deaths.

Explain to me how they could possibly accomplish that if they weren't still very much alive themselves.

Explain to me that there's still no proof of life after death.

Chapter Eight

PSYCHIC ATTACKS: RECOGNIZING THEM AND BANISHING THEM

I first wrote about psychic attacks in Lindsay's and my first book together, *The Other Side and Back*. That was in 1999. On one hand, it doesn't seem that long ago. On the other hand, the more Lindsay and I talked about it when we began this chapter, the more we realized that in a lot of ways, it was longer ago than we can measure with traditional watches and calendars.

In 1999, September 11 was nothing more than the day that came between September 10 and September 12. People worked and ate dinner in the twin towers of the World Trade Center seven days a week without giving it a second thought. I doubt if one out of ten people had ever heard of Osama bin Laden. Airport security was that silly inconvenience between the ticket counter and your gate where they asked you if you'd packed your own suitcase and what you intended to use your nail clippers for. We'd never heard the terms "Operation Shock and Awe," "mother of all bombs," or "hanging chads," we thought the President of the United States was the one who gets the most votes, and there was no such thing as SARS. Watching the bombing of Baghdad would have involved a lot of special-effects postproduction work, and only their family and friends had a clue who Chandra Levy, Elizabeth Smart, and Laci Peterson were, as it always should have been.

It's not as if we were all skipping around in 1999 marveling over how negativity-free our lives were, but I'm not a big believer in feeling guilty over not knowing how good we had it. Actually, I'm not a big believer in feeling guilty over much of anything. What's past is past, and where we've fallen short, instead of wasting energy beating ourselves up over it, we have to invest that energy in making up for it. But the time will never come when there's no negativity in our lives at all. That's part of what life on earth is about, and learning to overcome it is part of why we occasionally choose to come here. Unsuccessful lives perpetuate negativity. The most successful lives avoid it and reject it as best they can, even at its most deceptively seductive.

Psychic attacks are born and take root in the darkness, fear, and divisiveness of negativity. The more negativity thrives, the more the danger of psychic attacks grows and spreads.

Psychic attacks are almost literally imprints on the air we breathe and, if we're not careful, imprints on our overworked, overinformed, overthreatened, overwhelmed, underinspired, underspiritualized, underconfident minds.

And so the combination of these rough times and this particular book seem like a perfect opportunity to revisit the subject of psychic attacks, expand on it, and assure you that while you might not always be able to protect yourself from them completely, I can help you understand what they are, how to put up the best guard you can against them, and how to get rid of them if one settles in against your best efforts.

I don't know anyone, including me, who doesn't go through their share of depression from time to time, those flat feelings that nothing matters much, that there's nothing to look forward to, that we're in a rut we don't have the energy, the motivation, or the inspiration to get out of, and that we can't remember what it's like to be excited about something, or even just to laugh and really mean it. Those depressions aren't fun, but they come and go through life in varying degrees, and we either learn to rely on the fact that they'll pass or we get professional help for what can sometimes turn out to be a chemical imbalance that's easily treated and controlled.

But then there's this other nightmare that almost makes depression look like a trip to Disneyland. (And believe me, I emphasize the word "almost." I happen to take depression very seriously.) In my case, it was the early 1990s, and while I have the impression this hit very suddenly, I know that's not true. I'm sure I just managed to stay busy enough to avoid noticing that I was slowly sliding off an emotional and spiritual cliff. You've heard me say a hundred thousand times that I'm not psychic about myself, and I'm here to make the same mistakes and learn the same lessons you all are. That can include being crystal clear about the lives of my clients and thick as mud about my own, with toxic dark entities eating right there at my table, gaining my trust and eroding my soul while I dutifully locked my doors every night, years away from catching on that I was locking the enemy in, not out.

So I don't doubt for a moment that this negative atmosphere I chose for myself, as we always do, no matter how much we wish we could blame someone else, created an irresistible target for the psychic attack that hit me like a ton of bricks and virtually paralyzed me. Unlike the depressions I was familiar with and was pretty good at riding out, which involved varying degrees of low-energy apathy, boredom, and tedium, this was frighteningly personal, aimed right between my eyes, my heart, and my relationship with God, which is often the one thing that keeps me going when nothing else can.

Basically, what I woke up very early one morning to hear, playing over and over in my head, in my own voice, sounded like some version of this:

"I don't know who I thought I was kidding for all these years, but the joke's over. It's time for me to admit how useless I am, not as a psychic, but as a human being. I've been given this gift, but what have I really accomplished with it after all these years? What difference have I really made? No difference that counts, that's for sure, and I know why. Because as a woman, as a person, I don't deserve this gift, or any of the attention and admiration that come with it. If all those people knew what an insignificant, worthless, undeserving person I really am, they wouldn't ask me for advice about laundry detergent, let alone advice about their lives and their spirituality. Who in the world did I think I was, and how in the world did I have the nerve to run around pretending I had answers that mattered? If I had answers, I wouldn't feel so empty. And worst of all, I wouldn't feel so sure that I've let God down, and I have no idea how I'm supposed to live with that."

Those thoughts kept replaying in my head day and night for what seemed like, oh, about a century, while I did my best to go about my business and act as if nothing was wrong. I remember a constant fear that I might burst into tears at any moment and that if I started crying I might not stop. I also remember averaging maybe an hour or two of sleep and spending the rest of the night thinking those same thoughts over and over and over again and wondering if this is what a nervous breakdown felt like. Yes, I told myself, God must really be patting Himself on the back for choosing me of all people to give people guidance, when the best I could probably offer them was a perfect example of how *not* to live your life.

As luck would have it, I was scheduled to speak to a large congregation at my church just a couple of nights after that thought occurred to me, and I ended up deciding that if any group should be the first to hear what a dismal failure of a human being I was, it was these dear, loyal, trusting people who'd stuck by me for decades and had more than earned the truth, no matter how it would break my heart to tell them.

I'm sure they'd never seen me nervous before, and I know they'd never heard my voice so quiet, especially with a microphone in front of me. The room got very quiet very quickly when I began to speak. There was no doubt about it, something was up, they knew that, and rather than build dramatic tension, I got it over with as quickly as possible and confessed right up front just exactly what I'd been feeling, every negative thought about myself, every self-doubt, every crushing wave of certainty that after having such high hopes for me, I was sure they, and God, must be so disappointed.

I scanned those faces I knew so well, expecting looks of disillusionment, betrayal, mistrust, and a whole lot of sadness.

Instead, to my growing amazement, I found understanding, nods and smiles of what looked like relief and some tears of the most loving, overwhelming empathy. It touched me and confused me, and my voice broke as I said, "I need all of you to talk for a while. Tell me what's going on with you."

One by one at first, and then almost in unison talking over each other, every other person in that room that night stood up and announced that at some point in their lives, they'd gone through a period in which they'd felt everything I'd described, just as diminished and empty and unworthy of any love and admiration they'd been given. They'd felt the same grief I was feeling, and "grief" was the perfect word—it did feel exactly like my essence, my spirit, that part of me where my pilot light burns, had died. The only difference was, they hadn't known how to talk to anyone about it because they couldn't imagine how to put it into words, let alone find anyone who'd have the first clue what they were talking about. I had the advantage of a captive audience and a congregation I felt emotionally, morally, and spiritually responsible to, whether they could relate to what I was saying or not.

It was an unforgettable night for me, for several reasons.

It was the night my congregation and I became even closer than we had been before, which I didn't know was possible.

It was the night the awful darkness of self-doubt I'd been going through began to lift, thanks to the openness and honesty that embraced me and everyone else in that room, proving how important it is that we really talk to each other. We'd all gone through a terrible emotional crisis, a kind of spiritual desert. Each of us as we went through it thought we were alone, that it was just us. That night we found out it wasn't just us at all, and that fine, wonderful, kind, brilliant, spiritually and professionally successful people in this room had suffered and survived this exact same crisis. They certainly weren't failures or phonies, and there was no way they had let God down. If it wasn't true of them, maybe it wasn't true of me or the rest of us either.

Finally, it was the night my Spirit Guide, Francine, gave me the term "psychic attack" and I began researching and writing about what causes psychic attacks and what we can do about them. I don't mind telling you that the research was informal, but in this case the information I needed wasn't in books, it was in the hearts and psyches of the hundred or so clients from all over the world whom I talk to in any given week. By definition, the relationship between me and my clients involves a lot of confidentiality, which I treasure, so they were stunningly frank with me when I gently asked them about any periods of dramatic self-doubt they might have gone through. Every client I talked to over the age of thirty (and a handful of them younger than that, but only in very difficult circumstances), no matter what their religion, culture, country, or continent, no matter what their career or financial status or marital status or degree of success or lack of it in the eyes of the world at large, had experienced their own version of a psychic attack at some time or other. Every single one of them. And what became even more remarkable to me, as I jotted down the adjectives and phrases they used to describe them, was that the same words kept coming up over and over again— words that had kept me awake night after fitful night had plagued a financier in London years earlier, just as they had plagued a homemaker in Indiana and a movie star in the middle of a film in Rome. Somehow, it became fascinatingly apparent, when a psychic attack hits, *we're all listening to the same "tape."*

It doesn't take a genius, Scotland Yard, or the world's greatest psychic to figure out who's responsible for that "tape." At the heart of all negativity, at the core of every effort to disrupt our confidence in the unconditional love God has for us, and in the center of each attempt to extinguish the sacred white light that burns inside us as a birthmark from our Creator, lies the Dark Side, those Godless entities who've turned their backs on the sanctity of humanity, compassion, dignity, kindness, and life itself, and whose existence depends on the absence of light. Think of them as terrorists in spirit form— let's face it, if we white entities can accomplish astral travel, so can they. Every psychic attack they launch with that "tape" that manages to permanently pull one of us under is one more light they've managed to permanently extinguish and one more shard of darkness on this troubled earth where light used to be. And sadly, wars, no matter what their intentions, and grotesque horrors like September 11, can create enough fear and uncertainty that that "tape" is almost like an imprint in the air itself until we start to feel whole again. That imprint only has power until, inspired by the courage, faith, and sacrifice of thousands of men and women whose faces and names we'll never know, who stood up to the devastation in New York and Pennsylvania and Washington and Iraq because it was there to be done, our lights are back on and burning brighter than ever.

I've never had so many clients suffering from psychic attacks than I have right now. For them, and for any of you who might be going through one, let me remind you of something I didn't know when I went through mine. It's an imprint. A prerecorded tape, made by the Dark Side, full of all the negativity they could come up with, and then imprinted on the atmosphere to trick you into feeling as powerless and as separate from God as you possibly can. It's a good trick, I'll give them that, but like everything else the Dark Side tells you, all of those negative thoughts you're suddenly having about yourself are lies. Don't dignify them with a single moment of your time and energy. As you've probably learned from other circumstances in your life, even a lie can start to seem real if you concentrate on it too much.

Instead, at the very instant a negative thought about yourself flashes through your mind, I want you to do something that I'll tell you right now is going to feel really silly. I don't care. You've probably felt sillier for less worthy causes than this. I know I certainly have, and I'm sure I will again.

I want you to take the forefinger of your dominant hand and reach up to a spot on your forehead where your "third eye" would be—about an inch and a half above your eyebrows and right between them. Now, where that spot is, where that "third eye" would be, I want you to picture the "eject" button on a tape recorder. And I want you to push that eject button while saying, "I refuse this tape and all other input from the Dark Side, and I release its negativity from my mind into the sacred, loving purity of the white light of the Holy Spirit."

There's a marvelous feeling of satisfaction when you hit that "eject" button. It's like going from the awful sensation of a psychic attack that you didn't ask for and didn't see coming to reminding your-self that it's *your* mind, thank you very much, *you'll* be the judge of what goes into it, and you're not falling for this cheap trick twice in one lifetime. From "no control" to "in control" with one subtle push on a spot between your eyebrows. Like I said, I've felt a lot sillier for a lot less of a payback than that.

TOOLS OF PROTECTION

I do want to say a few words about Tools of Protection. I write about them a lot. I believe in them. I use them. And especially in this book, where there are some residents of the Dark Side and the after-life who can't be counted on to bring peace and comfort to your life, the subject of arming yourself with a Tool of Protection or two seems important.

Like the "eject" button gesture in the psychic attack discussion, Tools of Protection are simple images to remind you of far bigger, more complex concepts that most of us are too busy and over-whelmed to keep in mind every minute of every day. They don't re-quire meditation. They don't require time-consuming exercises. All they require is the ability to picture them. You can use any of mine that appeal to you or devise your own, whatever works for you. The details of the imagery aren't important, as long as you accomplish the goals that the Tools of Protection were created for in the first place: to reinforce the sacred, tangible, unconditional love that exists between you and God, and to repel the Dark Side and tell it to take its negativity elsewhere because it's wasting its time with you.

Every Tool of Protection should start with an image of yourself surrounded by the white light of the Holy Spirit. That's simply a gor-geous aura, cleansing and pure and divine, glowing around you from the top of your head to the bottoms of your feet, emanating from a brilliant white bulb that's the God-center deep inside you.

The Circle of Mirrors

This one in particular makes me so glad that the Tools of Protection are invisible, because I'd be embarrassed for people to know how often I use this one, particularly at large cocktail and dinner parties. There always seems to be one person at those parties who's figured out some despicable, underhanded way to get rich at my expense while trying to make it sound as if it's the most legitimate, charitable undertaking in the history of humankind and it would be amoral of me not to lend my name to it. If I'm not paying attention and don't get my Tools of Protection activated in time, the pitch invariably starts with some version of "Oh, my God. Sylvia Browne. I can't believe it. I've been dreaming of meeting you, and now here you are. Tell me there's no such thing as divine intervention, huh? Wait till the gang at [fill in name of phony charity no one's ever heard of] hears about this." And if you are one of those people, trust me, that never works. I'm many things, but I'm not an idiot.

But when I am paying attention, what happens on my end from the moment I arrive goes like this. First, as always, I surround myself with the white light of the Holy Spirit. Then, in my mind's eye, up goes a perfect circle of mirrors, taller than I am, facing away from me, with me in the middle of them. White entities are either not bothered by the mirrors at all or they're actually drawn to them. Dark entities, on the other hand, can't maintain their vanity when faced with the repulsiveness of their own images and go out of their way to avoid mirrors at all cost.

I won't be a bit surprised if you find this hard to believe, but try it in a social situation or two, or in your own house if you've been having trouble with some of the more distressing ghosts we've talked about, and I think you'll appreciate the difference it makes, if only in the feeling that the choices and the control are in your and God's hands, where they belong.

The Security Sign

Any crime statistician will tell you that, given a choice, criminals want nothing to do with houses that feature prominent signs announcing that they're protected by an armed security company. Thinking of the Dark Side as a bunch of criminals, thugs, and punks is accurate and useful and a reputation they encourage, so using their psychology against them can't hurt.

Rather than using one of those boring metal poles most security companies use to post their signs, I strongly encourage you to mount your sign on a powerful, jewel-encrusted sword, its hilt strong across your chest, a cross of gold deflecting the cowards of the Dark Side from your heart and the brilliant light of your God-center. Lashed securely to the sword's hilt with fine gossamer threads as strong as steel, only hiding your face from those you don't want to see it, is a sign of gold and jewels that reads *This Child of God Is Protected by The White Light of the Holy Spirit and Armed with Eternal Love.*

Getting around this sign is far more work than the Dark Side wants to go to. Believe me, they'll move on.

The Bubble of Light

If you've seen *The Wizard of Oz*, you know this Tool of Protection without even having to picture it, and to give credit where it's due, I borrowed it from them, they didn't borrow it from me. Remember Glinda, the Good Witch of the North, who traveled around in the beautiful blue bubble? That's all the Bubble of Light is, with the two exceptions that it's too big a stretch to expect yours to float while you're stuck walking around, and since you've already surrounded yourself with the powerful white light of the Holy Spirit you might want your bubble to be white instead of blue as well. Whatever color makes you feel the most loved, protected, and connected to God and repellent to the darkness and negativity around you, outside your home and inside it as well, that's the color you should use. And whichever one you choose, it will work, I do promise you that.

Hard as it is to believe sometimes, there is far more light than darkness in this world, and that's never more apparent than when we all stand together. Never doubt that, and never forget it. If the Dark Side tries to put out your light with a psychic attack or any of its other insidious tricks, don't suffer in silence like I did for longer than I should have. Haul out every Tool of Protection in your arsenal and yell for help at the top of your lungs. It's time for us all to start helping each other. We need every light we've got.

Chapter Nine

TO FIND A GHOST AND PROVE A GHOST: THE MOSS BEACH DISTILLERY

O ne of the haunting investigations I'll always treasure the most was that of the Moss Beach Distillery, which I explored for the TV series *Unsolved Mysteries* and without which I would never have had the great pleasure of meeting Robert Stack.

As most of you know, Robert Stack died of heart failure in his home in Los Angeles on May 14, 2003. I'm sure it won't surprise his family and friends to hear that he was on The Other Side before his body had even completely come to rest, that he says he felt so healthy on the very morning he died that if someone had offered him a movie that day he would have said yes, and that he was as much in love with Rosemarie on the fourteenth of May, 2003, as he was on the day he married her in 1956.

We didn't spend much time together on the set of *Unsolved Mysteries*, since we each had more than enough of our own work to focus on and a very tight shooting schedule to maintain on the unpredictable northern California coast. But in the few hours we did share in each other's company, it was apparent that I was in the presence of a gentleman. A rare experience these days, a rare word, and a rare man.

To Rosemarie, Elizabeth, and Charles, my deepest sympathy and my heartfelt hope that there's comfort in knowing he's Home, he's ecstatically happy, and he visits you often.

The Moss Beach Distillery

It wasn't *Unsolved Mysteries* that got me interested in this particular haunting investigation. In fact, the show didn't come along until later, and in the meantime, I was on record as being officially *dis*interested. The owner of the Moss Beach Distillery had been calling my office for almost a year, trying to convince my staff that what was going on at his establishment was both legitimate, with a line of witnesses a mile and several decades long, and unique. By the early 1990s, when those particular calls started coming, I'd heard those words a thousand times from people who insisted I come check out their "legitimate, unique, no-seriously-you've-never-seen-anything-like-this" ghost invasion. Too often I'd found either a deliberate attempt at a hoax that was meant to fool me, or a hoax that I was encouraged to participate in, which enraged me even more. Please don't ever doubt that I'm friendly with law enforcement all over the country for a reason. I've never been shy about reporting a hoax, especially in my own area of expertise. Where some pinhead would get the idea that I'd knowingly be part of a hoax I'll never understand. Maybe it's the "if some psychics are crooks, then they all must be" mentality. All I can say to that is, ask me to help scam someone and watch what happens.

Incidentally, there have been a few haunting investigations I've wanted very much to tackle but still had to say no, and occasionally it gets back to me that the people involved assumed they either didn't offer me enough money or their case wasn't "important" enough for me to be bothered with. Please let me clear that up right now by repeating a conversation I had with an old friend of mine who happens to be a retired highly ranked police officer. There's a famous series of unsolved murders in his city from several decades ago, and he used to be asked on a regular basis how he could resist going back, digging through those files with today's forensic technology and seeing if he could finally solve those murders once and for all. What he said to me was "Let's say you're the mother of some kid who got murdered yesterday, and you call me up, wondering if I've got any leads, and I tell you I'm sorry, but I'm flying to a DNA lab back East, I've got some blood samples from an important case I'm working on from 1969. I'll call you the minute I get back. You'd hate my guts, and you'd be right." I know how he feels. At any given time, I have about 250 files on my desk from law enforcement, some of which involve missing children, and it doesn't get more urgent than that. I enjoy haunting investigations. But for every one I say yes to, that pile of files on my desk gets ignored for several more crucial hours, and I mean this from the depth of my soul, I would rather find a missing child for free any day of the week than find a ghost, no matter what the size of the paycheck.

Which leads me back to one of the reasons I finally said yes to the owner of the Moss Beach Distillery. All the missing children files on my desk had been cleared away for the moment. I also had to give the man points for persistence after almost a year of calls in which he was always unfailingly courteous and respectful, and it didn't hurt that the place he wanted to show me was an easy drive from home.

The Moss Beach Distillery, it turned out, is an utterly charming restaurant perched on a cliff of Half Moon Bay in northern California. The walls are blue, with a darker blue trim, and there's a ceiling of pressed tin. The Pacific Ocean crashes away beneath not one but two sides of the restaurant. Diners take full advantage of the panoramic windows so that the view of sunsets from the upstairs dining room or the gliders on the downstairs patio is stunning and deceptively peaceful.

The Moss Beach Distillery was officially established as a business named Frank's Roadhouse in 1927, although it was most certainly popular a good ten years before that without all those messy inconveniences like paperwork and licenses. Frank's Roadhouse was apparently quite proud of its reputation as the northern California coast's most thriving speakeasy. It was a melting pot of sorts, where the film world, the political world, and the underworld could meet with complete discretion and engage in deals and activities they would have denied under oath in any court of law.

After it was Frank's Roadhouse it became the Galloway Bay Inn for a while, owned by a man named Mike Murphy. I'm sure it came as a surprise to absolutely nobody when Mike Murphy transformed Frank's Roadhouse into an unapologetic homage to Ireland, complete with a menu of traditional Irish cuisine. Nobody seemed quite clear on exactly when that happened, or when it was renamed the Moss Beach Distillery, and to be honest I wasn't on the edge of my chair to find out either.

But everyone seemed to know that it was haunted by a ghost whose nickname was the Blue Lady, and stories of her activities in the restaurant and the surrounding area have become legendary. On a small scale, furniture gets rearranged and showers get turned on in the middle of the night with no one there to accomplish either task. Light switches shamelessly click from off to on to off again by themselves right before people's eyes. Checkbooks float from the top of a desk to the top of a bookcase while an incredulous accountant watches helplessly. A supposed "virus" once changed all the dates in the computer to 1927 (coincidentally the year the building itself first legally opened for business), but the technician sent to repair the problem never could find what had caused it to happen in the first place. Waiters and waitresses hear their names whispered or feel taps on their shoulders when they're alone in the restaurant closing up for the night, only to turn and find there's no one anywhere near them. One woman took a lovely posed photograph of a friend at their table in the dining room, the magnificent view of the Pacific Ocean behind her. When the picture was developed, everything was exactly as it had been, from the other guests in the restaurant right down to the place settings on their table in the foreground, except for one small detail—the friend was nowhere to be seen in the photograph, as if she'd just dematerialized as the camera's shutter clicked. Another customer was innocently tending to business in the downstairs ladies' washroom when, right before her eyes, both water faucets turned on full blast. She stared at them, frozen in place, part of her frightened and part of her wondering if they might turn themselves off again. When, after several moments, they didn't, she turned them off herself, left the ladies' washroom, quickly paid her dinner tab, and never returned to the restaurant again.

Employees and customers alike have reported countless sightings of a woman in a blue dress walking alone along the steep cliffs below the Moss Beach Distillery, and countless disappearances as well when they try to call someone else's attention to her. Former owners Pat and Dave Andrews routinely found themselves locked out of their residential quarters in the restaurant from the inside, and they grew so tired of hearing the Blue Lady's footsteps on the hardwood floor of the dining room in the otherwise silent predawn hours that they finally had carpeting installed.

Children, especially little boys, seem to be of particular interest to the Blue Lady. She reportedly warns them away from the cliffs so that they won't fall, and she's been seen by many boys in the men's room, frightening some of them who can tell immediately that she's from some world other than this one.

One of the most locally famous Blue Lady stories happened in 1978, when a séance was held at the Moss Beach Distillery to try to contact the spirit or spirits who were so clearly wreaking havoc on the restaurant and anyone who came through its doors. Attending the séance and more than a little embarrassed about it were two hopelessly curious officers from the San Mateo County Sheriff's Department. It was bad enough that two proud members of the law enforcement community had shown up at a paranormal event. But when absolutely nothing happened at the séance, these two men felt like the most gullible idiots in town. They were headed home on Highway 92 in a white Jaguar, taking turns swearing to each other that they would never mention a word of this to their wives and coworkers, when suddenly, inexplicably, their car veered off the road and over the side of a hill. Later, a concerned tow-truck driver at the scene asked the deputies what happened to the young girl in the blue dress.

The dazed, slightly injured officers gaped at each other for a moment before turning to the tow-truck driver.

"What girl?" one of the officers managed to ask. "There was no one else here but us."

"Sure there was," the tow-truck driver replied. "I saw her myself. A young girl, she had on what looked like a blue dress, and she was covered with blood. Wherever she went, she looked like she was hurt bad, and she needs help."

Try as they might, the two officers couldn't seem to explain away or laugh off that ending to an otherwise uneventful séance, and they never set foot in the Moss Beach Distillery again.

By the time I arrived in the spring of 1992, the Moss Beach Distillery was owned by a wonderful and, as I'd certainly learned by then, persistent skeptic named John Barbour. He bought the restaurant thinking it would be a good business investment, nothing more, and he believed in ghosts exactly as much as I believe I could have been a great opera singer. He clung to that position for as long as possible despite a lot of strange reports from a lot of employees he knew and trusted, until the inevitable happened—he himself had an experience he couldn't explain.

"We were doing our routine monthly inventory," he told me. "Uneventful, just business as usual, until we got to the storage room and the door wouldn't budge. I mean, it might as well have been part of the wall, it was so impossible to move that door even a fraction of an inch, and we'd never had trouble with it before. So we rounded up the biggest guys we could find who happened to be at work at the time, and eventually we managed to get the door open enough to squeeze into the storage room. Once we got in there it was easy to see what the problem was. Someone had stacked boxes and boxes and boxes of wine right against the door, from the inside. Now, I'd love nothing more than to write that off as a practical joke by a few employees with too much time on their hands, except for one thing: that blocked door is the only way into and out of the room. See what I mean? At this point I almost have to believe in ghosts. I saw that with my own eyes, and I know it was humanly impossible."

The Moss Beach Distillery segment of *Unsolved Mysteries* originally aired on October 28, 1992, and it's been rerun in syndication approximately a trillion gazillion times. I still get calls about it, and it still makes me smile. But because it was only one of several segments on that particular episode, and because commercials are just a fact of network television life, *Unsolved Mysteries* was only able to deal with the highlights of the Blue Lady and the Moss Beach Distillery hauntings. Not having to make room for commercials or anyone else's segments but my own, I get to take all the time I want and give you the whole story.

The Séances

As you undoubtedly noticed many, many, many pages ago, I don't usually conduct séances unless I think the situation calls for them. When I do conduct a séance, I can't be bothered with making a bunch of people sit around a table holding hands with their eyes closed. Maybe it works for some psychics, but I'd last about two minutes before this laugh would come snorting through my nose and it would take me an hour to stop snickering and make my sides stop hurting and get back to business again. I'm much more comfortable just sitting in a relaxed position with relative quiet around me, focused and describing what comes through.

John Barbour was willing to put up with whatever my version of a séance was, as long as I held one of some kind to try to contact this alleged Blue Lady ghost who'd been making such a nuisance of herself for decades. And so, on March 5, 1992, I held the first of what would turn out to be three séances at the Moss Beach Distillery. In attendance of particular importance was a researcher named Jan Mucklestone, who would end up spending literally hundreds of hours tracking down the information I gave her, whether it led to a pot of gold or a brick wall. She seemed to think I was amazing. I think *she's* amazing for the work she did.

Again, I knew nothing more as I arrived for that first séance than the ghost's popular nickname, the Blue Lady. Stories or no stories, I was wide open to the possibility that there was no ghost there at all.

As it turned out, there were four.

But I don't want to get too far ahead of myself, and this all revealed itself to me over a series of weeks, not hours.

I have a transcript of the first séance. You'll be so glad that I'm only giving you a few of the highlights. No, I'm not editing it to make myself look good. I'm just sparing you the get-acquainted material, in which I explained to these people who Francine is, and talk about Johnny Johnson, the Toys"R"Us ghost, and the two caretaker ghosts at the Winchester Mystery House, things like that. Do you really want to read all that again? I didn't think so.

Transcript: The First Séance

. . . the woman in blue wears a hat with a filmy scarf. And there's a man. Dark-eyed man, tall, almost a Valentino figure. Have you come across the name Marian Moseley, or Mary Anne Mosley, Morley? Because the name Marian Moseley, or Morley, comes in so strong. Also the name Contina, I think it is a John Contina, C-o-n-t-i-n-a. There's a third man, too, younger, totally opposite of Contina, light haired, I can't get what his involvement is with all this, and he's not in residence here, he's just part of the story. There's also the name Reed involved. Anyway, you've definitely got a woman and two males. The woman is short, five feet two, maybe five three, with long hair and a very slight build. There is some conflict between the two men. She was married to one of them, but not to the one she was in love with.

I'm getting a woman in the water, tangled up in the seaweed. Jan, see if you can find this John, I know that his last name is absolutely Contina. Once we have all the last names on this it will be much easier to check. This woman wants to be heard, and it's a dramatic story. A lost love, a bad marriage, walking out by the beach, going into the water, drowning.

As often happens once I get involved in a haunting investigation, I became preoccupied with the Moss Beach Distillery story without even realizing it, jotting down notes in the middle of the night, interrupting dinner to scribble initials on a napkin, or turning to my poor housekeeper who learned years ago to just humor me no matter what and saying, "I'm not sure Moseley is quite it." "*Sí,*" my housekeeper would nod pleasantly, as she did at anything and everything I said, and bolt for another room as quickly as possible. So I did call Jan on April 4 to give her the name Anna Lee Philbrick, who I thought was also in residence at the Distillery, and to tell her that I felt Marian Moseley's, or Mosley's, or Morley's, injuries were to her head and chest. "Morley" was coming in more strongly, as was a break in the name Marian, so that it was sounding much more like Mary Ann, or Mary Ellen. Mary Ellen Morley. And just to complicate things even more, in addition to an Anna, I was also picking up a Hannah, no last name. I didn't know how she was connected to these other people or *if* she was connected to them, but I definitely felt she was hanging around the Distillery with them. I started keeping in constant touch with Jan as more and more details came into focus, and I was so relieved on her behalf that computers had come along by now so she wouldn't have to set up a cot and her own coffeemaker at the San Bruno Archives.

Somewhere along the way someone at the Moss Beach Distillery, I assume, contacted *Unsolved Mysteries.* Their producer, Cindy Bowles, was later quoted as saying, "When we heard that Sylvia Browne was interested in the case, we knew it was a verifiable sighting, and worthy of our attention." I still count it as one of the nicest compliments I've ever received.

Transcript: The Second Séance

On April 23, 1992, we gathered at the Moss Beach Distillery again. This time, in addition to my staff, John Barbour, and Jan Mucklestone, we were joined by a reporter from the *San Francisco Examiner* and approximately forty guests. The transcript of the second séance will be even more liberally edited than the first. Not only is a whole lot of it repetitious, but there are long stretches where I'm asked inaudible questions by someone in the room, leaving me with snappy answers like "Yeah, that's very valid," and "Not at all," and my particular favorite, "That's good, I didn't know that, thanks." (Doesn't that sound like I was just told something interesting? I wish I had a clue what it was.)

At any rate, here is the edited transcript of the second séance, with a report from our researcher, Jan Mucklestone, I think you'll find fascinating.

". . . She (the Blue Lady) is trying to tell us that we're going to have a fire here. She's predicting a future event. I don't think she's talking about this room, I think she's talking about the kitchen. She's worried about the grease trap in the kitchen.

"Anyway, this is the first triangle I've ever caught in a haunting. These women—Mary Ellen and this Anna—and this John Contina. He's here, but who cares about him? He's mean as hell, and we're invading his domain, and he doesn't like it. He's furious because he doesn't want us to talk (Mary Ellen) over. And there's not a doubt in my mind, by the way, it's Mary Ellen who's the Blue Lady. You can count on that.

"She keeps mentioning her child, her little boy. John, or Jack. She's calling him Jack. She's lost him, she can't find him. Making her way through a terrible storm, rain, she's very confused, very frightened, she just wants to get to Jack, but it's too far, or she's lost, so she comes here, she knows she can get help here. And she looks young to me. Maybe twenty-six or twenty-seven.

"This is in the present again. She says she's cold. Something has gone wrong with the heating and the air in here. I don't know what that means. What does that mean? . . . You just got air conditioning in here? That's it, that's why she's cold.

"Okay, she's worried about the oil fire in the kitchen again, she doesn't like the air conditioning and says she's cold all the time, and she wants someone to check on the floorboards, something about some boards in the hardwood floor that need to be checked so that someone doesn't trip on them.

"And she misses Jack. This boy.' Her child. She died when he was three. He's probably gone on and she's still here.

"Oh, great, now here's the dark-haired guy again. He's walking right through here now. Do you want to say anything to us? No. He doesn't like the idea that we're putting his life on display out here. Now he's leaving. She left, too, that way, but she says she'll be back.

"Anna came in for just a little while. She stood way over there in the corner and then left. Long blond hair, big blue eyes, almond shaped, where Mary Ellen is darker.

"Hannah seems to go in and out. She's the spokesperson. Kind of the mother superior to this whole group. Hannah Elder. Now, she's an older woman. Much older. Wears a little funny, like a Mennonite bonnet. Shirt dark little Eton jacket, big billowing skirt, big side pockets, and an apron. A little pinched, sharp white face. But sweet, like somebody's mother. From an earlier time, too, maybe 1898. (A SIGH) Oh, great, Hannah's a chatterbox. (AUDIENCE LAUGHTER)

"Mary Ellen's coming back through again. Mary Ellen, please walk closer, I can hardly hear you. Can anybody see that bright light flash, or is it just me who's seeing it? Sometimes it's so aggravating when nobody sees what I see.

"Mary Ellen, I'm glad you came back. Do you know that your son is not alive? That he's on The Other Side? Do you know that if you leave this place, you can go to your son, you can find your son, your mother, your father, everyone you want to see? (TO AUDIENCE) She says she's tired, and she has to go look for Jack. (TO MARY

ELLEN) But if you go, you'll find him. He'll find you. He's probably looking for you right now. (TO AUDIENCE) No, she says she has to stay here and keep everybody in line, whatever that means, and she's gone back out through the door again. I have a feeling she'll go one of these days. She's weakening, because she keeps coming in and out.

"Now, the man, on the other hand. I'm not too thrilled about this man. I don't like his energy. He's a very selfish human being, and I think he's keeping these women here for his own satisfaction. Ego. Nothing sexual, just ego."

(FROM THE AUDIENCE) "Was his other girlfriend married, too, this Anna Philbrick?"

"Anna Philbrick was married. She was married to an Edward Philbrick. Now, that information is coming from 'Chatty Hannah,' who is still right over here. There was also a mother. Bushnell was her maiden name, maybe. But Anna's husband was Edward L., Edward Leon Philbrick. I really hope we can get a coroner's report or a death certificate on her, because I'm getting that she drowned. She was despondent, and she drowned. She said something to me like 'I went down to the water and I got tangled in the seaweed.' But then she said, 'I didn't care to go on,' which makes me think there wasn't any seaweed, she just didn't want to admit that she killed herself. I think Anna Philbrick was in love with John Contina, and she found out about his relationship with Mary Ellen Morley, and because she was heartbroken or jealous or feeling guilty about being unfaithful to her husband . . .

"I'm sure Mary Ellen Morley died in an accident, by the way, a car accident, and her injuries were to her head and chest. I hope it specifies 'head and chest' on her death certificate, because that would help validate her.

"Oh, and, Jan, 'Chatty' over here says to try looking for John Contina in Utah.

"Now here's Mary Ellen again. We know, Mary Ellen, thank you, the kitchen fire and something about grease."

The tape clicked off at that moment. Before the transcription of Jan's comments I do want to mention, to be fair to Mary Ellen, that one week after this second séance, there was a kitchen fire that closed the restaurant for an evening.

The tape picked back up on Jan, who stepped up to the microphone with a folder of papers in her hand. At my own insistence, she hadn't shown any of them to me. After giving the guests a history of the Moss Beach Distillery, the activities and sightings of the Blue Lady, and an overview of the first séance, she continued.

(JAN) "Sylvia gave me the name Mary Ellen Morley. She also mentioned that Reed fit in there somehow. So I went to the San Mateo County Records, and I found a Mary Ellen Morley, whose maiden name was Mary Ellen Monica Reed. She was married in 1914, and she was tragically killed in an auto accident on November 5, 1919. At the end of the evening you're welcome to look at a copy of the death certificate and the front page articles about her death. And by the way, according to some of the articles, there apparently was a blinding rainstorm on the night Mary Ellen Morley died. I hadn't heard Sylvia mention anything about a storm until tonight.

"Sylvia also gave me another name, Anna Lou Philbrick, kind of an unusual name. I was allowed to go through the records in San Francisco and I found an Anna D. Philbrick, born in Pismo Beach in 1907. And I have a copy of her birth certificate, but I've not found anything more on her.

"John Contina, I've not been able to locate yet, but I'm just getting started."

Needless to say, I grabbed that folder away from Jan and practically tore into it with my teeth. Sure enough, there was Mary Ellen Morley's death certificate. Wife of Frederick Morley. Born May 1, 1891, died November 5, 1919. Age at death, twenty-eight years, six months. Cause of death, fracture of skull from automobile accident.

An article entitled "City Grieves Over Death of Beloved Young Woman" in the November 6, 1919, issue of the *Redwood City Star* read, in part, "Mrs. Morley remained conscious for fully half an hour after the accident, until finally when she realized the end was coming, she clasped her husband's hand and in a feeble gasp whispered, 'Good-bye. Take care of little Jack,' their three-year-old son."

I don't mind one bit admitting, I was blown away. My first ghost love triangle was amazing enough to keep me going. But for a ghost to communicate with that much clarity was so rare I was humbled by it. This poor woman, looking for her three-year-old son, having no idea he'd long since died, probably of old age, and was waiting for her on The Other Side by now—no wonder she was so concerned for children's safety on the cliffs outside the Moss Beach Distillery, and kept talking to little boys in the men's room. She undoubtedly kept hoping one of them would be Jack.

Even her appearance at the accident site of those two off-duty sheriff's deputies made sense, assuming the story and the tow-truck driver's memory were accurate. We'd all heard Mary Ellen warning that night about upcoming grease fires and needed repairs on the hardwood floors so that no one would trip. This woman had some psychic sense, and she was nothing if not compassionate. If she anticipated that those two officers had a car accident in their immediate future on the way home from the séance in 1978, I have no trouble believing that she would have followed them to try to help if she could when they went through an experience that she herself hadn't survived.

Now if I could just get these other three ghosts to be half as articulate and candid as Mary Ellen. Anna seemed willing to talk if she were approached properly, Contina was just mute and nasty, and the trick with Hannah would be getting her to stop gossiping about the other three, slow down, and talk about herself.

However it turned out, there was no way that séance number three was going to be dull.

Transcript: The Third Séance

Another forty guests gathered for the third séance on May 19, 1992, along with John Barbour, my usual staff, Jan Mucklestone, and three special added members of the "team": producer Cindy Bowles of *Unsolved Mysteries*, historian June Morrow, and the brilliant paranormal photographer Bill Tidwell, with whom I'd had the pleasure of working before and leapt at the chance to do it again.

By the time the third séance came along, I'd given Jan more information to check out, thankfully not as obscure as some of the other assignments I'd handed her, and seemingly not of any earth-shattering importance. But I had a strong sense that there had once been a large addition to the restaurant, and that the addition had been destroyed. I was close but not 100-percent accurate. In the early 1900s there had been what was politely called a "hotel" but was just as often used as a brothel, immediately adjacent to the restaurant on the land that was now the Moss Beach Distillery parking lot. The hotel, known at least for a while as the Marine View Hotel, was generally believed to have burned down. That was good enough for now and probably forever. I told Jan not to dig any deeper on that subject unless it started to look like a more significant piece of the puzzle than I believed it was.

I'd also been told by one of the guests who was at the second séance that there was a fairly large Mennonite community in that area at around the turn of the century. It was news to me, and Jan was able to confirm it. One more tiny bit of information about Hannah's story, but not nearly enough to fill in the blanks about her. Who in the world was little Mennonite chatterbox Hannah Elder, and what was she doing at the Moss Beach Distillery with this smarmy Valentino wanna-be and the two married women who bought into his act?

The audiotape clicked on.

"You know, there's always a fear in a psychic's heart of holding a séance—actually, I hate that word—but holding a séance and the ghosts you know are there don't show up. It's depressing to say, 'Are you there?' and no one comes. But thank God I know the Blue Lady, Mary Ellen, is here, I've seen her twice already tonight. What I'm really hoping is that we can get ahold of Hannah, who's sort of our unknown commodity, but I'm not going to push away whoever we get, I'll be happy to talk to any of the four of them.

"Before I start with them, though, I'm picking up something I didn't pick up last time, and I'm hoping that since we have an historian here tonight, June Morrow, she can help with this. Right down below these cliffs there is a cave, or a boarded-up cave, or a cave covered up somehow, and years ago this cave was used to hide bootlegged liquor. At one point someone tried to dig a pathway underneath, coming up into this house. I don't know how far they got, if it was ever finished, or if you'd ever actually find a trapdoor in the floor or anything like that, but I'm getting that cave or that boarded up area very strongly. June, or maybe our researcher Jan, see what you could find out about that, would you, because it's really strong? Thanks.

"Okay, now, back to our four ghosts here. I'm not doing this to make things spooky, but can we dim the lights a little bit? Because my friend Bill Tidwell is here, who took the most incredible authenticated photograph of Johnny Johnson, the Toys'R'Us ghost, I've ever seen in my life, and I want him to get any shots he can tonight on infrared film.

"Now, Hannah? I want to call Hannah Elder toward me. Mary

Ellen is coming toward me, still dressed in blue, fiddling with her scarf. Bill, she is almost approaching the table right now.

"Oh, Anna is coming right behind her. With seaweed all over her. What a mess. Anna, enough with the seaweed, will you come toward me? We're all concerned about you, we all want to know what happened and why you went in the water. (LISTENS, REPEATS) You wanted to make John sorry. Is that John, the dark-haired man? Yes? Do you think it made him sorry? (LISTENS, REPEATS) I don't know, either, Anna.

"Can you tell us something that will validate, uh, let me use another word, something that will prove to the people who know this building well that you are in residence here? (LISTENS, REPEATS) The locks are funny? I don't understand that. The locks don't work right? All right. The doors stick? Well, yes, but this is an old place. (LISTENS, REPEATS) The doors will really stick. The locks will really stick. Okay. I've got that. A shift in the foundation, and it needs to be propped up. We've all seen that, we can tell that, we're not stupid. (LISTENS, REPEATS) Termites. We're in California, Anna, all places in California have termites. (LISTENS, REPEATS) Not in the roof? I don't know about that. Look, what I'm saying is, I want you to do something or say something significant enough that we can catch it on film or have a sense that you're real to someone besides me. Is there anything else you can tell me? (LISTENS, REPEATS) The music cuts off and on, because the electrical makes it so. That doesn't mean anything to me.

"Yes, I know, I see Hannah coming up on the left. No, I'm not going to say anything to her unless she says something to me, she's been ignoring me all evening. (PAUSE) All right, Hannah, what is it? What do you want to say? Why are you bending down like that? Look up. Look at me. (LISTENS, REPEATS) A baby? Born to who? To you? You lost a baby? (LISTENS, REPEATS) Your name was Borden. That was your name before Elder. Old family. Borden. You had a child, and it died, and before your name was Elder it was

Borden. Is that it? You just wandered in here to tell us that, or do you have some relationship to these people?

"Of course I'll help you, if you'll tell me what to do for you. Why do you keep doing this? Does your stomach hurt? (LISTENS) You had a baby. I know. Did anybody know you had a baby? (LISTENS, REPEATS) The baby was born dead? And what happened to it? (LISTENS, REPEATS) Buried. And where did you bury it? (LISTENS) Oh, Hannah. Under here? Under this place? Oh, Hannah, were you here at the time of the brothel? I'm sorry. I'm so sorry. So you're from a different time. (LISTENS) Of course, no, that doesn't mean anything to you. Uh, what was the last year you remember? (LISTENS, REPEATS) 1901? 1901, and this place was what? (LISTENS, REPEATS) The Blue Cascade. And, what? At the same time? (LISTENS, REPEATS) Okay. A shingle outside that said 'Blue Cascade' and 'Martha's Kitchen.' Both names. I see.

"Hannah, I want you to listen to me, you know your baby is gone. What are you here for? What are you coming around for? (LISTENS, REPEATS) Because you did something evil, and you don't think that God will forgive you. God forgives everybody, Hannah. Besides, I think you have paid long and hard enough for whatever you have done. You said the child was stillborn. It was not alive. You had to bury it. You didn't kill anything. I mean, you didn't. Yes, Hannah, I will come see you again. I promise. (LISTENS) Yes, God bless you too. (TO AUDIENCE) Hannah's gone.

"Now Mary's back, moving all over the place, John's still standing over there glaring at all of us, oh, here's Anna. Anna, what exactly is John's problem? Does he have to look so cross all the time? (LISTENS, REPEATS) *He's* skeptical? Does he have any idea how skeptical *we* are? (AUDIENCE LAUGHS) Well, I guess skepticism on both sides can be healthy. (LISTENS, REPEATS) Yes, I will come back and talk to all of you, but I think a lot more would be accomplished if we could all sit down and maybe talk together. (PAUSE) Okay, fine, never mind, then, sorry I mentioned it. Good night to you too. (TO AUDIENCE) Well, we can turn the lights on again. They're all gone. I hope you followed that. I'm sure it's hard when you only hear one side of a conversation.

"So poor little Hannah, this little Mennonite-looking person, had a child. A stillborn baby. Bless her heart. I'll bet she wasn't part of the bordello, I'll bet she was one of the servants and someone just decided to help themselves to a free bonus one night or something and she got pregnant. So sad. Borden, right? Her name was Borden, and she said they were a known family, or old family, in the area?"

(JUNE, HISTORIAN) "There was a Borden family in Half Moon Bay, as a matter of fact."

"Were they prominent, or well to do?"

(JUNE, HISTORIAN) "Yeah, Borden and Hatch was the name of the lumbermill just south of Half Moon Bay. Actually, the Hatch name was more well known. The Bordens kind of died out, but the word you said she used was 'old,' an 'old family,' and that was true. Around 1900 they would still have been in the area too.

"And before I forget, at the beginning of the evening you were asking about a cave, that they might have used to hide bootlegged liquor in?"

"Yes. Thanks for remembering. Do you know anything about that?"

(JUNE, HISTORIAN) "Absolutely. There are a lot of caves all up and down the coast that rumrunners used to hide booze that landed here. And I know a lot of the caves along this whole Half Moon Bay coastline have been barricaded, for the safety of people who might be walking along the shore and decide to explore one and not know to get out of there before the tide starts rolling in. Now, not to say a few bootleggers wouldn't have tried, but considering the amount of rock they would have had to cut through to build a tunnel up into this building, it couldn't have been worth it. I'll bet they gave up almost as soon as they got started. But the caves themselves, with bootlegged liquor hidden inside? You're right about that."

"Fascinating. Thanks, June, I knew that was coming in strong for a reason. By the way, John, Anna was carrying on about sticking locks and sticking doors and electrical problems, I don't know, I guess trying to take credit for them. Do you know anything about that?"

(JOHN BARBOUR, OWNER) "I've got to tell you this! In fact, I want the microphone. I have to be classified as a major skeptic, as some of you know. But I've got to tell you, tonight is really wild. I swear to God on my father's grave, these things happened to me in the last two weeks.

"We have two new doors in this place, amongst half a million dollars of other things we've done. One of them is the door that goes down to the Seal Cove patio. We had that installed about a year ago, and the key for that door became so difficult to open, it was almost impossible. About a week ago, I had the contractor who installed that door stop by and file it away so that it would finally unlock again. It's still a little tough even now, but a week ago I almost broke a key trying to open that door.

"The second thing is the front door. A year and a half ago we installed a brand new up-to-code door, which of course means it costs three hundred thousand dollars a door, it has to be pushed only from the inside, etc., etc., etc., we all know that routine, right? Well, anyhow, what happened was, swear to God, the door would not shut. Okay? Because theoretically the building has shifted, but who cares, the point is, I had a three-hundred-thousand-dollar front door that wouldn't shut, and I had to have it shaved off to get it to close. Nobody in this room, no person in this room, and may God strike me dead, I'm telling the truth, no person except me knew about this."

A perfect time for the tape to click off, don't you think?

Saying Good-bye

There were still a lot of loose ends to be tied up, if possible, and I'd promised Hannah, Mary Ellen, and Anna that I'd come back. (John Contina had silently made it clear that he couldn't care less if he never saw me again.) This last time, though, I thought it might be more productive and less emotionally turbulent if it was just me, Jan to take notes for her research, and my assistant to sit discreetly nearby and take notes for both of us.

And sure enough, we did make some progress.

John never did say a word to me, but I finally got Mary Ellen to open up to me about him by asking about the ascots and scarves he constantly wore around his neck. His throat was cut, she told me, and he was thrown off a boat a few years after her car accident. (She never did acknowledge that either she or John was dead.) John had told her the two men who "cut" him were brothers whose last name was Bordeaux.

Jan spent several weeks researching coroner's records of deaths up and down the California coast and did find a possible match. In a year that was consistent with John Contina's story, the decapitated body of a John Doe had washed ashore on the San Gregorio Beach, less than five miles from the Moss Beach Distillery. She was never able to find a single record, though, of the Bordeaux brothers he'd named as his killers.

As for Anna Philbrick, the birth certificate Jan provided was indeed for a child of that name, but that child would have only been twelve years old at the time of the Anna Philbrick/John Contina affair. To thoroughly confuse us, though, the mother of the Anna Philbrick whose birth certificate we had was also named Anna Philbrick, and she would have been thirty-two at the time of the affair. That sounded much more like it, especially since the Anna Philbrick we were looking for was married at the time she was fooling around with John Contina. We had proof she existed, thanks to her name on her child's birth certificate, but Jan was never able to find either a birth certificate or a death certificate for the elder Anna Philbrick.

Hannah told me, once and only once, that she "ran" the bordello. She wouldn't discuss it further, tell me what it meant, or even acknowledge that she'd said it. Her guilt about the tragic burial of her stillborn child was never referred to again except by the euphemism "that evil thing."

A Postscript

As Jan and my assistant and I were leaving the Moss Beach Distillery that day, Mary Ellen Morley stepped close to me and said quietly, "Can I tell you something?"

"Of course," I told her.

"My husband wasn't driving."

"What? Are you talking about the car accident that killed you?"

She put her finger to her lips. "He's not the one who was driving," she whispered. "It was me."

She turned away and quickly disappeared before she even reached the door.

I told Jan about it during the drive home. "I don't get it," she said. "You read the same articles I did. They all said Fred Morley was driving, it wasn't even an issue, or an implied cover-up, or a hint that there was anything deliberate about the accident, so why would the press have bothered to lie about who was driving the car?"

"Beats me," I shrugged. "I'm just passing along the information, because I think she wanted me to. I didn't get the feeling I was supposed to keep this to myself, and for whatever reason, it seemed important to her."

Jan suddenly looked very tired as she turned away to stare out the car window, probably wondering how to go about reopening the investigation of a car accident in November of 1919 because a ghost told a psychic that the newspapers got it wrong.

A few weeks later I was in my office, reaching for my keys and purse, ready to leave for home after a long day, when the door flew open and I turned to see Jan standing there, a little out of breath and grinning from ear to ear.

"She was driving," she blurted out before I could say a word.

Like I said, a few weeks had passed. "Who was driving? What are you talking about?"

"Mary Ellen Morley," she beamed. "She was right. Fred Morley wasn't driving when the accident happened, Mary Ellen was."

Now I was grinning, too, and within seconds my office door was closed and we were both sitting.

"I won't bore you with all the details," Jan told me, "but after going blind reading obituaries and newspaper articles and even a document or two I had to pull some strings to look at for ten seconds, I was more convinced than ever that Mary Ellen Morley lied to you and Fred Morley was driving that car after all. But then I realized there was one more source I should probably check out before I gave up, even though it was a long shot. So I picked up the phone, and what do you know? It wasn't such a long shot after all."

"Who did you call?" I asked, loving her tenacity.

"Believe it or not, I managed to track down Mary Ellen Morley's granddaughter. Who literally gasped when I asked if it was possible that Mary Ellen was driving when the accident happened. She said it wasn't only possible, it was true, she was just so surprised that anyone outside the family knew. Apparently Fred Morley was pretty up front about it."

"If he was so up front about it," I said, "why did article after article after article claim that he's the one who was driving?"

Jan smiled. "Because, Sylvia, at the time, it wasn't considered proper for a lady to be operating a motor vehicle."

It took me a few minutes to stop laughing and calm down. Not until then did it hit me. "You realize what this proves, don't you?"

"What?"

"It proves that the ghost of Mary Ellen Morley is alive and well at the Moss Beach Distillery," I said.

She was confused. "I thought we already knew that."

"I already knew that. I had the advantage of being able to see her and talk to her. But did you really *know*, or did you think it was just amazingly probable?"

"I'm not sure," she answered honestly.

"Do you know now?" I asked.

She thought about it a moment, then replied with a definite "Yes."

I asked her what had made the difference for her between "probably" believing and absolute certainty. Of course, I knew what the answer was before I asked the question. So did she. So do you. But she was polite enough to say it anyway.

"Just that little thing of who was driving. It doesn't even matter, you know, but I get chills thinking about the fact that this woman who's been dead for more than seventy years would tell you something she couldn't possibly know unless she really is who she says she is."

"Exactly," I said. "That's called validation. What other possible reason could she have had for telling me she was driving that car? Because you're right—in the overall scope of things, it really doesn't matter who was driving, it's trivial."

"It's not trivial if it proves she has to be who she says she is. And the person she says she is is dead."

"And that," I said, "is called eternity."

Chapter Ten

VOICES OF A GHOST

It was March of 1995, and I was on a vacation to the southwest with my family and a few members of my staff. One day our trip took us to the stunning, almost mythical-looking cliff dwellings in New Mexico. The rest of the group had already moved on ahead of my assistant and me as we stepped inside an arched stone opening into a small bare stone space. My assistant started to step back out again. I touched her arm to stop her and shook my head, silently telling her to wait. I felt something. Someone.

"Is anyone here?" I asked.

The clarity of the response was so remarkable that I gestured to my assistant to take notes. Like I said, it's a good thing my staff has been with me for so long. Nothing I throw at them surprises them or has to be explained. I was confident, without having to ask, that everything that was about to be said would be written down word for word. The following is that conversation, verbatim, with my repeating what I heard for my assistant, who throughout the whole experience never could hear anyone else's voice but mine. I wish that weren't the case, but that's the truth and that's what we're stuck with. Obviously that leaves open the possibility that I had a sudden whim while hiking around in these cliff dwellings to just make all these things up and have my assistant go along with the joke. I'm flattered if anyone thinks my imagination is as colorful as it would have to be to come up with this:

"My name is Meta. I lived in 836. We are a proud people that came from Latia, the far north. We settled here in caves. They were protection from the wild boar and big cats. I made clothes and tended the fire. We met in the hunsa. We did not go out at night, because night air can poison people. Besides, the shadow people wait to take your soul."

"Why?" I asked.

"People who go out don't ever come back."

"Who do you pray to?" I asked.

"The White Mother Bear that protects us. If you make her mad, she scolds you. My father is very wealthy. He rules the village. His name is Katsu. Water dried up and we went south for a while, but we came back. I lived in the large house. The poor people lived in the little caves. The priests lived in bigger caves. Every third day, except when the moon was full, we gave offerings to Mother Bear, Amu. We roasted bricks and brought them in on wood planks very quick."

"Why bricks?" I asked.

"No smoke. Eagles soared too. Good luck to have it fly between your face and the sun."

"Are you an Indian girl?" I asked.

"No, I am Latia girl. Do not know Indian. I am four thousand new moons old. We brought dry seeds and grain from the north and planted here. I loved Semi. He was killed by a rock by Simu, who wanted me for his wife. I did not marry. I gave food and medicine to all people who traveled to see me. Do you need health and protection?"

"I would like health and protection for my family," I said.

"You are a wise woman, because by asking for health and protection for your family first and then you, you will get wealth. Father wind lives in the caves and when you make a good wish, whatever it may be, it is carried on the eagles' wings to the High God and He grants it."

"Why did you choose to talk to me?" I asked.

"You asked is anyone here. I came. I am now keeper of the village, and I will be here until the earth goes away. It is my duty for not having children. I am very powerful, and I am never alone, but I will be glad when I can meet Semi. I know he waits for me."

I know he does too. I also know that if you visit the cliff dwellings in New Mexico and quietly say into various arched stone openings, "Meta? Are you here?" some of you will absolutely hear a voice answering, "Yes, I am here," and you'll have paid your well-deserved respects to a very old, very lonely Latia woman who just wants very much to go Home and be with the man she loves.

Hearing a ghost or a spirit speak is a truly spiritual moment for me. I feel the connection to The Other Side very strongly, and I always feel there is a chance I can help someone. Sometimes, though, when I hear a ghost talking, it can be chilling. Not because I am afraid, but because of what they are saying. Sometimes they will confess to a crime. Other times they will solve a crime, or divulge a long-held secret. These make for intense encounters. One of the most intense encounters with a ghost occurred a couple of years ago. The ghost spoke directly to Francine. I'll never forget her words:

I was born in Hyde Park, Suffolk County, Massachusetts, on July 29, 1924, and grew up in Medford, about fifteen miles away. People from Medford always say, "You know. Medford,

Massachusetts? As in 'Paul Revere's Ride' Medford, Massachusetts?" As if they're important because Paul Revere rode his horse through their town once about a million years ago. I'm sorry. There are a lot of nice people in Medford, I'm just not too happy with a few of them right now. But I'll get to that later.

My mother's name was Phoebe. She was a housewife and then got a regular job outside the house when there was no money. She worked hard, and she was a good woman. She and I didn't always get along very well. She was tired a lot, and I needed more attention than she had the time and energy to give me. It wasn't my fault, it wasn't her fault, it was just the way it was. It never meant I didn't respect her and love her. I did, very much. She deserved a happier life than she had, that's for sure. I was very young when I decided mine was going to be different than hers.

My father's name was Cleo. He built miniature golf courses. I had four sisters, two older than me and two younger. We used to watch out the window for his car when he was coming home from work so we could tell our mother he was on his way, because he didn't like to be kept waiting for his dinner no matter what time he got there. I remember presents from him, and I remember him expecting us all to look nice when he took us places, but I don't remember him hugging us or kissing us or telling us he loved us. Maybe he did, but I don't remember it.

One day in 1930, when I was six years old, my father didn't come home. His car was found abandoned in another town a few miles away, and he just never came back. Some people thought he killed himself. Some people thought he ran out on us. Either way, he was gone, and our mother was left alone with no money and five daughters to raise. It was hard for her, but I had health problems, so I couldn't help as much as my sisters did.

I didn't care very much about school, but I liked being there. I wasn't invisible there. I wasn't just one of six females trying to live together in the same house. And I don't care how much those six females love each other, or how hard they try to get along with each other, females are just too competitive and too moody and too territorial for six of them to spend that much time together, so getting dressed up and going to school every day was an adventure for me. I liked finding out I could have an effect on boys just by walking past them a certain way, or letting them catch me looking at them, or smiling at them from across the room but leaving before they could get too close to me. Even then I liked being noticed, but I was never, ever promiscuous. For that I was labeled a tease, for my whole life, really. No one ever showed me a rule that said enjoying attention from men meant I was promising to be a whore.

There was also the school part of school, too, though, which I thought was pretty pointless and embarrassing. Why go to so much trouble to prove in front of a whole classroom of kids that I wasn't very good at math and science and all those other subjects when I could have told them that on the first day? So I dropped out my freshman year and never regretted it once. Girls didn't need school as much as boys did anyway. That was just a known fact.

The most memorable day of my teenage years, I guess, was in 1942. I was eighteen years old, and one day, it doesn't even matter how, I found out my father was alive and well, living three thousand miles away in Vallejo, California. No new family, doing okay for himself, not even the decency to have committed suicide out of guilt or died penniless in a snowdrift. Doing okay for himself, probably with a tan, in Vallejo, California, which I imagined was about a mile from that fantasy land called Hollywood. Back then I imagined every town in California was about a mile from Hollywood.

I was furious with him. He had to be the coldest, most irresponsible, selfish person on earth to not have at least sent money to help us. I never told my mother and sisters that he was alive and I knew where he was. It was the biggest secret I ever kept in my life.

I also wanted desperately to see him, and I started corresponding with him, having him use a fake name and return address and send his letters to me through a friend. It seemed like a miracle that I might get a second chance to be close to him. I'd spent a lot of time thinking about him in all the years he'd been gone, and I'd decided that, like it or not, the truth was, of my two parents, I definitely took after my dad. I thought he'd be proud of that, and that he'd understand me when so many other people seemed to find me difficult. I never meant for that to happen. Frankly, I found myself difficult sometimes. I wasn't good at middle ground when it came to my emotions. I was high or I was low. I was hot or I was cold. I was in or I was out. Laughing or crying, with you or against you, black or white, no gray areas with me, and I felt like my emotions controlled me a lot more than I controlled them. I wish I'd been more even tempered. Maybe I would have learned as I got older. If I'd been given the chance to get older.

Anyway, I was so full of hope when my father sent me the money to move to Vallejo to live with him. I was nineteen, free, and off on a whole new adventure, and I couldn't wait to surprise him with what a head-turner his middle daughter had become. I was pretty, everyone said so, with black hair and blue eyes and pale white skin, and I loved wearing dark clothing and a single flower in my hair to make myself look mysterious and set myself apart from all those blondes and redheads who were trying to look like Lana Turner and Rita Hayworth. Like most girls my age, I dreamed of going to Hollywood, and I imagined my father and me driving there together from Vallejo one day and just being too successful and too popular from the moment we got there to ever turn around and go back.

I guess I was a big disappointment to him. Or he didn't really want a daughter, he just wanted a free live-in housekeeper. Almost from the day I got there he was furious with me for going out and having fun instead of staying home scrubbing the floors and starch-

ing his shirts or something. I was nineteen. What was the big surprise? We fought a lot. During one of our worst fights he called me
lazy, irresponsible, and worthless, and I said, "Then I guess the ap-
ple really doesn't fall far from the tree, does it?" So much for my
touching reconciliation with my father. He kicked me out of his
house in 1943, and we never had a civil conversation again.

Somewhere people got the idea that I moved straight from my
little hometown back east to seek fame and fortune in Hollywood,
pitifully thumbing rides from movie studio gate to casting couch to
soda fountain counter, willing to sacrifice it all for that one big
break, that one moment when I would be discovered and achieve
the stardom that had always been my one and only dream.

The truth is, after my father threw me out, I felt lost and completely abandoned, and I didn't know where to go or what to do. I
had my looks and nice clothes but no money. I headed south, and as
some of you may know, I got arrested in Santa Barbara, which has
been blown completely out of proportion. I wasn't arrested for
underage drinking, because I wasn't drinking. And I certainly wasn't
arrested for soliciting or any of those other obscene rumors that
have gone around. I was arrested for being in a bar that I was too
young to be in. That's all it was. It was still scary and embarrassing,
though, and the police even took my fingerprints and a mugshot.
In recent years I've seen people try to pass off my mugshot as a picture from their personal pocket photo album, to imply some sort
of connection between us. I don't understand that.

I got sent back to Medford from Santa Barbara, and then I took
off and started traveling again. I ended up in Florida, where I'd
spent some earlier winters with family friends because of my
asthma. Everything changed in Florida. I fell in love. I'm not sure I
knew I could. I didn't think I took men seriously enough for that to
happen. But it did. What was even more amazing was, he fell in
love with me, and he wasn't just some drunk, blushing, drooling
loser with no future either. He was a real live military hero. A

major. A pilot. Young and sweet and a great dancer, and so handsome I couldn't stop staring at him. Someone took a picture of us that you should see. We even kind of looked alike, and we were so happy. This was a good man. You could tell. This was a man who would never abandon his car a few miles from home and just disappear.

He got sent overseas, and we were going to get married as soon as he got back. But his plane went down in India and he was killed in 1945. I can honestly say that when I heard the news, I felt like I died too. I went from being the luckiest girl in the world to the emptiest in the time it takes to say two words: "Matt's dead." It was too long and fast a fall, and if I had some problems before, I was definitely never the same after that.

There was no one around for me to grieve with, or ask for details, so I called his parents. Later they said that Matt and I were never engaged, and that I asked them for money. It's true, I did ask them for money, and maybe I shouldn't have, but I was broke and alone again, only this time I was also trying to deal with losing someone I genuinely loved, and I'll be the first to say I didn't deal with it very well. As for claiming we were never engaged, that's not true. We were, and I think it was cruel to deny it just because of what ended up happening to me. We'd all like to rewrite history, you know, but that doesn't make it an acceptable thing to do.

I didn't really "settle," if you can call it that, in Hollywood until the summer of 1946. I've heard about people I supposedly had ongoing affairs with in Hollywood before then, but I have no idea how I managed to accomplish that from all the way across the country. A friend introduced me to her friend Mark, who owned a nightclub with rooms in the back where girls could stay when they needed to, and he was helpful, as were lots of other people. But Hollywood's a funny place. Everyone you meet knows someone who knows someone who knows someone who knows a famous producer or director who's about to make a movie you'd be perfect for. Along the way you find out that half of those someones don't really know the someone they said they did, they know that someone's cousin's gardener, and the other half of those someones expect a much higher price for an introduction than you're willing to pay. You don't know who to believe, so you pretend to believe everybody but you're a fool if you believe anybody.

Including me, to be fair. I told my share of stories, and, no, I couldn't always be counted on to tell the truth. I didn't have the kind of life that afforded me the luxury of honesty very often. Not a week went by when I didn't write to my mother, for example. What harm was there in letting her think her middle daughter just might be a star any minute now? She deserved better than the truth from me.

In late 1946 I went to San Diego. You could ask why, or you could ask why not, and the answer would be the same. I ended up staying with a very nice family, and they thought I was nice for a while too. But I had a talent for wearing thin on people without meaning to, so right after the holidays they asked me to leave.

In the meantime I'd met this sweet, helpful guy, Red, from Los Angeles who'd offered me a ride back up there if I needed one. Rather than tell him I'd been kicked out of this family's house, I told him I had to meet my sister from out of town back in L.A., and I'd love to take him up on his offer if it was still open. I knew it would be. He was very attracted to me, but I could also tell he would never push his luck. I was right too. We stayed in a motel one night after he picked me up, and he never came within five feet of me. He slept on the bed, I slept on a chair, both of us were completely dressed the whole time, and it couldn't have been more innocent.

I had everything I owned with me, which wasn't very much, just a couple of suitcases, my identification papers, a newspaper article about Matt I still carried for good luck two years after he died, and a few other personal things. I didn't have a clue where I was going or what I was doing, so I had Red help me drop off my suitcases in a bus station locker and then take me to the Biltmore Hotel. He thought that's where I was meeting my sister. The truth is, it's the best place I could think of where he'd feel okay about leaving me, and I really did think it was time he moved along now. I don't mean to sound cold. He was a nice man. But he had a wife and baby, and I wasn't interested beyond the time we'd already spent together, so why linger over it as if it was anything more than it was—an innocent drive to Los Angeles, thanks a lot, good meeting you, have a nice life?

The lobby of the Biltmore was busy as usual, and I kind of pretended to look for my sister until I was sure Red was gone. Then I started calling around looking for someone who could help me out with a little money or a place to stay until I could get my bearings and figure out where on earth to go from here. Not where on earth to go from the Biltmore. Where on earth to go from square one. Again. For the millionth time.

I had a friend's old address book, and I was meticulous about writing down phone numbers. I mean, everybody's phone numbers, because you never knew when they might come in handy. Like now, for instance. I started making calls, but it was 6:30 at night. A lot of people weren't home. Out to dinner, probably. Other people's lines were busy, and a few of them just hung up.

Finally a man answered at what I had written down as his office number.

"Hello, Walter?" I said. "We've never actually met, but your daughter Barbara is one of my favorite people, and my sister Virginia West told me that if I'm ever in Los Angeles and don't get in touch with Walter and Ruth I'm missing a real treat." So often with men if you talk fast enough and drop enough names they're familiar with, they forget that they're talking to a complete stranger, have you ever noticed that?

He was courtly on the phone, as older men often are. My sister and his daughter really were friends too. I was sure Virginia had said that he and his wife were good solid Christian people, and that he was a well-respected surgeon. He was friendly but not inappropriate when he agreed to meet me. He didn't want me to come up to his office, which was in a building just around the corner from the Biltmore, so we met at his car that was parked not far away.

He drove me to a yellow frame house only a few minutes from his office. Three steps led to a modest front porch, nothing nearly as grand as I would have imagined for a doctor who'd undoubtedly been in practice for several decades. And there were no hints that life ever spilled from inside the house onto a porch that shouldn't have been so bare. No potted plants were being nourished there, no comfortable glider sat waiting for someone to come out after dinner and relax as the heat in the Los Angeles basin lifted. I couldn't picture a happy family ever having lived here.

It didn't get any easier when we stepped inside. The furniture was sparse and mismatched, someone else's leftovers, a table, a few chairs, a sofa, things you justify keeping by claiming they're "better than nothing." Walter had been quiet and sullen as we drove to this house, not the same friendly man I'd talked to on the phone. I started adding things up and came to an obvious conclusion I didn't know how to put politely, so instead I asked, "How is your wife, Walter?"

I expected him to say, "She passed away."

But he didn't. He said, "We're separated. My lawyer's serving her with divorce papers this week."

I said, "I'm sorry to hear that."

He said, "Don't be."

There was an edge in his voice, and a whole lot of stress. He looked at me, and I remember seeing his eyes and thinking, "Something's very wrong with him." I almost panicked for a second, but then I realized I was being ridiculous. The man was a renowned surgeon, for God's sake. He was going through a hard time, he'd just finished a long day's work, I'd be in a bad mood, too, if I were him, there was certainly nothing to be afraid of.

And then, of course, there was the fact that I hadn't eaten since early that morning, I was feeling a little weak and dizzy myself, I had maybe a dollar at most to my name and nowhere to go, and I wasn't even exactly sure where I was.

So when he took my hand in both of his and asked, "Would you join me for a glass of wine?" and his voice sounded okay again, I convinced myself that I'd just imagined the sickness in his eyes and said, "That would be lovely, thank you." He tightened his hands around my hand before he let go. I guess it was supposed to be some little romantic gesture, a lingering touch or something. I didn't like it. I didn't like how surprisingly strong his hands were, and I didn't like the way he was staring at me. As far as I was concerned, he and his wife and I should have been sitting down to dinner in their lovely home right about then, and she might have even been insisting that they wouldn't hear of me staying in a hotel when they have such a nice cozy guest room going to waste. Instead, I was in this almost vacant house, forcing myself to smile at this man who was nothing to me but my sister's friend's father, who was suddenly too friendly and much too tightly wound.

The wine was strong, and I drank it too fast on an empty stomach in my hurry to just ask for some money and get out of there.

I remember him coming toward me, and pushing him away, and him hitting me across the face.

I remember something about him blocking the door, and being on a bed crying with him on top of me and seeing those eyes again and realizing he really was completely insane.

I remember being bound, with sheets or something, not always, but maybe he left sometimes, I'm not sure, and a feeling that a lot of time had passed, not hours, but maybe a day or two or more. I wasn't always conscious, and when I was awake I felt weak, often too weak to move. I think there was a bottle of red pills beside the bed. He might have given me some of those.

There were moments when he'd look at me and suddenly start to cry, like his sanity and compassion had just come flooding back into him. But then just as quickly he'd turn violent again. Some of what he did to me was unspeakable, things I can't even let myself remember.

One night a woman walked in on us. I only got a glimpse of her. She was thin and severe, and she spoke with a thick accent. It wasn't his wife, whose name I knew was Ruth. He called this woman Alexandra. She was in a rage, and he seemed frightened of her. They fought, and I felt her hit me very hard on top of my head. Then she said something like "Finish it and get rid of her."

The next thing I remember was waking up in a vacant lot in a residential area. There were men around me, and one of them was kneeling down having his picture taken with me, not the way you do for a shot of two people posing together but the way you do when you have your picture taken beside some freakish dead thing that's washed up on the beach and you can't wait to repulse everyone back home with your snapshot of it. It was chaos, and everyone was yelling and going crazy, and there were cops running up from all directions, so I jumped up and looked to see what on earth everyone was in such a panic about.

I don't know how to describe what it's like to stand staring down at your own body. Thank God I knew it couldn't possibly be real. For one thing, no one could have survived what everyone else and I were staring at. My body had been cut exactly in half at the waist and then posed there like a mannequin. I was naked, with my breasts and everything else perfectly intact for the most part, except for some cuts and bruises on my face and a gouge on my thigh. Which was the other thing that proved that this was just some nightmare or something. All that vicious, brutal carnage, and there was not a drop of blood to be seen, anywhere near my body. Anybody knows that's impossible.

The crowd of people just kept growing and growing, and the police and the reporters were practically having screaming and shoving matches like a bunch of wolves over a fresh piece of raw meat, so I finally just turned around and walked back to the Biltmore because I didn't quite know where else to go. I'm still there for the most part, watching for a familiar face who might offer me dinner or a place to stay. Every once in a while, though, I walk over to Thirty-ninth and Norton again and try one more time to make sense of that awful dream I had on that January morning in 1947.

Obviously a lot of other people are as confused about it as I am, too, because I keep hearing things about it, and about myself, that are simply not true. And people thought I was a storyteller?

Apparently more than fifty people confessed to killing me back then, and on top of that, several books have been written claiming to solve my "murder" once and for all. Two different authors have even named their own fathers as having killed me. With a father like Cleo, I relate to the temptation, it's just that they've all been wrong so far. The truth hasn't come out yet. I've given you a little of it, and who would know better than I do? The rest will come in good time, if you insist on believing I'm dead at all, which seems to be a popular myth.

There seems to be no end of fascination with the subject of my private parts. As I understand it, the most irresistible twist is the one in which I constantly threw myself at men, only to frustrate them at the last possible moment by revealing that I had "infantile genitalia" and was unable to have any kind of normal sexual intercourse. I hate to ruin a great story, but the truth is, there was absolutely nothing "infantile" about my "genitalia" at all. My female parts were as intact and ordinary as they could possibly be. It was hard to find a lot of men who slept with me because I wasn't promiscuous. It's that simple. Dull but true.

My poor personal hygiene has been widely publicized, too, which is embarrassing. Not one of those things you ever imagine the whole world discussing at dinner parties, you know? But I suppose I can't get too indignant, since fair is fair, personal hygiene wasn't something I excelled at. The truth about me in general, I guess, was that whether you were talking about my looks, or my character, or my supposed "Hollywood dreams," or my life in general, your best bet was to take me in from a distance. The closer you started to get, the less I could hold up under scrutiny. If you think that's an easy thing to know about yourself, you're sadly mistaken.

I did love my mother and my sisters always, though, very much. Not very well sometimes, but very, very much. That's the truth.

I mentioned at the beginning being annoyed with a handful of people in Medford, Massachusetts. What happened was, someone donated a plaque acknowledging that I grew up there, and there were some fine, upstanding citizens, I guess, who objected to it and wanted it taken down. Something about Medford "values" and only wanting "positive figures" to be memorialized. Mind you, the plaque doesn't say that everyone from Medford is just like me, or that everyone from Medford admired me and continues to hold me up as a role model to this very day. It only says that I grew up there. That's the truth. I thank the majority of citizens who saw to it that the plaque stayed, and to those who objected to it, I just want to remind you: I didn't do something horrible. Something horrible was done to me.

I still don't understand how I walked away from it.

My name is Elizabeth Short.

They called me the Black Dahlia.

Epilogue

MY FAVORITE
GHOST STORY

It was 1990, and my life was busier than ever. I was in my twentieth year of television appearances on everything from talk shows to *In Search Of* and more network specials than I can remember. I was touring the country giving lectures, I was averaging twenty private readings a day, and I was devoting countless pro bono hours to my consultation work with both law enforcement and the medical community. In fact, looking back, I might have been trying to stay too busy to think. I was just recovering from a serious personal crisis, proving once again that I don't have a psychic bone in my body about my own life, and I tend to compulsively run myself ragged when I'm fighting my way out of a depression.

So when an invitation came out of nowhere to do a haunting investigation of the *Queen Mary* in the Long Beach, California, harbor, I said yes before I even had time to realize that my schedule and I were already on serious overload. I wasn't even quite sure who'd issued the invitation. I caught the name "Herman," and something about a brother and a Halloween show, and a reference to CBS, with whom I'd enjoyed a long-standing relationship. I also noticed that the date they wanted me happened to coincide with a trip to Los Angeles I'd committed to anyway, so I had nothing to lose but a few hours I couldn't really spare. And when you're in the middle of compulsive workaholism, it doesn't get much more irresistible than that.

Stepping onto the *Queen Mary*, if you've never had the experience, is like stepping into a beautiful, gleaming, elegant past-life dream. There is dark polished inlaid mahogany everywhere, with gorgeous brass railings and massive crystal chandeliers, history preserved in exquisite craftsmanship. I was wondering why such stunning surroundings felt so oppressive when a young production intern dashed up, welcomed me, and offered to show me to the cabin where I would be spending the night. With apologies, she explained that "Our Host" wouldn't be joining us until the next day, as if I might be terribly disappointed about a delay in meeting someone I'd never heard of. I kept my apathy to myself and simply assured her that I was too preoccupied with the idea of meeting the ghosts on board, if there were any, to worry about when Our Host was arriving.

My cabin was as lovely as the dinner I was served, and throughout the meal I kept my antennae up for any ghosts or spirits who might be hanging around trying to get my attention. Nothing. I smiled to myself, a little perversely, as I pictured a Halloween special in which I walked Our Host around this huge ship for an hour on film saying over and over again, "Nope. Sorry. There's nothing here." But Halloween special or not, if I came to the conclusion that the *Queen Mary* wasn't haunted, there was no way I would ever claim it was just for the sake of ratings, or to feel that I gave these people their money's worth. This was their bright idea, after all, not mine.

I hadn't realized until I sank into bed how exhausted I was. In fact, I was almost too exhausted to realize that I'd become a banquet for swarms of mosquitoes that were flying in and out through the open porthole of my cabin. I finally swatted my way to the porthole, slammed it shut, and went back to bed, only to discover after a few minutes that with the porthole closed, the cabin was sweltering hot and the still air was so stifling I could barely breathe. Great choice, I thought, feeling sorrier for myself by the minute. Being eaten alive by mosquitoes, or smothering to death. I finally opted for the mosquitoes and stomped over to open the porthole again.

It was at that moment, well past midnight, that I heard footsteps running up and down the hall outside my door. I didn't think much about it at first. There was a whole television production team and crew on board, so it could easily have been any one of them. But the more I listened the more I realized that these sounded like awfully tiny feet, taking awfully tiny steps, to belong to any of the production staff. I crept to the door and very quietly opened it. And there in the hallway, playfully dashing around all over the place, was the very real but indistinct ghost of a little boy. He was filmy, more like a figure made of white smoke than anything solid, but I could make out knickers and a newsboy cap on his small frame. He didn't talk to me, didn't even notice me, just kept right on playing what looked like a solitary game of tag, and after watching him for several minutes I left him to his private illusions and fell into bed among the mosquitoes again, thinking as I drifted off to sleep that maybe this Halloween special wouldn't be completely uneventful after all.

I was sleepy, cranky, and very itchy the next morning when I told the production team about the little ghost boy in the hallway, and you've never seen a less impressed group of people in your life. I had no details to offer, since the boy never spoke to me and I couldn't get a clear enough image of him to come up with any psychic facts I could rely on, and there were certainly no witnesses, so the reactions ranged from polite patronizing to blatant eye-rolling. The crew was wondering what kind of lunatic they were stuck with and I was wondering if any of them cared how miserably tired and mosquito-bitten

I was when the young intern I'd met the day before flew by to suggest we start the tour without Our Host.

"He'll catch up with you shortly," she excitedly assured me.

Who cares? I muttered silently to myself.

We followed orders and started our tour of this gorgeous ship—or, as I was now thinking of it thanks to my mood, this stupid boat. Audiotapes were rolling and cameras were at the ready to capture my every encounter with every ghost and spirit we ran into along the way. The problem was, there weren't any. Cabin after cabin, deck after deck, from the dining rooms to the ballroom to the magnificent captain's quarters, there wasn't even a hint of the afterlife to be found. Not even the little ghost boy from the night before put in an appearance. My fear of being part of the dullest Halloween special in history, kind of the Sylvia Browne version of Geraldo Rivera unearthing Al Capone's vault, was becoming more and more real by the minute.

After what seemed like weeks, we reached the lowest deck on the ship, where it looked as if a swimming pool used to be. And suddenly, to my complete surprise, a ghost, as real and distinct and in full color as the rest of us, materialized from out of nowhere. I stopped cold, then stepped forward. The crew stayed where they were, not seeing a thing but rolling their cameras on the off chance I wasn't crazy.

She was young, maybe nineteen or twenty. She was wearing a midcalf-length white party dress, a sleeveless sheath with heavy beading at the hem, a long strand of pearls around her neck, very much like a flapper from the 1920s would wear. She had on opaque white stockings and white low-heeled Mary Jane shoes. Her hair was short and jet black, in finger waves framing her face. Her eyes were dark, dramatic, and slightly Indian looking, reminiscent of Merle Oberon, the strikingly lovely actress whom I've probably watched fifty times in the classic *Wuthering Heights* with Laurence Olivier. She was dancing, arms high in the air, and when I stepped toward her she changed course and began twirling in circles around and around me. There was no joy in her wild, whirling dance. Instead, it looked frantic and driven, and the incessant smile on her face seemed much more insane than happy. All ghosts are desperately confused and disoriented, of course, but I'd never seen one as manic as this one.

I asked her what her name was.

"Mary," she said, spinning closer, pleased to be noticed and acknowledged. She looked up and down at me and added, "You're dressed so oddly."

Any impulse I might have had to offer up the pot-calling-the-kettle-black cliché was lost immediately when, for the first time, I could see angry red open wounds on the inside of both her wrists. It didn't take a psychic to figure out that she had taken her own life, and I asked her if the cuts hurt her.

"Not anymore," she laughed, and then added defensively, "and they're not cuts, they're just scratches."

"No, they're deep cuts, Mary," I said quietly. "Tell me what happened."

She never stopped moving, never stopped her dizzying dance as she told me her story, her occasional giggling inappropriate for such a tragic chain of events. There was a man. His name was Robert. She was deeply in love with him and had ecstatically accepted his proposal of marriage. Then, with no warning and no apologies, he simply vanished one day, running off to marry another woman he'd decided might be more to his financial advantage, she later found out. Mary was disconsolate, and her parents, whom she called "Mommy" and "Daddy" in what sounded like a contrived childlike voice, virtually dragged her onto the *Queen Mary* as the first leg of a three-month trip to Europe they hoped would mend her broken heart and help her forget about this man they'd never approved of in the first place. As far as Mary was concerned, this was the third day of their cruise—

in other words, very probably the day she'd descended to the lowest deck of the ship and killed herself.

"You know what's going to happen?" She laughed, dropping her voice to a low, secretive murmur as she twirled by.

"What's going to happen?"

"He's going to leave her and come back to me. You'll see, he's going to wire me through the ship's captain and tell me he's waiting for me in England."

I wanted to tell her that Robert was dead. I wanted to tell her that *she* was dead, so that she could go Home and finally be at peace. I approached the subject gently, knowing how seriously disturbed she was. "Mary," I started, "you can be with Robert right now if you'll let me help. . . ."

I was interrupted by a quiet baritone voice behind me, asking, "Who in the world are you talking to?"

I turned around and found myself looking into the beautiful, sensitive face of a man who was so obviously charismatic I knew he had to be our long-awaited Host. My dear friend and cowriter Lindsay describes rare moments like that one, in which you meet a stranger who seems inexplicably familiar the instant your eyes meet, as a feeling of wanting to say, "Oh, *there* you are. I've never heard of you, but I've been waiting for you to come into my life." I actually blushed, partly because I realized that, from his point of view he'd just caught me having a rather emotional conversation with myself, and partly because his eye contact was so intense.

We introduced ourselves, and then I quickly began telling him about Mary and her tragic story, not sure if I was making myself less crazy or more as I explained that no, I wasn't chatting with myself, I was chatting with a ghost. She was twirling wildly around both of us now, and I noticed that she was listening intently and vain enough to love knowing that we were talking about her. Our Host listened intently, without judgment, the exact kind of open-minded skeptic I appreciate.

"She's here right now?" he asked.

I nodded.

"What's she doing?"

"She's whirling around us in a circle, like she's been doing since I got here," I told him. For some reason at that moment it occurred to me that she was in a sleeveless dress in the chilly air of that bottom deck, and I turned to her and said, "Aren't you cold?"

"Why do you think I'm dancing?" she answered. Her tone reminded me exactly of my granddaughter Angelia's tone when she thinks I've asked a stupid question. I decided Mary was probably a Scorpio too.

Our Host, in the meantime, was looking all around, clearly unable to see Mary but genuinely wanting to if, in fact, she existed. There was no way I could help make that happen, but if he was open to the idea of experiencing her, there was one thing I knew might be worth trying.

First, I told Mary to stand still. She loved all this attention so much that she actually did it. Then I took Our Host by the hand. He was brave enough not to hesitate, even though he didn't have a clue what I was about to do. And then, without a word, I simply walked him right through Mary's ghostly body.

I'll never forget how huge his eyes were after he'd stepped through her. "Oh, my God!" was all he said, clearly shaken.

"Did you feel that?" It was a rhetorical question. I could look at him and tell he'd felt it.

"Feel it? How could I *not* feel it?" he replied. "Whatever it was, it was freezing cold."

I decided to play the devil's advocate. "Well, to be fair, it is chilly down here."

He shook his head. "Not like that. That wasn't any kind of cold I've ever felt. It went all the way through me, right down to my bones, and just in that one spot you walked me through."

"Anything else?" I asked.

"Absolutely," he said, shuddering a little. "It was like walking through a wall of cobwebs. I can still feel them all over me."

I'd had that same feeling myself during ghost encounters, and I knew that even though the sensation itself would pass quickly, he would never forget it. I smiled and kept my response to a simple "So now you've met Mary."

He just nodded and looked at me. All the skepticism was gone from his eyes. He believed. I didn't convince him. Mary did.

Mary had lost all interest in us by now and went whirling away into her own lost world again. The producer and several members of the crew were excited to tell me that it was on this lowest deck, in this exact spot, where the employees of the *Queen Mary* had heard the most unexplainable noises, seen the most unexplainable visions of something filmy white, and been the most frightened. I wasn't surprised, and I appreciated the validation.

Our Host suggested we go find a place to sit. I'm sure he needed a chance to regroup, and I was grateful for a chance to quietly and privately learn more about this handsome, charismatic, oddly familiar stranger. We settled onto a bench on an upper deck and started talking.

To this day, all these years later, we haven't stopped.

As most of you probably figured out pages and pages ago, our host's name was Montel Williams.

That's how we met.

And that's why the *Queen Mary* is and always will be my favorite ghost story.

About the Author

Sylvia Browne is the #1 *New York Times* bestselling author of *The Other Side and Back; Life on The Other Side; Past Lives, Future Healing; Sylvia Browne's Book of Dreams;* and *Blessings from The Other Side*. She has been working as a psychic for nearly half a century. She is a regular guest on *The Montel Williams Show*, and has appeared on *Larry King Live, Good Morning America*, CNN, and *Entertainment Tonight*. She lives in California.